When Kristy and her friends set up the Babysitters Club, they little think it will be so successful. The idea is simple – parents make a single phone call and reach a team of babysitting experts, ready and willing to look after their children for them. The parents are happy, the kids are happy, everybody's happy! And if things don't always go according to plan, at least there's a lot of fun to be had on the way!

The Babysitters Club

COLLECTION 4

Book 10
LOGAN LIKES MARY ANNE!

Book 11
KRISTY AND THE SNOBS

Book 12
CLAUDIA AND THE NEW GIRL

Ann M. Martin

Hippo

Scholastic Children's Books,
Commonwealth House, 1–19 New Oxford Street,
London, WC1A 1NU, UK
A division of Scholastic Ltd
London ~ New York ~ Toronto ~ Sydney ~ Auckland

Logan Likes Mary Anne!
Kristy and the Snobs
Claudia and the New Girl
First published in the US by Scholastic Inc., 1988
First published in the UK by Scholastic Ltd, 1990
First published in this edition by Scholastic Ltd, 1998

ISBN 0 590 19880 7

Typeset by Rowland Phototypesetting Ltd,
Bury St Edmunds, Suffolk
Printed by Cox & Wyman Ltd, Reading, Berks.

1 2 3 4 5 6 7 8 9 10

CONTENTS

The Babysitters Club

LOGAN LIKES MARY ANNE!

1st CHAPTER

It was the last day of the summer holiday. I couldn't believe more than two months had sped by since the end of school. One day the weather had been fresh and cool with the promise of summer and fun, and now it was stale and hot with the promise of autumn and school. Tomorrow my friends and I would become eighth-graders. An awful lot had happened over the summer. In fact, it had been a more eventful summer than usual. Something important had happened to every single member of the Babysitters Club.

I guess that, first of all, I should tell you what the Babysitters Club is, in case you don't know. The club consists of me (I'm Mary Anne Spier) and my friends Kristy Thomas, Dawn Schafer, Claudia Kishi, and Stacey McGill. The five of us run a business, which Kristy started. We baby-sit for the kids in our neighbourhoods, and we have a lot of fun – and earn quite a bit of money, too. We meet three times a week to take calls from people who need baby-sitters, and also sometimes to gossip and fool around. But we're very professional about the way we run our business.

Anyway, here's what happened to us over the summer. I'll start with Kristy, since she's the chairman of the club, and since her event was the biggest and most exciting of all. Her mother got married again and Kristy was her bridesmaid! Honest. She wore a long dress and her first pair of shoes with heels. Claudia and Dawn and Stacey and I were guests at the wedding. And *then* Kristy and her family (her two older brothers Sam and Charlie, and her little brother David Michael) moved out of their old house, which was next door to mine, and across town to her stepfather's mansion. Kristy's really got a good deal in her new place – she has anything she wants (within reason) plus built-in baby-sitting charges. Andrew and Karen, her little stepbrother and stepsister, spend every other weekend (and some inbetween time, too) at Watson's. Watson is Kristy's stepfather.

Then there's Claudia Kishi. Claudia is the vice-chairman of our club. We always hold our meetings in her room, since she has her own phone and even her own private phone number. Claudia's summer event was the saddest of all, but it has a happy ending. Her grandmother Mimi (who lives with the Kishis, and who's a favourite of the Babysitters Club) had a stroke one night in July. She had to stay in the hospital for a long time and she still has to have physical therapy, but she's getting better. She can walk and talk, and someday (maybe) she'll be able to use her right hand a little more.

Dawn Schafer is my new best friend. She's the official alternate officer of the club, which means she can take over the duties of anyone who has to miss a meeting. Her family used to live in California, but her parents got divorced, so her mother moved Dawn and her younger brother Jeff all the way across country to Stoneybrook, Connecticut. Claudia and Kristy and I grew up here, but New England has been kind of an adjustment for Dawn. Anyway, over the summer, Dawn and Jeff got to fly to California to visit their father, and (after they'd come back) Dawn discovered a secret passage in the old farmhouse she lives in!

The fourth member of the club is Stacey McGill. She's our treasurer, and also sort of a newcomer to Stoneybrook. She moved here exactly one year ago from big, glamorous, exciting New York City. Stacey, by the way, is sort of glamorous and exciting herself. That's why she and Claudia are best friends. They're both sophisticated and love wearing flashy clothes and weird jewellery and doing things to their hair. The two of them really stand out in a crowd, and I've always been envious of them.

Anyway, Stacey's summer excitement was mine, too. We got jobs as mother's helpers with one of the families we sit for and went with them to the beach – Sea City, New Jersey. We stayed in Sea City for two weeks and not only had a great time, but found boys we liked! I guess that wasn't such a big deal for Stacey, but it was a big deal for me. I'm kind of shy and tend to be on the quiet side, I'd never been very interested in boys, either. This wasn't because I didn't like them; it was because I was afraid of them. I used to think, What do you say to a boy? Then I realized you can talk to a boy the same way you talk to a girl. You just have to choose your topics more carefully. Obviously, with a boy, you can't talk about bras or cute guys you see on TV, but you can talk about school and movies and animals and sports (if you know anything about sports).

When Stacey and I were in Sea City, Stacey started out by being a real pain. She fell in luv (as she always writes it) with this gorgeous lifeguard who was years too old for her, and left me on my own. With no one my age around, I started talking to this nice-looking boy who was hanging around on the beach because he was a mother's helper,

too. We really hit it off. We talked about lots of things, and by the time I had to leave Sea City, we had exchanged rings with our initials on them. We bought them on the pier. I don't know if we'll really write to each other (as we promised), but it's nice to know boys aren't aliens from the planet Snorzak or something.

Ding-dong. The doorbell. I wasn't sure how long I'd been lying on my bed day-dreaming. I looked at my watch. It was almost time for our last Babysitters Club meeting of the summer.

"Coming!" I called.

I ran out of my bedroom down the stairs, and through the hall to the front door. I peered through the window. Dawn was standing on the steps. She sometimes comes to my house before a meeting, and then we walk over to Claudia's together.

"Hi!" she greeted me. Dawn was fussing with her hair. She has the longest hair of anyone I know. It's even longer than Claudia's. And it's pale, pale blonde. Dawn was wearing a pretty snappy outfit – hot-pink shorts with a big, breezy island-print shirt over a white tank top.

"Hi," I replied. "You look really terrific. Is that shirt new?"

Dawn nodded. "Dad sent it to me from California."

"Ooh, don't tell Kristy," I said.

"I know. I won't."

Kristy never hears from her real father. He hasn't been very nice to her, or to her brothers. He doesn't even send them birthday cards any more. I'm glad she's got Watson now. If she'll just let herself like him a little more . . .

"We better go," said Dawn.

"Okay, I'm ready. Let me make sure I have my house key." I found my key and locked the front door. I'm usually the only one home during the day. My dad is a lawyer and he works long hours, I don't have any brothers or sisters, and my mother died when I was little. I barely remember her. Sometimes it's lonely at my house. I wish I had a cat.

Dawn and I crossed my front yard, and I stopped to check our mailbox.

"Aughh!" I shrieked when I opened the box. "It's here! It came!"

"What did?" asked Dawn, looking over my shoulder.

"*Sixteen* magazine. Oh, no! I'm dying! Look who's on the cover. It's Cam Geary! Isn't he adorable? The last issue had an article about him, but here's his gorgeous picture – " (I gasped) "– and a poster of him, too. A free poster!"

Dawn looked at me, amazed. "You sure have changed this summer, Mary Anne," she said. "I've hardly ever heard you talk so much. And I've *never* seen you go this crazy over a boy."

I flinched, remembering how, not long ago, I'd been accusing Stacey of talking about boys too much. But Dawn didn't seem annoyed.

We crossed the street and Claudia's lawn. Dawn rang the Kishis' bell.

"But Cam is *ador*able," I said, hugging the magazine to me. "It's those eyes of his. They're so . . . so . . ."

"Hello, girls," Mimi greeted us, speaking slowly and clearly. The Kishis are Japanese and Mimi has always spoken English with an accent, but she isn't hard to understand. She speaks slowly now because of the stroke. "The other girls are here. They are in Claudia's room," she told us.

"We're the last ones?" I cried. "We'd better hurry. Come on, Dawn." I paused long enough to give Mimi a kiss. Then Dawn and I raced upstairs. As we ran by Janine's room (Janine is Claudia's older sister), we called hello to her, but we didn't stop. We didn't stop until we were in Babysitters Club headquarters. We closed the door behind us and flopped on the floor. The good spots were already taken – Stacey and Claudia were lying on the bed, and Kristy was sitting in the director's chair as usual. (She loves being in charge.)

"How did you get over here so early?" Dawn asked Kristy. Now that Kristy lives across town, she depends on her big brother Charlie to drive her to and from meetings.

The Babysitters Club pays him to do that. It's part of running our business.

Kristy shrugged. "Charlie wanted to leave early. He was on his way to the shopping centre . . . Well, let's get started."

"Oh, Kristy," said Claudia. "We don't have to be in a rush. This is our last meeting of the summer. Nobody has to go anywhere. Let's have some refreshments first."

I grinned. Refreshments to Claudia are junk food. She's addicted to the stuff and has it hidden all over her room. I watched her reach inside her pillowcase. Then her hand emerged with two bags – one of gumdrops, one of crisps. The crisps were for everybody. The gumdrops were for herself and Kristy and me. Dawn won't eat them because she says they're too unhealthy, and Stacey can't eat them because she has diabetes and has to stay on a strict diet – no extra sweets.

While Claudia passed around the food, Kristy got out our club record book and our notebook. She handed the record book to me. As secretary, it's my job to keep it up-to-date. I write down our baby-sitting appointments on the calendar pages and keep track of all sorts of things, such as our clients' addresses and phone numbers. Stacey, the treasurer, is in charge of recording the money we earn.

Our other book, the notebook, is a diary in which we write up every job we go on.

Each of us is responsible for reading the book once a week or so. It takes a lot of time, but it's helpful to know what's happened at the houses where our friends have baby-sat.

"Any club business?" Kristy asked.

The rest of us shook our heads.

"Have you all read the notebook?"

"Yup," we replied.

"Okay. Great. Well, we'll just wait for the phone to ring."

The club meets three times a week – Monday, Wednesday, and Friday – from five-thirty until six. Our clients know that they can call Claudia's number at those times and reach the five of us. They like the arrangement because they're bound to find a sitter.

I leant back against Claudia's bed, opened *Sixteen*, and gazed at the free poster.

"Who's that? Cam Geary?" asked Stacey, peering over the edge of the bed at the picture.

I nodded. "Mr Gorgeous."

"You know who he goes out with?" said Claudia.

"Who?" replied Stacey.

"Corrie Lalique."

"Corrie Lalique?" she shrieked. "The girl from 'Once Upon a Dream'? Does he really?"

"I read it in *Young Teen*," said Claudia.

"I read it in *Sixteen*," I added.

"But she's too old for him," Stacey protested.

"No she's not," Kristy spoke up. "She's fourteen."

Now it was my turn to be surprised. "You're kidding! Have you noticed the size of her – the size of her . . ."

"Chest?" supplied Claudia. "Well, she is kind of big, but believe me, Kristy's right. She's only fourteen. And she *is* going out with Cam."

"Boy –" I began, but I was interrupted by the phone.

Dawn answered it. "Hello, Babysitters Club," she said. "Oh, hi! . . . When? . . . Okay . . . Okay. I'll call you right back . . . 'Bye."

Dawn hung up the phone, I was already holding the record book in my lap, opened to the appointment calendar.

"Mrs Prezzioso needs someone for Jenny on Saturday afternoon, from four until about six-thirty," said Dawn.

This was met by groans. "I'll just check my own schedule," I replied. I'm the only one who likes Jenny at all. The others think she's bratty. It's a club rule that a job has to be offered to all the club members (not snapped up by the person who takes the call or something), but I didn't even bother to see if Kristy or Stacey or Claudia or Dawn was free. They wouldn't want the job. "Tell Mrs Prezzioso I can sit," I said to Dawn as I noted my job in the appointment book.

Dawn called Mrs Prezzioso back. When she got off the phone, Kristy's mother called needing a sitter for David Michael one afternoon when Kristy had a dentist's appointment. Then Dr Johanssen called needing a sitter for Charlotte, and Mrs Barrett called needing a sitter for Buddy, Suzi, and Marnie. It was a busy meeting. With school starting again, business was probably going to pick up a little. Everyone's schedules seemed to become more crowded.

The meeting was supposed to be over at six, but we all kind of hung around. No one wanted to end our last summer meeting. Finally I had to leave, though. So did Kristy. "See you in . . ." (gulp) ". . . school tomorrow!" she called, and I wanted to cry. Summer was really and truly over.

2nd CHAPTER

Claudia and Stacey and I walked to school together the next morning, since the three of us live in the same neighbourhood. It was the first time ever that Kristy and I hadn't walked off together on day number one of the school year. But Kristy had to take the bus from her new home. (Dawn, who lived not too far way, often took a different route to school, and sometimes her mother drove her there on the way to work.)

I was all set for eighth grade. My brand-new folder was filled with fresh paper; I had inserted neatly labelled dividers, one for each subject, among the paper; and a pencil case containing pens, pencils, a rubber, a ruler, and a pack of chewing gum was clipped to the inside front cover. My lunch money was in my purse, the photo of Cam Geary was folded and ready to be displayed in my locker. (That was what the chewing gum was for. You're not allowed to tape things up in the lockers of Stoneybrook Middle School, so a lot of kids get around that rule by sticking them up with bits of freshly chewed gum.) The only thing about me not ready for eighth grade was my age. I had the latest birthday of all my friends and wouldn't turn thirteen for several more weeks.

Starting eighth grade seemed like a breeze to me. I'd been a chicken when we'd begun sixth grade, and I was going to be one of the youngest kids in the school. I hadn't been much better when we'd started seventh grade the year before. But now I felt like king of the hill. The eighth-graders were the oldest kids in school. We would get to do special things during the year. We would have a real graduation ceremony in June. After that, we would go on to the high school. Pretty important stuff.

But I couldn't decide whether to be excited or disappointed about the beginning of school. When we reached Stoneybrook Middle School, Stacey and Claudia and I just looked at each other.

Finally Claudia said, "Well, goodbye, summer."

Then Stacey started speaking in her Porky Pig voice. "Th-th-th-th-th-th-th-that's all, folks!" she exclaimed, waving her hand.

Claudia and I laughed. Then we split up.

There were three eighth-grade classrooms, and we were each in a different one. I went to my locker first, working half a piece of chewing gum around in my mouth on the way. "Hello, old locker," I said to myself as I spun the dial on number 132. I opened the door. This was the only morning all year that my locker would be absolutely empty when I opened it. I pulled the poster of Cam Geary out of my folder and set the folder and my purse on the shelf of the locker. Then I unfolded the poster. I took the gum out of my mouth, checked the hall for teachers, and divided the gum into four bits, one for each corner. There. The poster stayed up nicely. I could look at Cam's gorgeous face all year.

I picked up my folder and purse, closed my locker, and made my way upstairs. The corridors were already pretty crowded. Kids showed up early (or at least on time) for the first day of school.

My classroom was 216, about as far from my locker as you could get. I entered it breathlessly, then slowed down. Suddenly I felt shy. Dawn was supposed to be in my classroom but she wasn't there yet. The room was full of kids I didn't know very well. And where was I supposed to sit? The teacher, Mr Blake, was at his desk, but he looked busy. Had he planned on assigned seating? Could we sit wherever we wanted? I stood awkwardly by the door.

"Mary Anne! Hi!" said someone behind me.

Oh, thank goodness. It was Dawn.

I spun around. "Hi! I just got here," I told her.

Mr Blake still wasn't paying attention to the kids gathering in his room.

"Let's sit at the back," suggested Dawn.

So we did. We watched Erica Blumberg and Shawna Riverson compare tans. We watched a new kid creep into the room and choose a seat in a corner without looking at anyone. We watched three boys whisper about Erica and Shawna.

At last the teacher stood up. "Register-call," he announced, and the first day of school was truly under way.

This was my morning schedule:

First Period - English
Second period - maths
Third period - gym (yuck)
Fourth period - social studies
Fifth period - lunch.

My afternoon schedule wasn't so bad: science, study hall, and French class. But I thought my morning schedule was sort of heavy, and by lunchtime I was starving.

Kristy (who was in my social studies class) raced down to the dining hall with me. We claimed the table we used to sit at last year with Dawn and some of our other friends. (Stacey and Claudia usually sat with their own group of kids.) In a moment Dawn showed up. She settled down and opened her lunch bag while Kristy and I went through the lunch line. Last year we'd brought our lunches, too. This year we'd decided brown bags looked babyish.

When we returned to the table with our trays, we were surprised to find Stacey and Claudia there with *their* trays. Since when had they decided to eat with us? We were good friends, but last year they always thought they were so much more sophisticated than we were. They liked to talk about boys and movie stars and who was going out with whom . . . Had Stacey and Claudia changed, or had Kristy and Dawn and I? I almost said something, but I decided not to. I knew we were all thinking that eating together was different and nice – and also that we weren't going to mention that it was happening.

I opened my milk carton, put my napkin in my lap, and took a good long look at the Stoneybrook Middle School hot lunch.

"What *is* this?" I asked the others.

"Noodles," replied Kristy.

"No, it's poison," said Dawn, who, as usual, was eating a health-food lunch – a container of strawberries, a yoghurt with dried fruit mixed in, some dried apple slices, and something I couldn't identify.

"I don't see any noodles here," I said. "Only glue."

"According to the menu, that glue is mushroom and cream sauce," said Claudia.

"Ew," I replied.

"So," said Dawn, "how was everybody's first morning back at school?"

"Fine, Mummy," answered Stacey.

Dawn giggled.

"I have third-period gym with Mrs Rosenauer," I said. "I hate hockey, I hate Mrs Rosenauer, and I hate smelling like gym class for the next five periods . . . Do I smell like gym class?" I leant towards Kristy.

She pulled back "*I'm* not going to smell you . . . Hey, I just worked something out. You know what the mushroom sauce tastes like? It tastes like a dirty sock that's been left out in the rain and then hidden in a dark cupboard for three weeks."

The rest of us couldn't decide whether to gag or giggle.

Maybe this was why Claudia and Stacey didn't sit with us last year. I changed the subject. "I put the poster of Cam Geary up in my locker this morning," I announced. "I'm going to leave him there all year."

"I want to find a picture of Max Morrison," said Claudia. "That's who I'd like in my locker."

"The boy from 'Out of This World'?" asked Stacey.

Claudia nodded.

I absolutely couldn't eat another bite of the noodles, not after what Kristy had said about the sauce. I gazed around the lunch room. I saw Trevor Sandbourne, one of Claudia's old boyfriends from last year. I saw the Shillaber twins, who used to sit with Kristy and Dawn and me. They were sitting with the only set of boy twins in school. (For a moment, I thought I had double vision.) I saw Erica and Shawna from my class. And then I saw Cam Geary.

I nearly spat out a mouthful of milk.

"Stacey!" I whispered after I'd managed to swallow. "Cam Geary goes to our school! Look!"

All my friends turned to look. "Where? Where?"

"That boy?" said Stacey, smiling. "That's not Cam Geary. That's Logan Bruno. He's new this year. He's in my class and my English class. I talked to him during registration. He used to live in Louisville, Kentucky. He has a southern accent."

I didn't care what he sounded like. He was the cutest boy I'd ever seen. He looked exactly like Cam Geary. I was in love with him. And because Stacey already knew so much about him, I was jealous of her. What a way to start the year.

3rd CHAPTER

The next day, Friday, was the second day of school, and the end of the first "week" of school. And that night, the members of the Babysitters Club held the first meeting of eighth grade. Every last one of us just barely made the meeting on time. Claudia had been working on an art project at school (she loves art and is terrific at it), Dawn had been baby-sitting for the Pikes, Stacey had been at school at a meeting of the dance committee, of which she's vice chairman, Kristy had had to wait for Charlie to get home from football practice before he could drive her to the meeting, and I'd been trying to get my weekend homework done before the weekend.

The five of us turned up at five-thirty on the dot, and the phone was ringing as we reached Claudia's room. Dawn grabbed for it, while I tried to find the club record book.

Everything was in chaos.

"I love it!" said Kristy when we had settled down.

"You love what?" asked Claudia.

"The excitement, the fast pace."

"You should move to New York," said Stacey.

"No, I'm serious. When things get hectic like this, I get all sorts of great ideas. Summertime is too slow."

"What kinds of great ideas do you get?" asked Dawn, who doesn't know Kristy quite the way the rest of us do. I was pretty sure that Kristy's ideas were going to lead to extra work for the club.

I was right.

"Did you notice the sign in school today?" asked Kristy.

"Kristy, there must have been three thousand signs," replied Claudia. "I saw one for the Remember September Dance, one for the Chess Club, one for cheerleader tryouts, one for class elections –"

"This sign," Kristy interrupted, "was for the PTA. There's going to be a PTA meeting at Stoneybrook Middle School in a few days."

"So?" said Stacey. "PTA stands for Parent Teacher Association. We're kids. It doesn't concern us."

"Oh, yes it does," replied Kristy, "because where there are *parents* there are *children*, and where there are children, there are parents needing baby-sitters – *us*. That's where we come in."

"*Oh*," I said knowingly. Kristy is so clever. She's such a good businesswoman. That's why she's the chairman of our club. "More advertising?" I asked.

"Right," replied Kristy.

The phone rang again then, and we stopped to take another job. When we had finished, Kristy continued. "We've got to advertise in school. We'll put up posters where the parents will see them when they come for the meeting."

"Maybe," added Dawn, "we could make up some more fliers and work out some way for the parents to get them at the meeting. I think it's always better if people have something they can take with them. You know, something to put up on their fridge or by their phone."

"Terrific idea," said Kristy, who usually isn't too generous with her praise.

Dawn beamed.

"There's something else," Kristy went on after we'd lined up jobs with the Marshalls and the Perkinses. "When we started this club, it was so that we could baby-sit in our neighbourhood, and the four of us – " (Kristy pointed to herself, Claudia, Stacey, and me) "– all lived in the same neighbourhood. Then Dawn joined the club, and we found some new clients in her neighbourhood. Now *I've* moved, but I, um, I – I haven't, um . . ."

It was no secret that Kristy had resented moving out of the Thomases' comfortable old split-level and across town to Watson's mansion in his wealthy neighbourhood. Of course she liked having a big room with a queen-sized bed and getting treats and being able to have lots of new clothes and stuff. But she'd been living over there for about two months, and hadn't made any effort to get to know the people in her new neighbourhood. Her brothers had made an effort, and so had her mother, but Kristy claimed that the kids her age were snobs. She and the Thomases' old collie, Louie, kept pretty much to themselves.

I tried to help her through her embarrassment. "It would be good business sense," I pointed out, "to advertise where you live. We should be leaving fliers in the mailboxes over on Edgerstoune Drive and Green House Drive and Bissell Lane."

"And Haslet Avenue and Ober Road, too," said Claudia.

"Right," said Kristy, looking relieved. "After all, I know Linny and Hannie Papadakis – they're friends of David Michael and Karen. They must need a sitter every now and then. And there are probably plenty of other little kids, too."

"And," said Stacey, adding the one thing the rest of us didn't have the nerve to say, "it might be a good way for you to meet people over there."

Kristy scowled. "Oh, right. All those snobs."

"Kristy, they can't *all* be snobs," said Dawn.

"The ones I met were snobs," Kristy said defiantly. "But what does it matter? We might get some new business."

"Well," I said, "can your mum do some more xeroxing for us?"

Kristy's mother (who used to be Mrs Thomas and is now Mrs Brewer) usually takes one of our fliers to her office and xeroxes it on the machine there when we need more copies. The machine is so fancy, the fliers almost look as if they'd been printed.

"Sure," replied Kristy, "only this time we'll have to give her some money for the xerox paper. We've used an awful lot of it. What's in the treasury, Stacey?"

Stacey dumped out the contents of a manila envelope. The money in it is our club subs. We each get to keep anything we earn baby-sitting (we don't try to divide it), but we contribute weekly subs of a dollar each to the club. The money pays Charlie for driving Kristy to club meetings and buys any supplies we might need.

"We've got a little over fifteen dollars," said our treasurer.

"Well, I don't know how much xerox

paper costs," said Kristy, "but it's only paper. How many pieces do you think we'll need?"

"A hundred?" I guessed. "A hundred and fifty?"

Kristy took eight dollars out of the treasury. "I'll bring back the change," she said. She looked at her watch. "Boy, only ten more minutes left. This meeting sure went fast."

"We couldn't come early and we can't leave late," said Dawn. "Summer's over."

There was a moment of silence. Even the phone didn't ring.

"I found a picture of Max Morrison," Claudia said finally. "It was in *People* magazine. I'm going to take it to school on Monday."

"Where is it now?" asked Stacey.

"Here." Claudia took it out of her desk drawer and handed it to Stacey.

"Look at his eyes," said Stacey with a sigh.

"No one's eyes are more amazing than Cam's," I said. "Except maybe Logan Bruno's." I'd seen Logan several more times since lunch the day before. Each time I'd thought he was Cam Geary at first. I wished I'd had an excuse to talk to him, but there was none. We didn't have any classes together, so of course he didn't know who I was.

"Logan Bruno?" Claudia repeated

sharply. "Hey, you don't . . . you do! I think you like him, Mary Anne!"

Luckily, I was saved by the ringing of the telephone. I took the call myself, and Stacey ended up with a job at the Newtons'.

By the time I had called Mrs Newton back and noted the job in our appointment book, my friends were on to another subject.

"Kara Mauricio got a bra yesterday," said Dawn.

I could feel myself blushing. I cleared my throat. "I, um, I um, I um –"

"Spit it out, Mary Anne," said Kristy.

"I, um got a bra yesterday."

"You *did*?" Kristy squeaked.

I nodded. "Dad came home early. He took me to the department store and a saleswoman helped me."

"Was it *awfully* embarrassing?" asked Dawn. "At least my mother helped me get my first one. She kept the saleswomen away."

Kristy was gaping at me. We've both always been as flat as pancakes, but I'd begun to grow a little over the summer. Kristy must have felt left out. She was the only one of us who didn't wear a bra now.

But suddenly she was all business again. She doesn't like us to get off the subject of the club for *too* long during meetings. "Let's try to get these fliers out next week. Business will really be booming. Who can help me distribute them?"

We looked at our schedules. A few minutes later, the meeting was over. Little did we know what we were getting ourselves into.

4th CHAPTER

"Emergency club meeting at lunch! Tell Kristy!" Claudia flew by me in the hall, her black hair flowing behind her. I caught a whiff of some kind of perfume.

"Wait! What –?" I started to ask, but Claudia had already been swallowed up by the crowd.

I thought over what she had just said. Emergency meeting . . . *tell Kristy*. That meant Kristy didn't know. But our chairman was usually the one to call emergency meetings. So who had called it? And what was going on? It was only the beginning of third period. I'd have to wait more than an hour and a half to find out.

I caught Kristy at the beginning of social studies class. "Emergency meeting at lunch today," I said urgently, leaning across the aisle to her desk.

"Who called it?" Kristy asked immediately, but before I could tell her that I didn't know, our teacher walked in the room.

I snapped back to my desk like a rubber band.

When the class was over, Kristy and I shot out of the room and ran to the dining hall. We dumped our stuff on our usual table, staking out five chairs at one end. Then we joined the hot-lunch line.

"I wonder what it is today," I said, breathing deeply.

"Smells like steamed rubber in car wax."

"Kristy, that is so disgusting. What is it really?"

Kristy stood on tiptoe, trying to see over the tops of kids' heads. She jumped up and down a few times. "I don't know," she said finally. "Maybe macaroni cheese. I can't really see."

She was right. It was macaroni cheese. Plus limp broccoli, a cup of tinned fruit salad, and milk. Kristy and I each bought a chocolate eclair, since we don't like macaroni or tinned fruit salad. Kristy even considered buying two since she doesn't like broccoli, either, but I stopped her. As it was, Dawn was going to die when she saw our lunches.

But when we got to our table we didn't have much time to talk about food. Stacey and Claudia had been not far behind us on

the line, and Dawn was already there. So as soon as we had settled down, Kristy said abruptly, "Who called this meeting?"

"I did," said Claudia. "I'm going crazy. I can't handle everything. I've been getting non-stop phone calls ever since that PTA meeting, and since we advertised in your neighbourhood, Kristy. I don't mind if people call during our meetings, of course, or once or twice in the evenings, but they're calling all the time. Look at this." She pulled a list out of her notebook. "These calls came last night. And this one came at seven-thirty this morning."

We leant forward to look at the paper. It was a list of seven names with phone numbers, and notes that said things like "3 kids, 2b, 1g" or "allergic to pets" or "6 yrs, 4yrs, 3 yrs". None of the names was familiar.

"I would have phoned you guys last night to offer the jobs around as they came in, but that would have meant more than twenty calls. Mum and Dad would have killed me. I'm already behind in my maths and English homework." (Claudia is a fabulous artist, but she's not a very good student. In fact, she's only allowed to be in the Babysitters Club if she keeps her grades up, which for her means Cs.)

"Anyway," Claudia continued, "my social studies teacher assigned a big project this morning, and I guess I just panicked.

That was when I called the meeting. I really don't see how I can take art classes, go to school, babysit, and be vice-chairman of the club, too."

Claudia looked near to tears, which was unusual for her.

Stacey must have noticed, because she put her hand on Claudia's arm and said, "Hey, Claud, it's okay. Really. We'll work everything out."

"Sure we will," said Dawn.

"We'll take it step by step," added Kristy. She forced down a mouthful of macaroni cheese. "First things first. What did you tell these people when they called?"

(Kristy really was feeling sorry for Claudia, but you could tell that, underneath, she was thrilled with all the new business we were getting.)

"I told them they would definitely have a sitter, but that I'd have to call them back to say who'd be taking the job."

"Perfect," said Kristy. "That was a good idea."

"Excuse me," I interrupted, "but we can save Claudia a little time if the *sitter* calls back. Claudia shouldn't have to do that."

"Right," said Kristy. "Now let's just hope we can schedule all those jobs."

"I brought the record book with me," said Claudia. She pulled it out from between her maths book and a reading book. "I know we're not supposed to bring it to school, but I wanted to get this straightened out today, even if we didn't have an actual meeting." (Once, months and months ago, we'd been bringing the record book to school, and Alan Gray, this big pest, had stolen information out of it and used the information to torment Kristy and Claudia.)

"That's all right," said Kristy. "Just be careful with it. Now let's see." She peered at Claudia's list, trying to read her sloppy handwriting. "The first job is on Friday, from six until eight, right?"

Claudia nodded. "A cocktail party."

We turned to the appointment calendar and began assigning jobs. It took some doing but we were able to take care of all of them. Stacey only had to miss one meeting of the dance committee, and Claudia only had to switch around a pottery class.

"Whew," I said, when we had finished.

"You know, that wasn't easy. I'm beginning to wonder if . . ." I paused and unwrapped my lolly thoughtfully.

"If what?" asked Dawn.

"If we're in over our heads. Maybe we have *too much* business. What happens if we start getting a lot of jobs we can't handle? What do we tell our clients?"

"Tell them we're busy," suggested Claudia.

"Once or twice, yes. But what if it happens a lot? We shouldn't advertise that we can babysit – and then not be able to do it," I pointed out.

"That's true," said Kristy, looking worried for the first time.

"And," I said, starting to feel a little annoyed with her for not having thought about these things in advance, "we definitely shouldn't do any more advertising. We were already pretty busy as it was."

Everyone looked at me. It wasn't the first time I'd criticized Kristy, but I don't do things like that very often.

Kristy bristled. "If you remember, we advertised in my neighbourhood so I could get some jobs nearby. Our regular clients would rather have one of *you* sit than *me*, because *somebody* has to drive *me* back to *your* old neighbourhood each time *I* have a job there." Kristy stuck her fork viciously into a spear of broccoli but couldn't bring herself to take a bite.

"Okay, okay," I said grumpily, "but we didn't have to advertise at the PTA meeting." Nobody could argue with that.

After an uncomfortable silence, Claudia, who had calmed down, said practically, "Well, we can't un-advertise, so we'd better just figure out what to do. We're too busy. How are we going to handle the problem?"

"I've done a lot of baby-sitting," spoke up an unfamiliar male voice.

The five members of the Babysitters Club swivelled their heads towards the

opposite end of the long table.

"In Louisville," the voice continued. "I've had plenty of experience."

I froze. I froze into an ice statue of Mary Anne. I couldn't even blink my eyes. The voice belonged to Logan Bruno, the wonderful, amazing Cam Geary look-alike.

He really did have a southern accent, too. It sounded as if he'd just said, "In Luevulle. Ah've haid plainy of expuryence."

My friends began to fall all over each other.

"*Really*?" asked Stacey, as if it were the most interesting thing anyone in the history of the world had ever said.

"You're a *sitter*?" exclaimed Claudia, tossing her hair over her shoulder.

"I don't believe it!" cried Dawn.

"Why don't you come and talk to us?" asked Kristy.

(I was tongue-tied. My mouth was still frozen.)

Logan was out of his chair in a flash, as if he'd been waiting for the invitation since the beginning of lunch period. The boys he'd been sitting with said (loudly) things like, "Go, Logan!" and "Whoa!" and punched him on the arm, grinning, as he walked to our end of the table. He sat down next to me.

If anything should have made me melt, it was Logan, but I was frozen solid. I couldn't even turn my head to look into his dark eyes. I was dying.

"Hi," said Logan lightly, as if he were used to plopping himself down with a bunch of strange girls. "I'm Logan Bruno." He looked around at us. "Oh, hi, Stacey," he added, and a little wave of jealousy washed over me.

"Hi," replied Stacey. "Logan, these are my friends." She pointed to each of us in turn. "Claudia Kishi, Dawn Schafer, Kristy Thomas, and Mary Anne Spier."

Logan smiled warmly at me, but I couldn't return the smile.

"I didn't mean to eavesdrop," he said, "but I did overhear you say that you were sort of in a jam."

"We are," said Kristy. "See, we run this business called the Babysitters Club." Kristy explained how the club had started and how it works. "So you've really done a lot of sitting?" she added when she'd finished.

Logan nodded. "I've got a nine-year-old sister and a five-year-old brother, and I sit for them a lot. And I used to baby-sit for our neighbours, too, when we lived in Louisville. I haven't found anyone to sit for here, though." Logan paused. "I've even taken care of babies. I don't like changing nappies, but . . ." He shrugged as if to say, "It's just part of the job."

"How late can you stay out at night?" asked Kristy.

(We were all staring at Logan. Not one of us could take her eyes off him.)

"Oh, I don't know. I guess about ten-thirty on a weeknight. Maybe midnight on Fridays and Saturdays."

"Super!" exclaimed Stacey.

We all nodded. (I was thawing out.)

"Want to come to our next meeting?" asked Kristy abruptly. "I mean, just to see what the club's all about?"

"Sure," replied Logan. Kristy told him when it was, and then he unfolded his long legs from under the cafeteria table and returned to the boys he'd been sitting with.

"Way to go!" exclaimed one of the boys.

"Yeah," added another. "All those girls. Are you ever lucky."

Suddenly I found myself beaming. The boys were *jealous* of Logan because of *us*. Not only that, Logan was going to attend our next meeting!

5th CHAPTER

Needless to say, I was a nervous wreck before the next meeting of the Babysitters Club. I was sitting for Jamie and Lucy Newton, and Mrs Newton had said she'd be back between five and five-thirty. When she showed up at 4.45, I had never been so glad to make an early getaway. I ran home, locked myself in the bathroom, and studied myself critically in the mirror. My hair is mouse-brown, but it looks okay if I let it flow down over my shoulders. My dad used to be really, really strict, and he made me wear it in plaits, but not anymore. Now I wear it loose. If I just brush it and leave it alone, it ripples nicely, kind of as if I'd had a body wave, which I haven't.

I brushed my hair one hundred times. I don't have any makeup, but I do have some jewellery, so I put on a pair of small hoop earrings and a gold chain bracelet that used

to belong to my mother. Then I took off the sweat shirt I'd been wearing and put on a bright tank-top over a short-sleeved white blouse. I looked . . . not bad.

When it was only five-fifteen I ran to Claudia's. I was not the first one there. We were all excited about Logan Bruno. I met Stacey and Kristy at the front door, and when we reached our club headquarters, we found Claudia and Dawn already lying on the bed. They were eating popcorn.

"I can't wait!" Claudia was squealing.

"I know," said Dawn. "He is *so adorable.*"

They were talking about Logan, of course.

Kristy practically bounced into the director's chair. I trailed after her, the last one into the room.

"Hey!" exclaimed Claudia. "You look nice, Mary Anne!"

"Thanks," I replied, blushing.

There was dead silence.

I didn't think I looked too different, but I must have, because all at once, everyone realized what I was doing.

"It's for Logan, isn't it," said Stacey softly, not even asking a question. She knew she was right.

"Of course not," I replied.

"Oh, come on, Mary Anne. You can tell *us*. We're your friends."

But just then the doorbell rang. Claudia

sprang off her bed and dashed out of the room, through the hall, and down the stairs. A few seconds later, we heard the front door open. Then we heard two voices, one male and one female.

Logan had arrived.

Now, I don't know about Claudia, but there has never been a boy in *my* bedroom. (I mean, a boy who counts. Kristy's little brother doesn't count.) What would a boy have thought of my horse books and Snowman, my white teddy bear? What would a boy have thought of my lacy pillow sham or Lila, my antique doll?

I looked around Claudia's room. There were the four of us, the bowl of popcorn, and this rag doll of Claudia's named Lennie. Before Claudia and Logan reached the top of the stairs, I stuffed Lennie under the bed. Then I checked Claudia's dressing table to make sure there was no underwear sticking out of drawers or anything. Her room wasn't too neat, but it seemed safe.

I cleared a spot on the floor for Logan.

I cleared it next to me.

"Hey, everybody," drawled Logan's familiar voice.

There he was, framed in Claudia's doorway. He looked more handsome than ever.

Claudia was settling herself on the bed again. "Come on in," she said. "Pull up a patch of floor." She began to giggle.

Logan grinned and sat next to me. "Mary Anne, right?" he said.

I nodded. But my tongue felt as if someone had poured glue on it and then covered it with sawdust.

"Let me make sure I have this right," Logan went on. He looked at each of us in turn. "Claudia, um, Kristy . . . Dawn?" (Dawn nodded.) "And Stacey. You, I know."

Stacey smiled charmingly.

"So," said Logan. "What do we do here?" (I loved his southern accent. I *loved* it!)

Kristy, Claudia, Stacey, and Dawn all began to talk.

"We answer the phone."

"People call in."

"We find the record book."

"We look in the treasury."

Logan glanced at me. "What do *you* do?"

The glue and sawdust just wouldn't go away. I tried clearing my throat. Ahem. *Ahem.* "I – " I croaked. "I, um –"

Stacey handed me the record book. She's our secretary," she spoke up. "Mary Anne sets up our appointments."

"Oh," said Logan. "I see." But he gave me a funny look.

At last the phone rang. The five of us jumped for it. Dawn got there first. "Hello, Babysitters Club," she said. "Oh, hi! . . . Yes . . . Monday? . . . Okay, I'll get back to you." She hung up. "That was Mrs Perkins. She has a doctor's appointment next Monday afternoon. She needs someone to watch Myriah and Gabbie from three-thirty till five-thirty." Dawn turned to Logan. "The Perkinses live right across the street. They've got two little girls, and Mrs Perkins is expecting another baby. That's why she has to go to the doctor."

"Okay," said Logan.

"Well, who's free?" asked Dawn, looking at me.

Why was she –? Oh, right. The appointment book. I picked it up, dropped it, picked it up, and dropped it again. Finally Logan handed it to me. I turned to the appointment calendar.

"What day did you say?" I asked Dawn.

"Next Monday."

"Um . . . I'm free and Claudia's free."

"You take it," said Claudia. "I've got to have a little time for my pottery."

"Thanks," I murmured, and pencilled myself in.

Dawn called Mrs Perkins back to tell her who the sitter would be.

"And that's how we work things," said Kristy to Logan as Dawn was hanging up.

"That's great," said Logan. "And you really get a lot of calls?"

As if in answer to his question, the phone rang three more times – Mrs Pike, Mrs Prezzioso, and a new client, a Mr Ohdner,

who needed a sitter for his two daughters. We assigned the jobs – but just barely. Claudia and Stacey were now busy with something every afternoon after school next week.

Claudia passed around the popcorn. Suddenly she burst out laughing. "You know what this reminds me of?" she said, patting the bowl.

"What?" we all asked.

"You know Dorianne Wallingford? Well, last weekend Pete Black takes her to the movies, and about halfway through, he reaches around behind her and snaps her br –" Claudia stopped abruptly.

I knew what she'd been about to say. *Her bra strap.* (Pete was always doing that, just to be mean.) Claudia had almost said *bra strap* in front of a *boy.*

Claudia began to blush. So did I. So did everyone in the room including Logan.

It was awful moment. Logan tried to cover up. "Here, have some," he said, passing me the popcorn.

I don't know how it ended up upside-down but it did.

"Oh, no!" I cried. I scrambled around, trying to put the kernels back in the bowl.

Logan and Stacey leaned over to help and knocked heads.

Somebody had better do something fast, I thought. Bring up a new subject . . . anything.

Claudia must have been a mind-reader because she turned to Logan then and said, "What was your worst baby-sitting experience ever?"

"Well," said Logan (only it sounded like *way-ull*), "let me see. There was the time Tina Lawrence flushed one of her father's ties down the toilet." (We laughed.) "And there was the time my brother got into Mum's lipsticks and coloured the bathroom pink and red. But I think the worst time was when I was sitting for this little kid named Elliott. His mother was trying to toilet-train him and she showed me where his special potty was and everything. All morning after she left I kept asking Elliott if he needed to go, and all morning he kept saying, 'No, no, no.' So finally I took him into the toilet and . . ."

"And what?" I dared to ask.

Logan was blushing again. "I just realized. I can't say that part . . ."

"Oh," I said lamely.

A horrible silence fell over Claudia's room.

I looked at my watch. Ten more minutes before the meeting was over.

"Anyone want some lemonade?" asked Claudia.

"I do!" we all said instantly.

Claudia got to her feet. Logan jumped up and followed her out the door. "I'll help you," he said.

As soon as they were downstairs, the other members of the Babysitters Club began moaning horribly. "Oh, this is so em*bar*rassing," cried Stacey.

"I *know*," said Kristy. "Can we really ask a boy to join the club? I didn't think about stuff like this. We're not even having a normal meeting. At least, it sure doesn't feel like it. We're hardly talking about club stuff at all."

My head was spinning. I wanted Logan to be in the club, but if he joined – would I ever speak again? Or would I have a sawdust-covered tongue for eternity? And would we ever have another nice, normal, businesslike meeting?

When Claudia and Logan returned, Logan sat down next to me and handed me a glass of Diet Coke, while Claudia handed glasses to the others. He smiled at me. "What was *your* worst baby-sitting experience?" he asked.

I'd had several pretty bad ones, but they all flew right out of my head. "Oh . . .I don't, um, know," I mumbled.

Logan nodded. What could he say to that? He turned to Kristy the chatterbox.

"Stacey told me the club was all your idea," he said.

Kristy nodded. "It just sort of came to me one evening," she replied loftily.

Ring, ring.

Kristy reached over and picked up the

phone, somehow managing not to take her eyes off Logan. (The things a cute boy did to our club . . .)

"Hello, Babysitters Club." We all listened to Kristy's end of the conversation. From the questions she was asking, I could tell the caller was another new client. When she hung up the phone, she said, "Okay, that was someone named Mrs Rodowsky. She has three boys. They're nine, seven, and four. They live way over on Reilly Lane. She picked up one of our fliers at the PTA meeing."

"Reilly Lane?" interrupted Logan. "Isn't that near where I live?"

"Yup," said Kristy. "A few streets over. And I'd like you to take the job. They'd be good clients for you, living nearby with three boys and all. The only thing is – I hope you don't mind – I'd kind of like one of us to, you know, see you in action first. I mean, I know you've done a lot of baby-sitting, but . . ."

"That's okay," said Logan. "I understand."

"Oh, good," said Kristy. "Well then, even though there's only going to be one of the Rodowsky boys to sit for next week – the seven-year-old – I want two baby-sitters to go on the job. Logan and someone who's free. Mary Anne?"

For I once I was on my toes. I picked up the record book. "What day?" I asked.

"Thursday. Three-thirty till six."

I looked at Thursday. I gasped. Then I clenched my throat. "I'm the only one free," I croaked.

Logan smiled at me. "I guess we've got the job," he said.

I nearly fainted. "I guess so," I replied.

6th CHAPTER

Kristy had called Mrs Rodowsky back and explained why two sitters would be coming for the price of one. Mrs Rodowsky had been very impressed and said we sounded responsible and mature.

Maybe that's how we had *sounded*, but I *felt* like I had spaghetti for bones. I'd felt that way ever since the club meeting. Now it was the day Logan and I were supposed to baby-sit.

I met him in front of the Rodowskys' at 3.25. As soon as I saw him, my legs and arms felt all floppy. The sawdust returned to my tongue. It was like this every time I got within a mile of him. Or even if someone mentioned his name.

"Hi!" Logan called.

I was going to have to shape up. I really was. This was a job. This was business. I couldn't have spaghetti-bones and a

sawdust-tongue while I was trying to baby-sit.

"Hi!" I replied brightly. I smiled. (There. That hadn't been so bad.)

"Ready?" asked Logan. He smiled, too.

"I hope so," I said. "How much trouble can one little kid be?" (Obviously, I wasn't thinking straight. Otherwise, Jenny Prezzioso would have come to mind, and I'd have kept my mouth shut.)

Logan and I walked to the Rodowskys' front door and Logan rang the bell. It was answered by a tall, thin woman wearing blue jeans and a denim jacket. She didn't look like most mothers I knew.

"Hello," she said. "You must be Mary Anne and Logan. I'm Mariel Rodowsky. Call me Mariel. Come on in." She held the door open for us.

Logan and I stepped inside.

"Jackie!" Mrs Rodowsky called. (I just couldn't think of her as Mariel. It's hard to call adults by their first names.) "Your sitters are here."

We heard footsteps on a staircase, and in a moment, a red-haired, red-cheeked, freckle-faced little boy bounded into the front hall.

"This is Jackie," said Mrs Rodowsky. "Jackie, this is Mary Anne, and this is Logan."

"Hi," Logan and I said at the same time.

"Hi," replied Jackie. "I got a grass-hopper. Wanna see him?"

"Honey," his mother said, "let me talk to Logan and Mary Anne first. Then you can show them the grasshopper." Mrs Rodowsky turned back to us. "Jackie's brothers have lessons at the YMCA today and I have a meeting. I've left the number of both the YMCA and the Stoneybrook Historical Society by the telephone. We should be back at six or a little before. I guess that's it. Jackie's used to sitters. You shouldn't have any problems. Just . . . just keep your eye on him, okay?"

"Oh, sure," said Logan. "That's what we're here for."

"Great," said Mrs Rodowsky with a smile.

(One point for Logan, I thought. He was good with parents.)

A few minutes later, Mrs Rodowsky left with two other redheaded boys.

Jackie began jumping on the couch in the playroom.

"Boing! Boing! Boing!" he cried. "I'm a basketball! Watch me make a basket!"

Jackie took a terrific leap off the couch, his knees tucked under his chin as if he were going to cannonball into a swimming pool. Logan caught him just before he crashed into the piano.

I'm not sure what I would have done if *I'd* caught Jackie, but Logan raised him in the air and shouted, "Yes, it's the deciding basket, fans! The Rodowsky Rockets have won the Interstellar Championship, and it's all due to Jackie, the human basketball!" Then he carried him away from the couch and the piano. (Another point for Logan.)

I hung back. This was really Logan's job, not mine. I was just along to watch.

Jackie giggled. He squirmed out of Logan's arms. "I gotta show you guys my grasshopper," he said. "His name is Elizabeth."

"You've got a grasshopper named Elizabeth?" said Logan.

"A *boy* grasshopper?" I added.

"Yup," replied Jackie. "I'll go get him for you. Be right back."

Jackie dashed up the stairs.

Logan glanced at me. "Whoa," he said. "That kid's got energy."

I nodded, feeling shy.

Logan wandered into the living room and waited. I followed him.

"Mr and Mrs Rodowsky must have their hands full," Logan commented.

"Probably," I managed to reply.

"Maybe they'll need sitters often," he added. "I wouldn't mind."

I gazed at the walls of the Rodowskys' living room. They were covered with the boys' artwork, professionally framed. Logan wandered over to one of the pictures – a house formed by a red square with a black triangle sitting on top of it. A green line below indicated grass, a blue line above indicated sky. A yellow sun peeked out of the corner.

"Well, what do you know," said Logan. "We've got a painting just like this at our house. Only it says *Logan* at the bottom, not *Jackie*. And all these years I thought it was an original."

I giggled. We had one of them, too. Why couldn't I say so? I looked at the other painting. Logan picked up a magazine.

"It's, um, it's – its' taking Jackie an awfully long time to – " I was stammering, when suddenly we heard a noise from upstairs.

KER-THUD!

The crash was followed by a cry.

Logan and I glanced at each other. Then we ran for the stairs. Logan reached them first. We dashed to the first floor.

"Jackie!" Logan bellowed. "Where are you?"

"Ow! . . . I'm in the bathroom."

Logan made a sharp left and skidded to a stop. I was right behind him. Jackie was sitting on the floor. The shower curtain was in a heap around him, and the rod that had held the curtain was sticking crazily out of the tub.

My first thought was to run to Jackie, give him a hug, and find out what had happened. But I hung back. This was Logan's job.

"Are you hurt?" exclaimed Logan.

"Nope," said Jackie. He stood up.

"Well, what happened?"

(So far, so good, I thought. But as far as I was concerned, Logan had made one mistake. After letting Jackie go upstairs alone, he had let far too much time go by. He should have checked on him after just a couple of minutes. Minus one point.)

Jackie looked a little sheepish. "Today in gym we were exercising. We were climbing ropes and chinning on these bars –"

"And you thought you'd try chinning on the curtain rod," Logan interrupted.

"Yeah," said Jackie. "How did you know?"

"I did it myself once."

Jackie nodded. (What was this? Some sort of boy's ritual I'd never heard of?) "I stood on the edge of the tub," said Jackie, "grabbed on to the rod, and as soon as I pulled myself up, the bar crashed down!"

"When I did it, I had to have six stitches taken in my lip," said Logan. "Look, here's the scar."

I shook my head. Logan hadn't checked Jackie for bumps or cuts, and he hadn't told him not to try chinning again. I waited a few moments longer. The boys were discussing gym class catastrophes. It was time to break in.

"Um, Jackie," I said, "I'm glad you're not hurt, but you better let us check you over, just in case."

Logan looked at me in surprise. "Oh, yeah," he said. "Good idea."

I checked Jackie's arms and legs while Logan rehung the curtain rod. A bruise was already coming out on the one of Jackie's knees, but it didn't look too bad. "Now let me feel your head," I said. "You wouldn't want a big goose egg, would you?"

"Goose egg?" repeated Jackie, giggling.

Logan smiled. "I should have thought of this, Mary Anne," he said. "Sorry. I'm glad you're here."

"Thanks," I said, and actually smiled. (*I* was glad *he* was there.) I decided the talk about not chinning could wait until later.

Jackie's head seemed fine. The three of us went downstairs. "I need some juice," Jackie announced. He made a beeline for the fridge and took out a jar of grape juice.

"Better let me pour," said Logan. (Score another point.)

"No, no. I can do it." Jackie got a paper cup and filled it to the brim. "I'll have it in the living room," he said, and before we knew what was happening, he ran out of the kitchen, tripped, and spilled the entire cup of juice on the living room carpet.

"Oh, no," I moaned.

But Logan kept his head. For one thing, the carpet was dark blue, so the juice didn't show – much. Logan sent Jackie into the kitchen for paper towels. He got busy with water, soap, and finally a little soda water.

When he was done, the rug was smelly and damp, but he assured me there wouldn't be a stain.

I was pretty impressed.

"Hey!" said Jackie. "I never showed you Elizabeth." He started up the stairs.

"We'll come with you," said Logan hastily. (I was relieved. He was doing okay after all.)

We followed Jackie into his bedroom. He removed a jar from the windowsill. "This is Elizabeth," he said softly. He reached into the jar, let Elizabeth crawl onto a finger, pulled his hand up – and found that his hand was stuck.

No matter how we pulled and twisted, Logan and I couldn't get the jar off Jackie's hand.

"Do you think we could break it without cutting Jackie?" I asked.

Logan frowned and shook his head. "I've got a better idea," he said. He went downstairs and returned with a tub of margarine. A few seconds later, Jackie's greasy hand was out of the jar.

"Good thinking!" I exclaimed.

Logan grinned. "What was it you said just before we rang the doorbell this afternoon?"

"I said . . . oh, yeah." (I'd said, "How much trouble can one little kid be?" but I didn't want to repeat that in front of Jackie.)

Before Mrs Rodowsky returned, Jackie

managed to fall off his bicycle, rip his jeans, and later to make *me* fall over backwards into Logan's arms. (Sigh.) I felt that Logan had earned every penny he was paid. I was really proud of the job he'd done – and I was glad the Rodowskys were going to be mostly *his* clients.

As Logan and I crossed the Rodowskys' lawn, the front door safely closed behind us, Logan said, "I'll never forget the look on your face when Jackie spilled that juice."

"I'll never forget the look on your face when the jar got stuck on his hand!"

"And," Logan added, "I'll never forget the look on your face when Jackie knocked you into me."

I blushed furiously.

"Oh, no," said Logan quickly. "It was a *nice* look. Really nice. You know, you have a pretty smile."

I do?

I was melting, melting away. I was turning into a wonderful Mary Anne puddle. And all because of Logan.

7th CHAPTER

Friday

I love ~~mase~~ ~~Myrih~~ Myriah and Gabbie. I really do. But that Chewy. What a dog! This afternoon I was suposed to hav a nise easy siting job at the Perkins but Chewy caused so many problems I can't believe it. Mrs. Perkins asked Gabie and me to meet Myriah when the bus from the comunty center ~~f~~ droped her off we did but we took Chewy whith us. What a mistake! Heres a tip for everyone in the club. Never ever let Chewey out of the bake yard! Im not kidding!!!!

Claudia really wasn't kidding. After her experience, no one will ever let Chewbacca Perkins loose again – unless we're told to walk him or something. He's a sweet, lovable dog, but he's so *big*. And he gets so ex*cit*ed.

Claudia went to the Perkinses' house right after school on Thursday. Gabbie answered the doorbell. "Hi, Claudee Kishi!" she cried, jumping up and down.

"Hiya, Gabbers." Claudia let herself inside.

Gabbie held up her arms. "Toshe me up, please."

Claudia picked her up and gave her a squeeze. Gabbie is very huggable. "Hi, Mrs Perkins," she called.

Mrs Perkins was frantically folding laundry in the living room. "Oh, Claudia, thank goodness you're here. It's been one of those days. The dryer just broke, although not till after I'd done this load, we have a leak in the bathroom, and Gabbie spent all morning gluing stickers to her bedroom door."

"Want to see, Claudee Kishi? My door is very beautiful."

"You did a nice job, sweetie," said Mrs Perkins, struggling with a sheet, "but stickers don't go on doors. They go on paper."

"My door is very beautiful," Gabbie repeated, looking serious.

"Where's Myriah?" asked Claudia.

"Oh, she's at the Community Centre." Mrs Perkins stood up, carrying a pile of folded clothes. "She takes Creative Theatre there on Thursdays after kindergarden. The Community Centre bus will drop her off at the corner of Bradford and Elm. I need you and Gabbie to meet her there at four, okay?"

"Sure," replied Claudia.

"I'll be back a little after five. I have a check-up with the doctor, and then I'm going to drop by a friend's house. Both numbers are stuck on the fridge. So's the number of the Community Centre, just in case."

"Okay. Where's Chewy?"

Mrs Perkins smiled. "You missed his galloping feet? He's out in the back garden. He's fine there."

Chewbacca is a black Labrador retriever. He has more energy than all eight Pike kids plus Jackie Rodowsky put together. The Perkinses have fenced in the entire back garden for him so he has a big safe area to run around in.

Mrs Perkins checked her watch. "Oh, I'm going to be late! Claudia, could you carry these clothes upstairs for me? Leave them anywhere. By the way, the girls can have a snack later. Myriah is usually starving by the time she gets home from the centre."

"Okay," said Claudia. "See you later. We're going to have lots of fun. Right, Gabbers?"

"Right, Claudee Kishi."

Mrs Perkins rushed off. Gabbie helped Claudia carry the clothes upstairs. When they'd finished, she took Claudia by the hand and led her to her bedroom.

"See my beautiful door?" she said.

Claudia smiled. It really was covered with stickers – wildlife stickers with gummed backs – from the floor to as high up as Gabbie could reach, which wasn't very high.

"You must have worked hard," said Claudia.

Gabbie nodded. "Yes," she agreed. "I did."

Claudia wondered what she would have done if Gabbie were her little girl. The door wasn't ruined, but it would take a lot of work to scrape off the stickers. Gabbie didn't think she had done anything wrong, though. She had only wanted to make her door "beautiful". It must be hard to be a parent, Claudia thought.

"Well," said Claudia, "what do you want to do? We don't have to meet your sister for a while."

"I want to . . ." Gabbie frowned. "I want to play with Cindy Jane." (Cindy Jane is an old Cabbage Patch doll. Myriah says her name is really Caroline Eunice.)

Gabbie found the doll. She placed her in a pram and wheeled her around the house, singing to her. By the time she got bored, Claudia was ready to meet Myriah.

"Let's go, Gabbers," she said. "It's almost four o'clock. Your sister will be getting off the bus soon."

Claudia and Gabbie left the house through the garage door. As they started down the driveway, Chewy barked at them from the back garden.

"Poor Chewy," said Claudia, turning around. "I bet you want to come with us, don't you?"

Chewy was standing on his hind legs, front paws resting on the fence. He whined pitifully.

"What do you think, Gabbie?" Claudia asked. "Should we take him with us? He looks like he'd enjoy a walk."

"Mummy doesn't walk him to the bus stop," Gabbie replied.

"But we could. Do you know where his lead is?"

"Yes," said Gabbie. "It's in the mud room."

Sure enough, Claudia found a fancy red lead hanging from a hook in the "mud room". It said *Chewy* all over it in white letters.

"Okay, boy. Here you go," Claudia murmured as she clipped the lead on Chewy's collar.

Chewy began wriggling with joy – tail first, then hindquarters. The wriggle slowly worked its way along his body until he was yapping and wagging and grinning. If he could talk, he would have been saying, "Oh, boyo, boyo, boy! What a great day! Are you guys really taking me for a walk? Huh? Are you? Oh, boyo, boyo, boy!"

Claudia grinned. "I wish *we* had a dog," she told Gabbie.

"Daddy says having Chewy is like having three dogs," remarked Gabbie.

Now that should have told Claudia something, but both she and Chewy were too excited for Claudia to pay much attention.

"Okay, boy. Here we go." Claudia took Chewy's lead in one hand, and Gabbie's hand in the other. They set off with a jerk as Chewy bounded out of the garden.

"Whoa, Chewy, slow down!" cried Claudia. She held him back, but he strained and pulled on the lead, whuffling and sniffing at everything he saw – rocks, patches of grass, cracks in the pavement.

Claudia and Gabbie passed a work crew repairing the road and reached the corner where they were to meet Myriah. A few moments later the yellow Community Centre bus pulled to a stop.

"There's your sister!" Claudia told Gabbie.

"Where?" Gabbie stood on her tiptoes

and craned her neck around.

"There. Look in the window."

Myriah was waving from a seat near the front, but Gabbie exclaimed. "I still can't see her."

So Claudia picked her up, dropping Chewy's lead as she did so. "Uh-oh," said Claudia.

As the bus door opened, Chewy bounded away. Claudia made a grab for the lead and missed. Myriah stepped off the bus then and Chewy ran to her with a joyous woof. But he didn't stop when he reached her. He snatched her schoolbag out of her hand and galloped away.

"Chewy!" Myriah screamed.

"Chewy!" Claudia and Gabbie screamed.

The bus drove off.

"Claudia!" cried Myriah. "He took my bag. Get him! There's a note from my teacher in there! And a permission slip and my workbook pages with stars on them!"

Chewy was halfway down the road by then, his lead trailing behind him. He tore along, every now and then looking over his shoulder at Claudia and the girls with a doggie grin, as if the chase were a big game.

"My bag's going to be all slobbery!" said Myriah.

"Well, come on, you guys!" shouted Claudia. She took off after Chewy, with the girls behind her.

Chewy ran into the Newtons' garden.

"Look out, Mrs Newton!" yelped Claudia.

Mrs Newton was working in a flower bed, with Jamie and Lucy playing nearby. When she saw Chewy, she dashed to Lucy and picked her up, whisking her out of Chewy's path.

"Help us catch Chewy, Jamie!" called Myriah.

Jamie joined the chase.

Chewy ran into Claudia's garden. Mimi, Claudia's grandmother, was taking a teetery stroll down the front path.

"Look out, Mimi!" cried Claudia.

Mimi stepped aside, but actually tried to grab Myriah's bag as Chewy flew by.

She missed.

"Thanks anyway, Mimi!" Myriah shouted.

Chewy galloped on, and Charlotte Johanssen, Stacey's favourite baby-sitting charge, rounded a corner. She saw Chewy coming at her full speed.

"Aughh!" she screamed.

Chewy put on the brakes to avoid her.

"Get the bag!" yelled Claudia.

And Charlotte did just that – but then Chewy sped up and tore away again.

"Oh, *thank* you," Myriah said breathlessly to Charlotte. "This bag is full of important stuff."

Well, the bag was back but Chewy wasn't. Claudia didn't know what to do. She couldn't catch Chewy, so she simply returned to the Perkinses' with Myriah and Gabbie, and waited. Mrs Perkins would be home around five. At 4.40, Claudia began to feel very worried. At 4.45, she was a bundle of nerves. At 4.50, the doorbell rang.

Claudia answered it. A workman wearing blue overalls was standing on the steps. "Hi," he said. "I'm fixing the road." He jerked his thumb in the direction of the road works that Claudia and Gabbie had passed earlier.

"Yes?" said Claudia curiously.

"Well," the man continued, "I really like your dog. He's very nice and all, but he won't give my cones back."

Claudia didn't have the faintest idea what the man was talking about.

"Go and look in your back garden," the man said.

Claudia left him at the door and ran through the house. She looked out the kitchen window. There was Chewy dragging a big orange plastic road cone over to a pile that he had gathered by the swing. Claudia sneaked outside and trapped Chewy on his next trip to the road works. The workman took his cones back. Mrs Perkins came home. Claudia told her what had happened while she was gone. But she wasn't sure Mrs Perkins believed her. Claudia couldn't blame her.

8th CHAPTER

"Ahem, ahem. Please come to order," said Kristy.

Every now and then our chairman becomes zealous and tries to run our club meetings according to parliamentary procedure.

We couldn't come to order, though. The rest of us were still laughing over the story of Chewy and the orange cones.

"Well, I guess I'll just have to decide about Logan by myself," said Kristy.

That brought us to attention. I'd been sprawled on Claudia's bed. I sat up straight. Stacey and Dawn stopped giggling. Claudia even forgot to look around her room for hidden junk food.

"Okay," said Kristy more casually. "We've all talked to Logan. He's come to one meeting. And now, he's gone on a job. Mary Anne, what did you think?"

"Well, for a while, I wasn't too impressed," I admitted. I told them about the shower rod incident. "But he was great with Mrs Rodowsky, and getting along with the parents is always important. Plus, he's good in a crisis, really level headed, and he's good at distracting kids from things they shouldn't be doing." I added the stories about the grape juice, the stuck jar, and the cannonball off the couch.

"Jackie Rodowsky sounds like a real handful," said Stacey incredulously when I had finished.

"Well, he is, but he doesn't mean to be," I told her. "He's just sort of accident-prone. He's really a nice little kid. You could tell he loved Elizabeth. He was very gentle with him."

"Would you say Logan is a responsible baby-sitter?" asked Kristy. "Could we safely send him to our clients?"

"Definitely," I replied, and I wasn't just thinking of being in love when I said that.

"And we all like him, right?" Kristy went on.

"Yes," we agreed. It was unanimous.

Kristy paused. "But do we want to ask him to be a member of the club?"

Silence.

Even I couldn't say yes to that. I had visions of one uncomfortable meeting after another, each of us trying not to talk about boys, trying not to mention things that were unmentionable, and of poor Lennie the rag doll spending the rest of her days under Claudia's bed.

"I thought so," said Kristy after a while.

We all began to talk at once:

"I really like Logan."

"Logan's great, but . . ."

"The Rodowskys need Logan."

"I was so embarrassed when . . ."

"Logan was so embarrassed when . . ."

"Okay, okay, okay," said Kristy, holding up her hands. "We've got a little problem here."

The phone rang and I answered it. I heard Mrs Rodowsky's voice on the other end. "Hi," I greeted her. "How's Jackie?"

"Oh, he's fine. As a matter of fact, he hasn't stopped talking about you and Logan. He had a wonderful time with you. And Mr Rodowsky and I need a sitter next Saturday night for all three boys. We have tickets to a play in Stamford."

"Okay," I said. "I'll have to check our schedule. I'll call you back in a few minutes." I hung up the phone. "That was Mrs Rodowsky," I told the others. "She needs a sitter next Saturday." I flipped through the record book to the appointment calendar.

"Who's free?" asked Kristy, leaning forward.

"Uh-oh. No one is," I said.

Kristy exhaled noisily.

"What about Logan?" asked Dawn.

"He really isn't a club member yet," Kristy replied.

"He might be free, though," spoke up Stacey.

"But we can't count on that," said Kristy. "And I don't want to start recommending him if he isn't a club member."

I didn't quite follow Kristy's reasoning on that, but I said, "Well, look, I'm busy that Saturday, but I'm not baby-sitting. These clients of Dad's are going to be visiting. He asked me to go out to dinner with them, but I know it's going to be really boring. I think Dad will let me baby-sit if I explain that we're in a tight spot. That way, I can call Mrs Rodowsky back now, tell her that either Logan or I will be able to sit, and after we decide what to do about letting Logan in the club, we'll tell her which one of us will be coming."

"Fine," agreed Kristy.

So I did that, and then Kristy said, "Okay, what about Logan?"

We all looked at each other. We just couldn't decide what to say.

Finally Claudia found some sweets and passed the bag around. The munching didn't help us make a decision, though.

"Well, look," said Stacey after a while. "I think Logan was embarrassed at the meeting, too. Maybe he doesn't even want to be part of the club."

"He went on the sitting job, though," I pointed out. "He must still be interested."

"He probably felt like he had to go," said Claudia.

"All right," said Kristy. "Here's what I think we should do. Call Logan and be completely honest with him. Tell him we think he's a great baby-sitter, but that the meeting was a little . . . awkward. Then just see what he says."

"I think that's a good plan," said Stacey. "Who should call him?"

"Well," Kristy said, and very slowly four heads turned toward me. Kristy, Claudia, Stacey, and Dawn were grinning mischievously.

"Me?" I exclaimed.

"Who else?" said Kristy.

"Well, at least let me call him in private."

I left the meeting a few minutes early that day. I wanted to make sure I had finished with the phone call before Dad came home from work. It was going to be a tight squeeze. Our meetings are over at six, Dad usually gets home between 6.15 and 6.30, and I'm responsible for having dinner started by then.

If I'd had any extra time at all, I would have delayed calling Logan. I might have put it off for a day, a week, a decade. But I was pressed. And I had an entire business to be responsible to.

I used the phone upstairs, just in case Dad should come home early. I sat in the armchair in his room holding a slip of paper in one hand. Logan's number was written on the paper. I took ten deep breaths. I was trying to calm down, but the breaths made me dizzy. I think I was hyperventilating. I stretched out on Dad's bed until I'd recovered.

All right. Okay. Time to dial.

K-L-five-one-zero-one-eight.

Maybe no one was home. Maybe the line would be busy.

Ring.

"Hello?"

Someone answered right away! I was so flustered I almost hung up.

"Hello?" said the voice again. It was a woman.

I cleared my throat. "Um, hello, this is Mary Anne Spier. Is Logan there, please?"

"Just a moment."

There was a pause followed by some muffled sounds. Then, "Hello?"

"Hi, Logan. This is Mary Anne." My voice was shaking.

"Hey," he said. "What's up?"

"Well, we just had a club meeting," I began, "and we agreed that you're a good sitter, someone, you know, we could recommend to our clients. So about joining the club –"

Logan interrupted me just as I was

getting to the most difficult thing I had to tell him, "Mary Anne," he said, "I don't know how to say this, but I – I've decided not to join the Babysitters Club."

He *had*? A funny little shiver ran down my back. I wanted to ask him why he'd decided that, but I was afraid. Hadn't we laughed together as we'd left the Rodowskys'? Hadn't Logan told me I had a pretty smile? Had I misunderstood everything?

I must have been quiet longer than I'd thought because Logan said, "Mary Anne? Are you still there?"

I found my voice. "Yes."

"I was wondering something, though. Would you come to the Remember September Dance with me?"

(*Would I*?!)

"Sure!" I exclaimed, without thinking of all sorts of important things, such as I don't like crowds of people, I don't know how to dance, and my father might not even let me go. "I'll have to check with my father, though," I added hastily.

I got off the phone feeling giddy. Logan liked me! Out of all the girls in Stoneybrook Middle School, he'd asked *me* to the Remember September Dance. I couldn't believe it. I'd have to learn to dance, of course, but no problem.

I was so excited, I just had to call someone and spread the news. I called

Dawn. When we got off the phone, I started dinner. I was walking on air. I was almost able to ignore the voice in the back of mind that kept saying, "Why doesn't Logan want to join our club?"

9th CHAPTER

Tuesday

Boy, is the Charlotte Johanssen I baby-sat for today different from the Charlotte I used to sit for last year. She has grown up so much! Skipping a grade was the right thing to do for her. She's bouncy and happy and full of ideas, and she even has a "best friend"-- a girl in her class named Sophie McCann. (Last week her "best friend" was Vanessa Pike. I remember when "best friend" meant almost nothing-- just whoever your current good friend was. Do you guys remember, too?)

Oh, well. I'm way off the subject. Anyway, there's not much to say. Charlotte's easy to sit for. I took the kid-kit over, and we had a great afternoon.

Actually, there *was* more to say, but Stacey couldn't write it in the club notebook because she didn't want me to read it! Something had happened that day that I wasn't going to find out about until my birthday, which was quickly drawing nearer.

Stacey showed up at the Johanssens' after school with her Kid-Kit. A Kid-Kit is something us baby-sitters invented to entertain the kids we sit for. We don't always take them with us (because the novelty would wear off, as Kristy says), but we take them along on rainy days or sometimes in between as surprises. A Kid-Kit is a box (we each decorated our own) filled with games and books from our homes, plus colouring books and activity books that we pay for out of the club treasury. Charlotte, especially, likes the Kid-Kits.

When Stacey rang the Johanssens' bell, it was answered by a bouncy Charlotte. "Hi, Stace, hi! Come on in! Oh, you brought the Kid-Kit! Goody!"

Dr Johanssen appeared behind Charlotte and smiled as Stacey walked through the doorway. "Charlotte's speaking in exclamation marks these days," she said fondly.

"Did you have a good day at school, Char?" asked Stacey.

"Yes." (Bounce, bounce, bounce.)

"We're learning fractions! And map skills. I love map skills!" (Bounce, bounce.)

"And how are you doing, Stacey?" asked Dr Johanssen. (Charlotte's mother knows about Stacey's diabetes. She's not her doctor, but she's helped her through some rough times. She's always willing to answer any questions Stacey has.)

"I'm fine, thanks," replied Stacey. "I was getting a little shaky before, but my doctor adjusted my insulin. Now I'm feeling okay again. And I've gained a little weight."

"Well, that's a good sign, hon."

"Stacey, is *Paddington Takes the Air* in the Kid-Kit?" Charlotte interrupted.

"Yes," replied Stacey. "And *Tik-Tak of Oz*, too."

Dr Johanssen smiled at her daughter. "I'd better get going," she said. "I've got a couple of patients to look in on at the hospital, and some work to do in the children's clinic. Mr Johanssen will be home around six, Stacey. You know where his office number is. Oh, and if you don't mind, could you put a casserole in the oven at five o'clock? You'll see a blue dish in the fridge. Just set the oven to three-fifty, okay?"

"Sure," replied Stacey.

As soon as Dr Johanssen was out the door, Charlotte took Stacey by the hand, led her into the living room, and pulled her on to the floor. She opened the Kid-Kit eagerly and began pulling things out: a colouring book, a dot-to-dot book, crayons, Magic Markers, drawing paper, Candyland, ("Too babyish," remarked Charlotte), Spill and Spell, a Barbie doll, and at last the Paddington book and the Oz book. Underneath them she found one more book, a Dr Seuss story called *Happy Birthday to You*.

"Hey, what's this?" asked Charlotte, opening the cover. "I've never seen this before."

"I just added it to the Kid-Kit," Stacey told her. "I liked that book a lot when I was younger."

Charlotte glanced at the busy pictures and the funny words. "Let's read this instead," she said.

"Instead of Paddington?" asked Stacey.

"Yes. I like birthdays." Charlotte settled herself in Stacey's lap, even though she's almost too big to do that, and Stacey began to read.

Now, Charlotte is perfectly capable of reading to herself. After all she skipped a grade. She's incredibly clever, but she loves to be read to. So Stacey read her the long, silly story.

When she had finished, Charlotte leant her head back and sighed. "That's just the way I'd like my birthday to be."

"When is your birthday?" asked Stacey.

"In June. I'll be nine. I can't wait."

"But you've just turned eight."

"I know. But nine sounds like a good age to be. It sounds so grown up."

Stacey smiled. She remembered when she longed to be nine. "It's almost Mary Anne's birthday," she told Charlotte. "She's going to be thirteen."

"Really?" squealed Charlotte, twisting around to look at Stacey.

"Yup."

"Gosh. Thirteen is *old*."

"She'll be a teenager."

"Is she going to have a party?"

"You know, I don't know," said Stacey. "Probably not."

"How come?" asked Charlotte.

Stacey shrugged. "Well, maybe she'll have a little party. Us baby-sitters will go over to her house or something."

"You guys should *give* her a party."

Stacey thought about that. But before she could say anything, Charlotte rushed on, "No, no! Hey, I've got it! You should give her a *surprise* party!"

"Oh, I don't know, Char."

But Charlotte was so excited that she didn't hear Stacey. She stood up and began jumping up down, "Really, Stacey! A surprise party. You invite all of Mary Anne's friends to come at one time, and you invite Mary Anne for half an hour later. Then everybody hides in the dark, and when Mary Anne comes over, you switch the lights on," (Charlotte made a great flourish with her hand), "and everybody jumps out and yells 'surpri-ise'!"

Stacey smiled. "Charlotte, that's a really terrific idea, but Mary Anne is shy. I don't think she'd like to be surprised that way."

"She wouldn't?"

"No. She doesn't like being the centre of attention – you know, having everyone look at her."

"Oh." Charlotte sat down again. "How'd she like just a little surprise?"

"What do you mean?"

"Well, maybe you could have an ordinary party but bring out a surprise cake for Mary Anne."

"You know, that's not a bad idea. I've been wanting to give a party anyway. I don't think Mary Anne would mind a surprise *cake*. After all, we're only doing it because we like her. She should feel flattered."

"Yeah," said Charlotte. "What kind of party would you tell Mary Anne it was?"

"Just a party, I guess. Back-to-school, or something like that. A chance for all our friends to get together after the summer."

What Stacey didn't tell Charlotte was that she was already thinking about the guest list – and the list included boys.

At home that night, Stacey began to make plans. My birthday was on a Monday, so Stacey asked her parents if she could have a party at her house the Friday before. Her parents gave her their permission. They especially liked the idea of the surprise cake.

Stacey started her guest list: Kristy, Claudia, Dawn, and me (of course), Dori Wallingford, Pete Black, Howie Johnson, Emily Bernstein, Rick Chow. She didn't worry about whether there were an equal number of boys and girls. She was going to tell each person to bring a date! Stacey's party would be one of the first boy/girl parties our class ever had!

The next day, Stacey made other lists:

Food – crisps and dips, twiglets, sweets, pizzas, coke, a big salad (more for Stacey and Dawn than anyone else) and a large birthday cake to be ordered from the Village Bakery.

Supplies – paper plates, cups, napkins, etc.

To do – start calling guests, check tape collection, buy me a birthday present.

Stacey's plans were elaborate. She told each guest except me that she was giving a party and was going to surprise me with a cake. The guests were supposed to buy a present and keep quiet about the cake. Stacey told me only that she was giving a party. She hinted (not very subtly) that I'd probably want to ask Logan.

I got so caught up in the idea of inviting Logan that it never dawned on me that the party would have something to do with my birthday.

And that, of course, was just what Stacey had been counting on.

10th CHAPTER

The Remember September Dance was on a Friday. Dad had not only given me permission to go with Logan, he'd seemed happy about it. In fact, he'd given me his Department Store charge card and told me I could buy a new outfit.

When he handed me the card, his eyes looked sort of teary. I hugged him tight.

A few days later, the entire Babysitters Club went shopping to find an outfit for me. We descended on the store after school. Everyone began pulling me in different directions.

"Shoes," said Claudia.

"Juniors," said Dawn.

"Underwear," said Stacey.

"Sportswear," said Kristy.

"*Sportswear*!" the rest of us exclaimed.

Kristy shrugged. "This isn't the prom, you know. You might find a nice sweater in

Sportswear. Or an accessory."

"We'll keep it in mind," said Dawn. "Let's go to Juniors first. You can find a dress there, Mary Anne. Then we'll buy shoes to go with it."

"And underwear," said Stacey.

"If necessary," I added.

In the junior department I tried on a green sweater dress that made me look like a mermaid, and a yellow sweater dress that made me look as big as a house. Then Claudia handed me a full white skirt with the words Paris, Rome, and London, and sketchy pink and blue pictures of the Eiffel Tower, the Tower Bridge, and other stuff scrawled all over it. She matched it up with a pink shirt and a baggy pink sweater. I would never, ever have tried on that skirt, but with the shirt and sweater it looked really good.

In the shoe department we found white shoes with pink and blue edging that matched the pink and blue in the skirt. I'd never have looked twice at those shoes, either, but with the rest of the outfit they were perfect.

I charged everything, and talked Stacey out of the underwear department and Kristy out of the sportswear department. I'm not that keen on shopping, and I'd spent enough of Dad's money already.

I might have felt calm and cool while we

were shopping on Thursday. I was even feeling okay while I did my homework that night. But the next day during school my stomach began to feel queasy, and by that afternoon I was a nervous wreck.

"I must be crazy," I told my friends as school finished. "I'm going to a dance and I don't know *how* to dance. And what if Logan and I can't think of anything to say to each other? What if I stomp on his feet while I'm trying to dance? What if I spill something on him?"

"You know what?" said Kristy. "I say we cancel today's club meeting and go over to Mary Anne's instead. We can pay Janine a couple of dollars to answer the phone for us. Then we can help you get ready for the dance, Mary Anne. I'll walk home with you guys, call Charlie, and tell him where I am so he can pick me up later."

That was just what we did. We gathered in my bedroom. Dawn inspected my outfit and ended up ironing the skirt and shirt for me.

Kristy looked at the soles of my new shoes, "Aughh!" she cried. "Mary Anne, scuff up the bottoms of those or you'll slip at the dance and fall flat on your face."

"Oh, no," I moaned. "Something else to worry about."

Stacey showed me a few easy dance steps.

Claudia gave me some tips on Logan. Things like, "Let him hold doors open for you and get you punch. If he brings you a corsage, wear it no matter what colour it is."

"What if it's dead?" asked Kristy, giggling.

Claudia scowled at her.

At 5.30, everyone left. My friends were all going to the dance, too. Kristy and Dawn were going alone, Stacey was going with Howie Johnson, and Claudia was going with Austin Bentley, whom she'd gone out with a few times before. I was glad they would all be there.

My dad volunteered to pick up everyone in the club and take us to the dance. Logan and I had arranged to meet at the entrance to the gym at 7.30. Dad dropped the five of us off at school at precisely 7.25. I leaned over and kissed his cheek. "'Bye," I said. "Thanks for driving us."

"Have fun, honey."

My friends and I got out of the car with a chorus of "thank you's".

"Remember," I called to Dad as I shut the door, "Mr McGill will drive us home. The dance is over at nine-thirty."

As I watched the taillights of the car disappear in the car park, part of me wished I were with my father, heading to our safe home where I could be alone and not have to worry about people and dancing and spilling punch and slipping in my new shoes. But the rest of me was excited.

I joined my friends and we walked to the

gym in a noisy bunch. We were all smoothing our hair and picking lint from our clothes and fussing with our jewellery. I thought we made a pretty good-looking group. Claudia was wearing short, tight-fitting black trousers and a big white shirt that said BE-BOP all over it in between pictures of rock and roll dancers. She had fixed a floppy blue bow in her hair. Stacey was wearing a white T-shirt under a hot pink jumpsuit. Dawn and Kristy looked more casual. Dawn was wearing a green and white oversized sweater and stretchy green trousers. Kristy was wearing a white turtle-neck shirt under a pink sweater with jeans. We just couldn't seem to get her out of blue jeans.

That evening while I was getting dressed, I'd imagined how Logan and I would meet at the door, I'd spot him from across the hallway and walk over to him ever so casually.

"Hi, Logan," I'd say softly.

"Hi, Mary Anne," he'd reply, and he'd hold out a sweet-smelling pink carnation.

As soon as we entered the hall, my dream was shattered. It was a mob scene, wall-to-wall laughing, screaming kids. I stood on my tiptoes and looked all around. After a few seconds I spotted Logan. He was across the hall. Twenty thousand people were between us.

"Logan!" I called. I jumped up and

down and waved my hands, but since I'm short, it didn't do any good.

"I see Logan," I told my friends. "I'd better try to get to him."

"Okay," replied Kristy. "See you later."

"Good luck!" added Dawn excitedly.

I elbowed and squeezed and shoved my way through the kids. When I finally reached Logan, I felt as if I'd just fought a battle. I was hot and sweaty, and the dance hadn't even started.

"Hi – *oof* – hi, Logan," I said as someone slammed into me from behind.

"Hi," replied Logan. Then, "Here," he said ruefully, handing me a smushed orange flower. "Sorry about that. I dropped it and someone stepped on it."

The flower (whatever it was) looked absolutely horrible againt my pink sweater, but I pinned it on anyway.

"Thanks," I said.

Logan smiled. "Mah play-sure," he drawled. "Come on. Let's dance."

He led me inside. The only really good thing I can say about the gymnasium was that it was less crowded than the hallway. I couldn't appreciate the decorations or the refreshments table or the band. I was too busy worrying.

There I was – actually at the dance. In a few minutes, the entire school would see that I had no business being there.

Luckily, Logan wasn't too keen on the

idea of dancing until a lot of other people were dancing, so we stood by the food for a long time. We drank three cups of punch each, and ate handfuls of cookies. I couldn't think of a thing to say to Logan. He kept asking me questions, and I kept answering them . . . and then the conversation would lag. I sneaked a peek at my watch. Eight-fifteen.

Finally Logan took my hand. "Want to dance?" he asked.

I nodded. What could I say? No? After all, we were *there* to dance.

By that time, the gym was so crowded that there was barely room to move around. I tried to remember the steps Stacey had shown me. Then I tried to imitate Logan.

Imitating Logan turned out to be fun. He smiled when he realized what I was doing, and began fooling around, dancing sort of the way I imagined King Kong would. I kept up with him. Logan started to laugh. He waved his hands in the air. I waved mine. He stomped his feet and spun in a circle. I stomped my feet and spun in a circle. Logan was laughing hysterically, and I was feeling pretty good myself. He put his arm across my shoulder and kicked his legs Rockette-style. I kicked my legs.

One shoe flew off.

It sailed through the air narrowly missing Mr Kingbridge, our deputy head. It hit a wall and fell to the floor. Mr Kingbridge picked it up. Leaving a speechless Logan behind, I had to limp through the crowd and claim my shoe.

Please, please, I prayed, let me wake up and find out that this is all a nightmare.

But it wasn't. A whole bunch of kids had seen my flying shoe and they were laughing. By the time I'd put it on and was winding my way back to Logan, he was standing with Stacey and Dawn, and the three of *them* were laughing, too. I had never, never, never been so embarrassed in my whole life. How could I have been feeling so happy just a few moments earlier? I should have known something like this would happen. I am not the kind of person who's cut out for boys or dances or parties. I'm just not. I *knew* this evening was going to be horrible.

"Well, *I* don't think it's so funny," I said stiffly to my friends and marched over to the benches which lined one wall of the gym.

"Mary Anne!" Logan called.

But I could hear Dawn say, "Let her go. I think she wants to be alone."

She was right. Except that I wanted to be more alone than by myself in a gym with twenty thousand people. I wanted to be by myself in my room . . . in bed . . . under the covers.

From my perch on the top row of benches I watched Logan dance with Dawn. When the song was over, he climbed the benches and sat down next to me. "Mary Anne," he said, "everyone's already forgotten about your shoe. Don't you want to dance?"

I shook my head. Logan brought us some more punch and we drank it while we watched the kids below. After three more songs, Logan said, "Now?"

I shook my head again. "But why don't you go and dance?" I really didn't mean it, but I felt I had to say it since Logan looked incredibly bored.

"Are you sure?" he asked.

"Yeah. Go ahead."

So Logan trotted down the benches. He danced with Stacey, then Claudia, then Kristy. Then he began with Dawn again. He even broke in on Austin Bentley the next time he wanted to dance with Claudia. In between dances he kept coming back to me, but I couldn't bear to leave the safety of the benches. I looked at my watch a million, billion times, waiting for nine-thirty to arrive.

When it did, Logan climbed the benches once again. "You'll come down *now*, won't you?" he asked with a little smile.

I smiled back, relieved that he wasn't mad. "Sure," I said.

As we approached the door to the gym I added, "Thank you for the flower."

"Thanks for coming with me. I'm glad you did."

"Honest?"

"Honest. Dancing with you was really

fun. No girl has ever fooled around with me like that. Most of them like to prove how well they can dance."

Really? I thought. Well, maybe I could try it again at the next dance . . . If there was a next dance with Logan.

11th CHAPTER

Friday

Neither Dawn nor I ever want to hear the word "memory" again. Karen, Andrew, and David Michael played that game all evening while Dawn was over to spend the night, and they drove us crazy with their arguing! I was glad Karen wasn't scaring everyone with her stories about Morbidda Destiny and the ghost of Ben Brewer, but— when she's telling her tales, there's no fighting. On the other hand, mum says she'd rather see Karen and David Michael fight than ignore each other. She says ignoring each other would be a much worse stepfamily problem -- at least when they fight they're interacting. But there must be something in between ignoring and fighting.... oh yeah - scaring each other.

Kristy's notebook entry was complete in terms of baby-sitting concerns, but not in terms of everything that happened that night. A lot of talking (especially about my birthday) went on, but I didn't find out about it until much later.

Let me start at the beginning, though. It was Friday night again. Logan hadn't seemed too upset about the dance, In fact, he'd called me the next morning to ask if I wanted to go over to school to watch the junior school football game. On Monday and Tuesday he'd sat with our club at lunchtime. On Wednesday, he and I had sat by ourselves (but we joined the club again the next day). On Thursday he had invited me to go to the movies on Friday.

Needless to say, I was ecstatic! We still had a little trouble talking sometimes, but Logan always seemed so *interested* in me, and in everything I did or said. It's hard to be shy around someone who thinks you're wonderful.

On Friday night, Kristy was stuck at home baby-sitting for Karen, Andrew, and David Michael, so her mother and Watson said she could invite a friend over. Usually she would have invited me, but since I was busy with Logan, she asked Dawn to come over.

Talk about ecstatic. Dawn still hasn't got over the days when Kristy was jealous of Dawn's friendship with me, and would barely speak to her. And Kristy had never invited just Dawn to sleep over. So Dawn gladly accepted. Her mother drove her to the Brewer mansion not long after Kristy's mum and Watson had left.

When Dawn rang the doorbell, she heard shrieks coming from inside, only they sounded like terrified shrieks, not joyful ones.

Nervously, Dawn turned around and looked at her mother who was waiting in the car until Dawn was safely inside. What should she do? She didn't want to call her mother to the door and then find out there was nothing wrong. That would be embarrassing.

Dawn rang the bell again. More shrieking. She screwed up her courage. With a shaking hand, she turned the knob and slowly peered around the door and into the front hall.

"Aughh! Aughh! Au – Dawn?"

"Karen?"

"Oh, I thought you were Morbidda Destiny, creeping into our house to put a sp –"

"Karen, that is enough." It was Kristy's impatient voice, "I don't want to hear another word about poor old Mrs Porter – or the ghost of Ben Brewer – tonight. And I mean it." Kristy appeared in the hall, followed by Louie the collie, and Dawn waved to her mother who waved back, then started down the drive.

"Okay, okay." Karen flounced off.

"Sorry about that," said Kristy. She reached out to help Dawn with her things. "I was in the kitchen. I could hear Karen screaming and I knew what she was doing, but I was too far away to stop her."

Dawn grinned. "That's okay." She held her hand out to Louie, who gave it a halfhearted lick.

"I don't think Louie's in top condition tonight," said Kristy. "He's getting old. Well, come on. We'll put your things upstairs. Then we'll have to keep an eye on the kids. After all, I'm baby-sitting.

"No problem. You know I like the kids."

Kristy and Dawn settled Andrew, Karen, and David Michael on the living room floor with the Memory set. Louie lay down nearby, his head resting mournfully on his paws. Then Kristy and Dawn retreated to a couch, where they sprawled out with a box of crackers – one of the few snack foods they'll both eat, since Kristy considers crackers semi-junk food and Dawn considers them semi-health food.

"I wonder what Mary Anne and Logan are doing right now," said Kristy.

Dawn looked at her watch. "The movie's probably just beginning."

"Yeah. The theatre's all dark . . ."

"Maybe they're holding hands . . ."

"Kristy!" shouted Karen. "David

Michael cheated. He just peeked at one of the cards." Karen stood indignantly over the blue cards that were arranged facedown on the floor.

(I guess I should explain here how Memory is played. It's very simple. The game consists of a big stack of cards. On each is a picture – and each card has one, and only one, matching card. The cards are laid out facedown. The players take turns turning two cards over. If someone gets a pair, he or she goes again. When all the cards have been matched up the winner is the one with the most pairs. Simple, right?)

Wrong!

"I did not cheat!" cried David Michael. "It's a rule. Each player gets one peeksie during a game."

"Show me where it says anything about a peeksie in the rules," answered Kristy, holding her hand out.

"Well, that's how we play at Linny's."

"Why don't you play by the rulebook?" suggested Kristy.

The game continued.

"Where were we?" Kristy asked Dawn. "Oh, yeah. In the dark theatre."

"Holding hands – maybe," said Dawn. "I wonder if they'll, you know, kiss."

"Ew!" exclaimed Kristy, looking disgusted, but then she grew quiet. "You know," she said after several moments, "maybe they will. Mary Anne seems more serious about Logan than Claudia ever was about Trevor."

"How do you mean?"

"Well, she's not silly about him. Remember how Claudia used to giggle about Trevor all the time? It was as if she liked the idea of going out with him better than she liked Trevor himself."

"Karen! No fair! You didn't let me finish my turn!" Now Andrew was shrieking.

"Woof?" asked Louie from his spot on the floor.

"Hey, hey!" cried Kristy.

"I got a match and Karen took her turn anyway! No fair! No fair!"

"Andrew, I just for*got*, okay? Finish your turn," said Karen.

"But you've already turned over two cards," said David Michael indignantly. "And Andrew saw them. He knows where two more cards are. So nothing's fair now. The game's ruined."

"Excuse me," said Kristy, "but did you *all* see which cards Karen turned over?"

"Yes," chorused the three kids.

"Then *every*thing's fair. You've all got an advantage. Think of it as a bonus or something. Andrew, finish your turn."

Kristy sighed. "You know," she said, picking at a tiny piece of lint on her sweater, "I was always the brave one and Mary Anne was always the scaredy-cat. Now everything's reversed. And suddenly she's . . . I don't know . . . ahead of me, and I've been left behind."

Dawn nodded. "But you're still her friend, one of her best friends."

"I know. I just have a feeling this is going to be an awful year. I moved away from you guys, and Mary Anne's moving away from me, if you know what I mean. And I haven't made any friends here in Watson's neighbourhood. My brothers have, but I haven't." Kristy stretched her hand towards Louie, but he wouldn't come over to her for a pat. He looked exhausted.

"It might help," said Dawn carefully, "if you stopped thinking of it as Watson's neighbourhood and started thinking of it as your own."

"Karen, you give those back!" This time, the indignant voice belonged to David Michael. "Kristy, she keeps hiding my pairs under the couch. Look!" David Michael pulled up the slipcover on the seat he and Karen were leaning against. He revealed a row of paired Memory cards.

"They're not his, they're mine!" squawked Karen.

"Are not!"

"Are, too!"

Kristy stood up. "The game is over," she whispered.

Karen and David Michael had to stop screaming in order to hear her.

"What?" they said.

"The game is over."

Kristy's patience had worn thin, although she kept her temper. Half an hour later, the three children were in bed, and Dawn and Kristy were seated side by side on Kristy's big bed. Louie was fast asleep at the end. The portable colour TV that Watson had given Kristy was on, but neither Dawn nor Kristy was paying attention.

"Clothes?" Dawn was saying.

"Tapes, maybe," Kristy suggested. They were trying to decide what to get me for my birthday.

"It has to be something she wants, but that she won't be embarrassed to open in front of boys."

"I really wish Stacey hadn't decided on a boy/girl party," said Kristy woefully.

"How come?" asked Dawn.

"Well, who are *you* going to invite?"

Dawn's eyes widened. "Gosh, I hadn't thought about it."

"Even if I could think of a boy I wanted to go with, I wouldn't know how to ask him," confessed Kristy.

"You know who I like?" Dawn said conspiratorially.

"Who?"

"Bruce Schermerhorn. He's in my maths class. You know him?"

"I think so."

"He's really cute."

"I *could* ask Alan Gray," said Kristy. "He's a pest, but we always end up doing stuff together. At least I'd know what to expect from him . . . I think."

Kristy and Dawn looked at each other, sighed, and leant back against their pillows. Louie sighed, too. Eighth grade came complete with problems nobody had counted on.

12th CHAPTER

Ring, ring, ring.

"Hello?"

"Hi, Mary Anne."

"Logan! Hi." (I was always surprised to hear his voice on the phone.)

"How're you doing?"

"Fine. How are you?" (It was four o'clock on a weekday afternoon. We'd just seen each other an hour earlier.)

"Fine. Guess what's on TV tonight."

"What?"

"*Meatballs*. Have you ever seen it? It's really funny."

"I don't think so. I mean, I don't think I've seen it."

"It's on at eight. Try to watch it."

"I will."

"So? What's going on?"

"I'm going to baby-sit for Jackie Rodowsky tomorrow. The last time I sat for him, he fell out of a tree, fell down the front steps, and fell off the bed. But he didn't get hurt at all."

Logan laughed. "That kid should wear a crash helmet," he joked.

"And carry a first-aid kit," I added.

There was a pause. I had no idea how to fill the silence. Why did this always happen with Logan? There were hardly any pauses when I talked to the members of the Babysitters Club. I knew I was blushing and was glad Logan couldn't see me.

"Want me to tell you about *Meatballs*?" asked Logan.

"Sure," I replied, relieved. A movie plot could take a while to explain.

And Logan took a while. In fact, he took so long that we reached my phone conversation limit. My dad still has a few rules that he's strict about, and one of them is that no phone conversation can last longer than ten minutes. Even though Dad was at work, I felt I had to obey the rule. For one thing, what if he'd been trying to call me for the last ten minutes?

Logan reached a stopping place, and I knew I had to interrupt him.

"Um, Logan?" I said.

"Yeah?"

"I hate to say this, but –"

"Your time's up?" he finished for me.

"Yeah. Sorry."

"That's okay. So are you going to watch *Meatballs*?"

"I'll try. If I get my homework done."

"Great. Well . . . see you tomorrow."

"See you tomorrow."

We hung up.

Whewwwww. I let out a long, slow breath. I love talking to Logan, but it makes me nervous.

Ring, ring.

Aughh! Dad *had* been trying to call! And I'd been on the phone for over twelve minutes.

"Hello?" I said guiltily. Excuses began flying around in my head: I'd needed a homework assignment explained. Someone else had needed homework explained. The phone had accidentally fallen off the hook.

"Hi, Mary Anne!" said a cheerful voice.

"Oh, Stacey. It's only you!" I exclaimed.

"*Only* me! Thanks a lot."

"No, you don't understand. I thought you were Dad. I mean, I thought you were going to be Dad. See, I've been on the phone for – oh, never mind."

"More than ten minutes?" asked Stacey, giggling.

"Yeah."

"Well, listen. I just wanted to make sure you were coming to my party – and that you'd invited Logan."

"Well . . ." The thing is, I'd been putting that party off a little. I was nervous about asking my father if I could go to a boy/girl party, and even more nervous about inviting Logan. How do you go about inviting a boy to a party?

"Mary Anne?"

"What?"

"Are you coming and have you invited Logan?" she repeated.

"I don't know, and, no, I haven't."

"Mary *A*-anne."

"Okay, okay. Sorry. Really I am." (I didn't know then why Stacey sounded so exasperated. I was the guest of honour at her party, but I had no idea.)

"Get off the phone and call Logan."

"I, um, have to call my father, too. I have to get permission to go to the party first."

"So call him, *then* call Logan."

"I've been on the phone since four."

"The rule is ten minutes per call. Just keep these calls short. It's the easiest rule in the world to get around. My mother put a five-minute limit on my calls to Laine Cummings in New York. So I just keep calling her back. If I call six times we can talk for half an hour."

I laughed. "All right. I'll call Dad."

"Call me back after you've talked to Logan."

"Okay. 'Bye."

I depressed the button on the phone, listened for the dialling tone, and called my father at his office.

His secretary put me through right away.

"Hi, Dad," I said.

"Oh, hi, Mary Anne, I'm in the middle of something. Is this important?"

I was forced to talk fast. "Sort of," I replied. "Stacey's having a party at her house. It's for both boys and girls. We're supposed to ask guests. Can I go? And can I invite Logan?"

"Will Mr and Mrs McGill be at home during the party?"

"Yes," I said, even though I hadn't asked Stacey about that. I was sure they would be at home, though.

"What time is the party?"

"It starts at six."

"You may go if you'll be home by ten, and if you *meet* Logan *at* the party."

"Oh, thanks, Dad, thanks! I promise I'll be home by ten! I promise everything!"

I called Logan with a bit more enthusiasm than I'd felt before. I punched his phone number jauntily – K-L-five-one-zero-one-eight.

Logan answered right away.

"Hi," I said. "It's me again. Mary Anne Spier."

"I know your voice!" he exclaimed.

"Oh, sorry."

"Don't apologize."

The call was already going badly. I wished I could rewind time and start over.

"Um . . ." I began.

"Hey," said Logan, more softly. "I'm really glad you called. You never call me. I always call you. I'm glad you felt, you know, comfortable enough to call."

(This was better, but still not the conversation I'd imagined.) "Well, I have to ask you something. Not a favour. I mean . . . Stacey's having a party. I wanted to know if you'd – you'd go with me. If you don't want to, that's okay," I rushed ahead. "I'll understand."

"Slow down, Mary Anne! Of course I want to go. When is it?"

I gave him the details.

"Great," he said. "I can't wait."

As long as I was doing so well, I decided to ask Logan one more question. "Have you thought any more about joining the Babysitters Club?"

Pause. "Well, I said I didn't want to join."

"I know, but . . ."

"I'll think about it some more, okay?"

"Okay." (After all, the rest of us hadn't decided that we *wanted* Logan to join.)

There was some muffled whispering at Logan's end of the phone, and then he said, sounding highly annoyed, "Mary Anne, I have to get off the phone. I'm really sorry. My little sister has a call to make that she thinks is more important than this."

"It is!" cried a shrill voice.

I laughed. "I better get off, too." I told Logan.

So we hung up. But I had one more call to make. "Hi, Stacey?"

"Hi!" she said. "Have you called Logan already? Did you call your dad?"

"Yes and yes."

"And?"

"And I can come and Logan's coming, too."

"Oh, great! Awesome! Fabulous! I can't believe it!"

Stacey was so excited that her excitement was contagious. My heart began pounding, and I was grinning.

We hung up.

Ring, ring.

"Hello?"

"Mary Anne! What on earth have you been doing? What happened to your ten-minute limit? I've been calling you for ages!"

"Kristy?"

"You ought to get call-waiting or something. Did your dad take away your limit? . . . Oh, yeah, this is Kristy." (*Click, click.*) "Oh, hold on, Mary Anne. We've got another call coming in over here." (Kristy put me on hold for a few seconds.) "Mary Anne?" she said, when she was back on. "That was Stacey. I'd better talk to her. Call you later. 'Bye!"

The plans for the birthday surprise were in full swing – and I suspected nothing.

13th CHAPTER

I dressed carefully for Stacey's party, even though I didn't have much choice about what to wear. My best-looking outfit was the one I'd worn to the dance, so I decided to put it on again.

By six o'clock I was ready and had to kill time. Stacey had originally said that the party would start at six, but that afternoon she'd called to say that everything was going wrong and could I come at six-thirty instead?

"Sure," I'd replied. "I'll call Logan and let him know."

"Oh, no. Don't bother," said Stacey quickly. "I'll call him. I have to call everyone else." She was talking very fast. I decided she must be nervous about the party.

So at 6.15 that night, dressed in my famous-cities skirt, the pink sweater, and the lethal white shoes, I was standing around in the kitchen while my father started his dinner. At 6.25, I flicked on the TV and watched the news. At 6.35, I decided not to leave quite yet because I didn't want to be the first to arrive at the party. Finally, at 6.40, I left for Stacey's. I wished I could have walked with Claudia, but she had told me that she and her mum were going to pick up Austin Bentley first. I sort of got the feeling that I wasn't wanted.

When I rang Stacey's bell at 6.45 I could hear an awful lot of voices inside. Stacey flung the door open. "Oh, you're here!" she cried. "Come on in!"

I stepped inside.

"Let's go downstairs. Everyone's in the rec room," she said giddily.

"Gosh," I replied, "it sounds like everyone else has already arrived." I glanced at my watch. "I'm sorry I'm so late."

"Oh, you're not – not late," said Stacey. "I guess the others were early."

All of them? I wondered. "Is Logan here?' I asked.

"Yup. You're the last to arrive."

That made me feel a little uncomfortable, but I tried to shrug the feeling off. I still wasn't suspicious. After all, I was used to feeling uncomfortable in a crowd.

Stacey and I descended the stairs to the playroom. On the way down, I thought of something important. "Stacey, your parents are home, aren't they?"

"Yes," Stacey answered, "but I made then promise not to come into the playroom. I think they're in the kitchen. That way, they can keep an eye on the food and an ear on the party."

From my vantage point halfway up the stairs, the start of Stacey's party looked a lot like the start of the school dance. Although the tape deck was playing loudly, no one was dancing. The girls were bunched up in a corner, and the boys were bunched up by the table where Stacey had put out twiglets, crisps, sweets, fizzy drink and salad.

Austin Bentley was tossing twiglets in the air and trying to catch them in his mouth. Mostly, he missed.

Alan Gray had put yellow smarties in his eyes and was going around telling the boys he was Little Orphan Annie.

Pete Black was dunking crisps in his coke before eating them.

Across the room, Dori Wallingford was showing her new bracelet to Claudia, who was pretending to be impressed, but who was really watching Austin toss the twiglets in his mouth.

Kristy was whispering to Dawn, who was giggling.

Emily Bernstein was saying loudly, "Alan Gray is *so* immature," and glaring at Kristy – for having invited him, I suppose.

As Stacey led me down the stairs it

seemed – for just an instant – that everyone stopped talking, that the entire room paused. But I decided it was my imagination. The room was as noisy as ever when I reached the bottom of the steps.

I looked for Logan. Before I found him, I felt a hand on my shoulder. I turned around and there he was.

"Hey," he said, giving me his wide, warm grin. "How ya doin?"

"Great," I replied.

"Boy, you look nice."

"Thanks, but this is the same outfit I wore to the dance."

"You still look nice."

A phone on the wall nearby began to ring. "Mary Anne, can you get that?" yelled Stacey from across the room.

I picked up the receiver. "Hello. McGills' residence."

With all the music and talking, it was hard to hear the person on the other end of the line, but I *thought* the voice said, "Hello, this is the Atlanta Pig Corporation. When would you like your pig farm delivered?"

"What?" I shouted.

"We have a pig farm reserved in the name of Stacey McGill. When would you like us to ship it to you?"

"Just a sec." I paused, putting my hand over the mouthpiece. "Stacey!" I yelled. "Come here!"

Stacey edged through the rec room. "What?"

"It's for you. Something about . . . a pig farm?"

Stacey got on the phone, frowning. "Hello . . . A *pig* farm? . . . Justin Forbes, is that you? You are *so* immature!" *Clunk.* She hung up. Stacey turned to Logan and me. "Justin's all bent out of shape because he wasn't invited to the party," she informed us. She went back to Claudia and the other girls.

Immediately, the phone began to ring again. "*I'll* get it this time," said Logan, reaching for the receiver. "Hello, Disneyland. Goofy speaking. How may I help you?"

I giggled.

"He hung up," said Logan, pretending to look surprised. "I can't imagine why."

Nobody was dancing and only the boys were eating. Logan steered me toward a couch. "Let's sit down," he said. "Wait, I'll be right back."

I sat, and a few minutes later, Logan returned with two cups of coke and a bag of crisps. We sipped our drinks in silence for a few moments but for the first time, our silence seemed comfortable, not uncomfortable. Then Logan asked me a question and we began to talk. We talked about school and our families. Logan told me about Louisville, and I told him about wanting a cat. We talked for so long I lost track of the time. I didn't even hear all the noise around me, except for when Alan Gray shouted, "Let's play Spin the Bottle!" and Emily Bernstein shouted back, "You are *so* immature, Alan!"

It was as if Logan and I were in our own world, and nobody and nothing else existed. A scary thought occurred to me. Was this part of being in love? Nah. I was only twelve-going-on-thirteen. I couldn't really be in love . . . could I?

"You know," said Logan, polishing off his coke, "I'm glad to be getting to know the real Mary Anne. This *is* the real Mary Anne, isn't it?"

"What do you mean?"

"Well, when I first met you, I liked you okay, but you were so quiet and shy. I've never known anyone as shy as you."

"Believe it or not, I'm better than I used to be."

"You're kidding!"

"No, really . . . Well, maybe I'm still not very good around boys."

"Yeah?"

"Yeah."

Logan considered that. "If you could just open up more – I mean, be the way you are right now – people would have a much easier time getting to know you. I almost didn't ask you to the dance, you know."

"Why *did* you ask me?"

"Because you're different from other girls. More . . . something."

"More what?" I asked, puzzled. I really wanted to know.

"More serious. Not serious like some old professor, but serious about people. You listen to them and understand them and take them seriously. People like to be taken seriously. It makes them feel worthwhile. But you have a sense of humour, too, which is nice. The only thing is, sometimes you're too sensitive. I really wasn't sure things would work out between us."

"I've always been too sensitive," I told him.

"AUGHH! AUGHH! HELP!"

The room was slowly darkening and everyone was screaming.

"Oh, would you guys grow up," said Stacey's impatient voice as the lights brightened again. "I was dimming the lights. I just wanted to make things more romantic."

I smiled at Logan and we looked around. While we'd been talking, the boys and girls had started to mingle. Claudia and Austin and some other kids were dancing. Alan was torturing Emily with his Little Orphan Annie eyes. Most of the food was gone.

"I'm sending Dad out for pizza now," Stacey informed me.

Mr McGill returned later with three pizzas (which he wasn't allowed to bring into the playroom) and they were eaten in no time. After Logan and I finished our slices, we sat on the couch again.

For the second time that night, the lights began to dim. Only this time, they went all the way out and nobody screamed. In the darkness, I heard only some muffled whispering and sensed that someone was coming down the steps.

Suddenly the lights were turned on full force, and everyone began singing "Happy Birthday".

I felt totally confused. What was happening? Stacey hadn't said this was a birthday party. Not until the kids sang, "Happy birthday, dear Mary Anne," did I understand. Then I saw that Stacey was at the bottom of the stairs carrying a big birthday cake that said HAPPY BIRTHDAY, MARY ANNE in pink frosting and glittered with lighted candles. Behind her were Kristy and Dawn, each holding a stack of gifts.

Stacey set the cake on a table next to Logan and me. Kristy and Dawn piled the presents on the floor near my feet. Logan held out a small box wrapped in silver paper and tied with a silver bow.

Silence had fallen over the playroom. The song was finished. Austin had paused in his twiglet-throwing. Alan was staring at me with his blind smartie eyes. Pete had stopped in the middle of a dunk, and the soggy crisp had fallen into his coke. Claudia, Dori, and Emily were standing in an expectant bunch, a safe distance from Alan, their eyes on me. All the guests were waiting for me to react, to blow out the candles, to cry, or *something*.

It was a nightmare. It was like one of those dreams in which you go to school naked, or study and study for an important test and then sleep through your alarm clock and miss it.

I had only one thought: I had to get out of there.

So I did.

I ran up the stairs, out the McGills' front door, and all the way home, leaving my nightmare behind.

14th CHAPTER

"Mary Anne," my father exclaimed as I barged into our house. "What are you doing home so early? I thought you were going to call me for a ride when the party was over."

"Sorry," I replied. I slowed down and caught my breath. I didn't want my father to know anything was wrong. I just couldn't explain this to him.

"Everything okay?" asked Dad.

"Oh, sure. The, um, party broke up early."

Dad looked suspicious. "Were Mr and Mrs McGill there?" he asked.

"Oh, yes. Stacey wouldn't let them go into the playroom, but they were right in the kitchen the whole time. Honest. It just wasn't a very good party. No one was having fun. So it kind of ended."

"I'm sorry," said Dad, and he really did look sorry.

"Me, too," I replied. "Well, I'm tired. I guess I'll go to bed."

I went slowly up to my room and stretched out on my bed, but I had no intention of going to sleep. I hadn't even taken my party clothes off. How dare Stacey have done that to me? I thought. She knows how I feel about parties and people and surprises and being the centre of attention. My other friends know, too. Especially Kristy and Dawn and Logan. But they had all let it happen.

I was beginning to put the pieces of the puzzle together. Everyone had known about the cake except me. I must have been the only one who was told to arrive at six-thirty. The others had probably come at six, as originally planned, so I wouldn't see them arrive with gifts. That's why Claudia hadn't wanted to go to the party with me.

I lay there, and the memory of the lights coming on flooded back: everyone singing, Stacey with the cake, Kristy and Dawn with the presents. I recalled that Logan had been grinning at me like a Halloween mask. How *could* he? Hadn't we just been talking about how I was shy and quiet? I took people seriously, but no one took *me* seriously.

I felt tears streaming down my cheeks, but I didn't bother to dry them. I had run away. I had humiliated myself. As mad as I was at Stacey and my friends, I realized that they had wanted to do something nice for me, and I hadn't let them. I'd spoiled everything.

But still . . . how *could* they?

I looked at my watch. I'd only left the party fifteen minutes earlier. Any moment now, Logan or Stacey would call. The thought cheered me. They would apologize for embarrassing me, and invite me back, and say they didn't know what they could have been thinking.

I tiptoed to my door and set it ajar so I'd be sure to hear the phone when it rang. Then I lay on my bed again.

When another ten minutes had gone by, I realized that Stacey (or Logan) was probably going to come over instead, to give things the personal touch. Of course. That was just like them.

I opened my window a crack so I'd hear them when they got to the front door. I hoped Dad had left the porch light on. I peeked outside. He had.

When an hour had gone by and my room was chilly with the night air, I knew that no one was going to call or come over. My stomach felt like I'd swallowed a brick. I'd really blown it this time. I should have seen it coming. My friends had finally had enough of my behaviour. I'd gone one step too far. No one likes a party-spoiler, no matter how well he tries to understand that person. And Logan had surely decided that I wasn't right for him after all. I really was just plain too shy.

Well, I was sorry I was different. I couldn't help it. But it was their fault for doing something they knew I wouldn't enjoy.

My anger was no comfort, though. All I could think was that I'd lost my friends. I tried to cheer myself with the thought that the last time that had happened I'd been forced to make a new friend – and I'd found Dawn. But the thought wasn't all that cheery. I didn't want any new friends now. I only wanted Kristy and Dawn and Stacey and Claudia and Logan.

Tomorrow might be a good time to ask my dad for a cat.

I fell asleep with my clothes on and awoke to a beautiful Saturday morning. But it felt bleak to me. As soon as I saw my famous-cities skirt, the awful evening rushed back. I realized that the brick was still in my stomach.

It was nine o'clock. Dad had let me sleep late. I felt as if I hadn't slept at all, though. I staggered to my feet, washed up, and changed my clothes. I found my father in the living room, drinking coffee and reading some papers for work.

"Morning," he greeted me.

"Can we get a cat?" I replied.

Dad raised an eyebrow. "What brought this on? . . . Oh, your birthday, right? I didn't forget, Mary Anne. We'll do something special on the big day. I was thinking of dinner at a restaurant in Stamford. Wouldn't that be fun? I've got some presents, too." Dad grinned. "And I had a little help picking them out, so I know you'll like them."

"That sounds great," I said, mustering a tiny smile, "but this doesn't have anything to do with my birthday. I just want a cat to keep me company. Then I wouldn't feel alone when you're not here."

"I don't know, Mary Anne. We've never had a pet before. We'd need a litter box and a basket. And what would we do with the cat if we went on holiday?"

"Get Mallory Pike to come and feed it?" I suggested.

"Well," said my father, I'll think about it. Do you know any vets? We'd need a vet, too."

"The Thomases go to Dr Smith," I told him. "They really like her."

Dad sipped his coffee and stared into space. At last he said, "Okay, I've thought about it. You may get a cat."

All I could say was, "What?" I couldn't believe he'd made the decision so fast.

"You may get a cat," Dad repeated. "If you'll use some of your baby-sitting earnings to buy dishes and toys and a litter box, I'll buy the basket and pay for food and the vet bills. Consider it an early birthday present. After all, thirteen is an important birthday."

"Oh, Dad! Thanks!" I flung myself at my father, giving him a fierce hug.

"We probably should have got a pet a long time ago," he said. "The only two things I ask are that *you* take care of the cat as much as possible –"

"Oh, I will, I will!"

"And that you get the cat, or a kitten, from the animal shelter. Give a home to a pet that really needs one. Most of the animals in the pet shop will eventually be sold, but the animals in the shelter are in a bit of trouble."

"No problem," I said. "I'd rather get a stray, too."

Suddenly I had an excuse to do something I'd sort of been thinking about ever since I woke up. I went into the kitchen, closed both doors, and called the Brunos' house.

Logan's little sister answered, shouted, "Logan, it's for you – a gi-irl!" and giggled nonstop until Logan got on the phone.

"Hello?" he said.

I cleared my throat. "Hi, it's me."

"Mary Anne?"

"I thought you always knew my voice," I teased him.

"I didn't expect to hear from you, that's all. I thought you were mad at me."

"You did?"

"Well, actually, we *all* thought you were mad at *us*. I'm really glad you called." Logan sounded relieved.

I bit my lip. "Is that why no one called me last night?" I asked.

"Well . . . yeah. We were sure you never wanted to speak to us again. We're really sorry about what we did. We should have known better."

"Wow," I said. "I thought all of *you* were mad at *me* – for being so, you know, ungrateful. And spoiling the party."

"Oh, boy," said Logan, letting out his breath. "Sorry."

"Me, too . . . But listen. I have some good news. Dad said I could get a cat! Want to meet me at the animal shelter and help me pick one out?"

"Sure! When? Today?"

"This afternoon. Dad and I have to buy a few things first."

So that morning my father and I went shopping for cat stuff, and that afternoon, we met Logan at the Stoneybrook Animal Shelter. Dad waited in the car so Logan and I could go looking alone.

The shelter was clean and the people were nice, but I sure wouldn't have wanted to be an animal stuck there. It was like an orphanage for pets. Row after row of wire cages, each holding a lost or homeless dog or cat. Most of them looked frightened and nervous.

A woman led Logan and me into the cat area.

"I think I'd like a kitten," I told her.

"Well," she said, "I'm afraid it's the wrong time of year for kittens, so we don't have many. Just one litter. They're over here. Someone left these four kitties outside the shelter a couple of weeks ago without their mother. We weren't sure they were going to make it. But now they're all healthy and frisky."

I peered inside a cage that was larger than most others. The four kittens were snoozing in a relaxed heap on an old blanket. There were two red tabbies, one splotchy, patchy calico, and a grey tiger cat.

"Are they old enough to be separated?" I asked.

The woman nodded.

"Then I want the grey one, please," I said.

Logan nudged me. "Don't you want to play with them first or something? Maybe you'd like one of the others better."

"Nope," I said. "I've always wanted a grey tiger cat, and I've always wanted to name it Tigger after the tiger in *Winnie-the-Pooh*."

This seemed to make sense to Logan.

The woman opened the cage, gently pulled the sleeping kitten from its litter mates, and handed it to me. "It's a boy," she said.

Dad and Logan and I took Tigger home in his basket, and he cried all the way. He didn't seem to want milk or kitten food or anything, and refused to leave the basket, so Logan and I left him in it and watched him fall asleep.

When Tigger was as limp as a little rag doll, Logan reached into his pocket, pulled something out, and handed it to me. It was the silver-wrapped box he'd had at Stacey's party.

"Happy birthday," he said. "I wasn't sure I'd ever be giving this to you. After last night, I thought we were through. I really didn't think things could work out between us. But you took the first step and called me today. I know that wasn't easy. Anyway, happy birthday."

While Tigger napped, I opened the box and found a delicate silver bracelet.

"Oh, thank you," I breathed.

"You're welcome," Logan said softly. "Want to come to the Fifties Fling with me next month?"

Did he have to ask? Of course I did!

15th CHAPTER

Saturday had turned out to be a pretty good day after all, what with Tigger, Logan's birthday present, and Logan's invitation to the dance. But I wasn't through with my apologies. I knew I had to call Stacey, too. So, late in the afternoon, with a now frisky Tigger playing in my lap, I picked up the phone and dialled her number.

"Stacey," I said, a lump rising in my throat, "it's me, Mary Anne."

"Oh."

I couldn't read that "oh" at all. Had it sounded surprised? Annoyed? Sarcastic? But before I could decide what to say next, Stacey mumbled, "I guess you're wondering why I haven't called."

"Well," I replied, "I thought *you* might be wondering why *I* hadn't called."

Then Stacey and I proceeded to have the same sort of conversation that Logan and I had had that morning. Each thought the other was mad, we both apologized, and then we cried a little. I promised to try to be more outgoing (after all, the kids at the party had been my friends), and Stacey promised to try to be more understanding.

"Ow!" I cried as she was finishing her promise.

"What? What?"

"Something bit me!" (Tigger, of course, with his baby teeth, which were like needles.)

I told Stacey all about Tigger then, and she suggested that we hold a special meeting of the Babysitters Club at my house the next day so everybody could see him.

It turned out, though, that she had another reason for wanting to hold a meeting at my house, but I didn't find that out until Sunday.

On Sunday afternoon at three o'clock, the doorbell rang.

"Time for our meeting," I told Tigger. I picked him up and carried him to the door so he could meet the first club member.

When I opened the door, though, I found the entire club on our doorstep, along with the remains of my birthday party – a chunk of cake, and all the presents.

"Surprise," whispered Kristy, Dawn, Claudia, and Stacey.

I giggled. "Come on in."

Tigger watched my friends with wide, bright eyes as they settled themselves in the living room. Dad stuck his head in the room, said hello to everybody, and then sensibly retreated to the study.

"You sort of missed the birthday part of your party," Stacey explained, "so we decided to bring it over. You can open your presents, and we'll meet Tigger."

"There are so many presents!" I exclaimed.

"Everyone at the party brought one. And they all wanted you to have them, even after you'd left. So here they are."

"Wow," I said. "Well, you can play with Tigger while I open them."

But Tigger didn't want to play with my friends. The wrapping paper was much more interesting. He rolled on his back, leaped in the air, and batted at the ribbon with his paws.

"He sure is lively," said Claudia.

"I know. We have to get the vet to look him over, though. I mean, since he was a stray and all. The shelter gave us this little book on cat care and it said the kittens should be checked for worms and mites. Plus, the vet has to tell us when he's old enough to get his shots."

"Are you going to take him to Dr Smith?" asked Kristy.

"Yes, I think so. Oh!" I had just opened Dawn's present. It was a blue shirt that matched my famous-cities skirt. "Thank you! This is perfect!" I cried.

I kept opening. I'd never seen so many presents. Kristy gave me a Smash tape. (They're our favourite group.) Stacey gave me a pair of famous-cities socks. (They were really wild.) And Claudia gave me some jewellery she'd made in her pottery class. "I can't believe you *made* this," I said. "It looks professional."

Most of the other gifts, especially the ones from the boys, were silly. Alan Gray gave me a wind-up dinosaur that shot sparks out if its mouth, and Austin gave me a brooch shaped like a cow. When I'd opened everything, Stacey said. "Well, let's kill the cake. You haven't even tasted your own birthday cake, Mary Anne."

I always feel bad eating sweets in front of Stacey, but she doesn't seem to mind. So I divided the cake into four small pieces and Kristy, Claudia, Dawn, and I ate every last crumb, while Stacey polished off a couple of rice cakes. (Yuck.)

"Maybe we'll turn you into a junk-food addict yet," Claudia said to Dawn.

"I don't think so." Dawn made a face. "Now that I've eaten all that sugar, the only thing I want to do is brush my teeth." She settled for rinsing her mouth out.

"You know what?" I said to the members of the Babysitters Club. "I think this has been one of my best birthdays ever – and it's not even my birthday yet!"

"Mew," announced Tigger. He was sitting up perfectly straight with his tail wrapped around his front feet, gazing at me with round eyes.

"And you," I said, picking Tigger up gently, "are part of what made my birthday so great."

Tigger looked at me for another moment and then yawned.

Everybody laughed.

"Come to order. Please come to order!" said Kristy. She was wearing a visor and she adjusted it on her head as she settled into Claudia's director's chair.

It was the next afternoon (my birthday), time for a real club meeting. Before she could say another word, the phone rang.

"Hello, Babysitters Club," said Stacey.

I listened as Stacey asked questions, and could tell she was talking to Mrs Pike. We fixed the Pikes up with a sitter, and the phone rang again immediately. It turned out to be one of those days.

After we lined up a sitter for Jenny Prezzioso, Mrs Barrett called. Then Kristy's mum, Mr Newton, and Mrs Rodowsky. By the time we hung up with Jackie's mother, our heads were spinning.

"Oh," groaned Kristy, and the phone rang again.

This time I answered it. "Hello, Babysitters Club."

"Hello, my name is Mr Morgan, I live across the street from Mariel Rodowsky. She recommended your group to me. I need a sitter on Saturday night."

"How many children do you have?" I asked.

"Four. All boys."

"And how old are they?"

Mr Morgan gave me all the information, and I hung up the phone with a sinking feeling – not because this new client had four boys, but because I knew none of us was free on Saturday.

"We've *got* to do something about this," I said. "We're in a jam. No one can take the job. Logan would be perfect for the Morgans. He's good with boys and he lives right nearby."

"But he doesn't want to join the club," said Kristy.

"I know. But couldn't we make him some kind of special member? Someone we could call when we need help, but who doesn't have to go to the meetings? That way everyone would be happy. Our club would look good because we'd be able to provide sitters instead of saying no one's available, Logan would get a job every now and then, and we wouldn't be embarrassed at the meetings."

"Well," said Kristy, "it really isn't a bad idea."

"Isn't a *bad* idea?! It's a great idea!" exclaimed Dawn. "Call him, Mary Anne."

"All right," I said. I waited for the usual nervousness to run through me, but I felt fine. I dialled Logan.

"Hello?" he answered.

"Guess who."

"I don't have to guess, I know," Logan replied. I could almost *hear* him smiling.

"Then guess where I am."

"At a Babysitters Club meeting."

"Very good! And guess what I'm going to ask you."

There was a pause. "To join the club?"

"No. I have a better idea. See, a whole bunch of people have called today and, as usual, we're really busy. A new client just phoned – a man who lives across the street from the Rodowskys. He's got four boys, and none of us can sit. We don't want to turn him down the very first time he calls, so I thought of you. Do you want this job?"

"Yes, but . . . Mary Anne, I've got to tell you the truth. I don't want to come to your club meetings."

"Why not?" I asked, my heart thumping.

"Because they're too embarrassing. I didn't like being the only boy. And Claudia told that story about the . . . you know."

So Logan didn't want to say "bra strap" either.

"I know," I replied. I was glad that was the *only* reason he didn't like the meetings. "Well, to be honest, we were embarrassed, too. So that's why I was thinking you could be some special kind of club member –"

"An *associate* member," whispered Kristy.

"An associate member," I said. "And we'll only call on you when we really need extra help. You won't have to go to the meetings."

"Really?" said Logan. "Hey, great!"

"So you want to do it?"

"Definitely."

I put my hand over the mouthpiece. "He'll do it."

"I'll make it official," Kristy announced, gesturing for the phone. "Hi, Logan," she said. "I hereby make you an associate member of the Babysitters Club . . . You do? Okay, sure. We'll need to meet them and stuff, but that's great."

Kristy handed the phone back to me, and I hung it up, wishing I could have said a more private goodbye to Logan.

"Guess what," said Kristy. "Logan knows a couple of other guys who might want to be associate members."

We all began talking. Then we called Mr Morgan with the news that Logan Bruno would be baby-sitting.

I sat back and let the excitement sink in. Our club had *boy* members. Well, one anyway. I had Logan. The Fifties Fling was coming up. It was my thirteenth birthday. And when I went home after the meeting, Tigger would be there to greet me.

The Babysitters Club

KRISTY AND THE SNOBS

1st CHAPTER

If there's one thing I can't stand, it's a snob. Well, actually, there are a lot of other things I can't stand. Cabbage, blood, people who chew with their mouths open, and squirrels are a few of them. But snobs are high up there on the list.

This is unfortunate since I have moved to a wealthy neighbourhood here in Stoneybrook, Connecticut, recently, and it is overrun with snobs. What happened was that my mum, who used to be divorced, got remarried to Watson Brewer, this rich guy. Since my mum had a little house for the six of us (Mum, me, my three brothers, and our dog, Louie), and Watson had this mansion all to himself (his two kids live with him every other weekend), it made more sense for us Thomases to move in with Watson than for him to move in with us.

So we did.

Watson's house is so big that my brothers and I, and Karen and Andrew (our step-sister and stepbrother, who live with us every other weekend), each have a room of our own. Mum and Watson share a room, of course, but their "room" is really a suite about the size of a landing field.

Anyway, to get back to the snobs — I'm surrounded. They're everywhere in Watson's neighbourhood. The teenagers around here get their own cars (fancy ones) as soon as they're able to drive. They spin along with the radios blaring, looking fresh and sophisticated. I am so *glad* my big brothers, Sam and Charlie, aren't like that. Charlie can drive now, but the only thing he drives is Mum's beat-up estate. And my brothers and I still go to state school, not to snobby private schools. Guess what most families on our street have: (a) a swimming pool (b) tennis court (c) a cook named Agnes (d) all of the above. The answer is (d) all of the above.

So far, Watson has (e) none of the above, which is one of things I'm learning to like about him. However, he's been talking about putting in a pool, now that Karen and Andrew are older, so we'll see.

I've hardly got to know any of the kids here. When we first moved into Watson's house it was summertime, the beginning of July. Most of the kids my age had been sent to fancy camps for the summer. (I would kill

Mum if she ever did that to me.) Plus, I'm chairman of a group called the Babysitters Club. All my friends are in the club, and they live way across town—where I used to live—so I spent a lot of time with them over in my old neighbourhood last summer. What I'm trying to say is that school had started again before I met any of the kids on my street.

My first encounter with the snobby kids was on a Monday morning. My alarm clock went off at 6.45 as usual. I rolled over and tried to ignore it.

"Please, please be quiet," I mumbled.

But the clock didn't obey. It went right on buzzing.

"Oh, all right, you win," I told it.

I reached over and turned it off, then sat up, rubbing my eyes.

"Louie!" I exclaimed. Our old collie was stretched across the foot of my big bed. Louie mostly sleeps with David Michael, but lately, he's been taking turns sleeping with all of us, even Karen and Andrew on the weekends they visit. I thought it was nice of Louie to share himself.

"You are such a good dog," I whispered, leaning over to him. I stroked the top of his head between his ears. The fur there is almost as soft as rabbit fur. Then I took one of his paws in my hand.

"Oh, your pads are cold," I told him,

rubbing the pink pads on the bottom of his paw. "It must be getting chilly at night. Poor old Louie."

Louie licked my hand and gave me a doggie smile.

"Thanks," I said.

I got up and looked through my wardrobe, as if I had a really big decision to make about what to wear. Ever since school began I've been wearing the same kind of outfit almost every day — a turtleneck, a sweater, jeans, and trainers. I don't care about clothes the way my friends Claudia and Stacey do. They always look really cool and well put-together.

After I was washed and dressed, I ran down the wide staircase to the first floor and into the kitchen. Mum and Watson were with Sam and Charlie. (David Michael, my seven-year-old brother, is a slowcoach. He's always the last one down).

Here's another thing about Watson that's not so bad. He helps around the house—with the cooking, cleaning, gardening, everything. I guess this comes from being divorced and having lived alone for a while before he met Mum. He and Mum share the workload equally. They both have jobs, they both prepare meals (Watson is actually a better cook than Mum is), they both run errands, etc. Twice a week, a cleaning lady comes in, and my brothers and I are responsible for certain chores, but basically

Mum and Watson run the show.

So I wasn't surprised when I stepped into the kitchen that Monday morning to find Mum making coffee and Watson scrambling eggs. Sam was setting the table and Charlie was pouring orange juice. It was a nice familiar scene.

"Good morning!" I said.

"Morning," everyone replied.

"Kristy, can't you wear something different once in a while?" Sam asked me, eyeing my jeans and sweater.

"Why do you care what I wear?" I replied, but I knew perfectly well why he cared. He cared because he was fifteen and girls were practically the only thing on his mind. He thought he was the girl expert of the world, and he was disappointed in my lack of fashion sense. Plus, he was interested in this *très* sophisticated girl down the street (one of the private-school girls), and he wanted everything about our family to be up to Monique's standards, which were sky-high.

"I think Kristy looks lovely," said Watson.

"So do I," added Mum, kissing the top of my head.

"But," Watson went on, "if you ever do want a few, um, new clothes, all you have to do is holler."

It was a nice offer, but leave it to Watson to use a word like "holler."

"Thanks," I said. "I'll remember that."

I absolutely adore Watson's kitchen. Although it has all the modern conveniences and appliances, it looks kind of like an old country kitchen. We eat at a big parson's table with two long benches. (Watson and Mum bought it when they got married.) Most of the surface tops are covered with blue and white tiles. Copper pots and pans hang from the walls. The curtains—tiny pink and blue flowers on a cream-coloured background—match the wallpaper. It's a wonderful, cosy room.

I plopped down on one of the benches, and almost at once Mum said, "Kristy, call David Michael, please, honey."

"DAVID MICHAEL!" I yelled.

"*Kristy,*" said Mum, giving me a look that was part smile, part exasperation.

"I know, I know." I got up, went to the bottom of the stairs, and called him again.

"Kristy, can you come up here?" he replied.

I ran up the stairs and into his room. "What?" I asked.

David Michael was sitting on the floor next to Louie. "Call Louie," he said.

"Why?" I asked.

"Just call him."

I got down on one knee. "Louie! Come here boy!" I clapped my hands.

Louie hobbled towards me. He was

limping. "Hmm," I said. "I see what you mean."

"I looked at all his paws," David Michael told me, "but I can't find any cuts or insect bites or burrs."

"Poor old Louie," I said for the second time that day. "Well, don't worry, David Michael. We'll tell Mum, but it's probably nothing."

I should mention here that although we got Louie right after I was born, he's really more David Michael's dog than anyone else's. We all love Louie, but David Michael has especially loved him, even as a baby, and he's always taken care of him. He's never complained about messy dog food cans or smelly flea collars. It was David Michael who discovered a rock song called "Brother Louie." (That's the one that goes "Louie, Louie, Louie, Lou*ee*".) Whenever he plays it, the real Louie howls joyfully each time he hears his name. One of David Michael's very first words was even "Yew-ee." (Louie still responds if someone calls him that.) And Louie has always loved David Michael back. Maybe he somehow sensed that David Michael was the only one of us Thomas kids who got cheated out of a father, since Mum and Dad got separated not long after David Michael was born. Who knows?

Louie followed David Michael and me down the stairs and into the kitchen.

"Mum," I said, "Louie's limping," but already his limp seemed less noticeable.

"I guess so," Mum said slowly, watching him. "It's hard to tell. We'll keep our eyes on him."

As soon as breakfast was over, things became hectic. Charlie and Sam got in Mum's car and left for the high school. Mum and Watson drove off, in separate cars, to their jobs. And David Michael and I waited at the end of the drive for our school buses. It was only 7.45, but I felt I'd been up forever.

David Michael's bus was right on time. He climbed on and waved good-bye to me from a window in the very back. He loves to sit in the back seat. My bus should have been just behind David Michael's, but it wasn't. By 7.55, it was later than it had ever been. It had better hurry, I thought. Registration starts at 8.30. Sharp.

For a while I worried about what to do if the bus didn't come at all. Call Stacey's house? Stacey's mum was one of the few I knew who didn't work and might be at home. Then I wondered how long I should wait before I called anybody.

Before I reached any decisions, something interesting happened. The front door of a house across the street opened and a girl about my age stepped out. She was carrying a knapsack, and wearing a blue tank top over a white short-sleeved blouse. She walked down her drive and stood across the street from me. She must have been waiting for a bus too, but not mine. I was the only girl in this neighbourhood who got picked up by the bus to Stoneybrook Middle School.

The girl and I eyed each other, but didn't say anything.

A few minutes later, three other girls joined the first one. They were all wearing the same outfit—a private-school uniform. They were slender, three of them had blonde hair, and they were wearing make-up and stockings. They looked sleek, sophisticated, and self-confident. They stood in a huddle, whispering and giggling. Every now and then one of them would glance over at me.

Where, oh, where was my bus?

I tried not to look at the girls. I pretended the cover of my notebook was absolutely fascinating.

But the girls would not allow me to ignore them. One of the blondes, who wore her hair in a cascade of thick curls, called to me, "You're Mr Brewer's new kid, aren't you?"

"I'm one of them," I replied warily.

"Are you the one who's been sending those leaflets around for some baby-sitting club?"

"Yeah," I said. (Every now and then our club tries to find new people to baby-sit for, so we send around advertisements. (We'd put one in every box in my new neighbourhood not long ago.)

"What does your little club do?" asked another blonde.

"What do you think?" I replied testily. "We baby-sit."

"How cute," said the blonde with the curls.

The others giggled.

"Nice outfit," called the one non-blonde, putting her hands on her hips.

I blushed. Too bad I'd chosen the jeans with the hole in the knee that day.

But if there's one thing to be said about me, it's that I have a big mouth. I always have. I'm better about controlling it than I used to be, but I'm not afraid to use it. So I put *my* hands on *my* hips and said, "Your outfits are nice, too. You look like clones. Snob clones."

Luckily, just at that moment, my bus finally pulled up. I chose a seat on the side of the bus facing the girls. I lowered my window. "Good-bye, snobs," I shouted.

" 'Bye, jerk-face," the curly-haired blonde replied.

I stuck my tongue out at her, and then the bus turned a corner and they were gone from sight.

2nd CHAPTER

"Thanks, Charlie! See you later! 'Bye!" I slammed the car door.

Charlie backed down the Kishis' drive as I ran to their front door and rang the bell. It was time for our Monday afternoon meeting of the Babysitters Club.

Janine Kishi, Claudia's older sister, answered the door. Janine has never been one of my favourite people, but lately she's seemed a little better than usual. The thing about Janine is that she's *so clever*. She's always correcting everybody.

But that day, all she said was, "Come on in. Claudia's upstairs. Dawn and Mary Anne are there, too."

"Thank you," I replied politely. But I didn't go straight upstairs. I stopped in the kitchen to say hello to Mimi, Claudia's grandmother. Mimi had a stroke over the summer, but she's getting much better. She can't use her right hand, so she's learning to do things one-handed. When I looked in on her, she was stirring something at the cooker.

"Hi, Mimi," I greeted her.

"Kristy. Hello. How nice to see." Mimi's native language is Japanese, and her speech was affected by the stroke, so she has a little trouble speaking. "How things in your new neighbourhood?"

"Okay, I suppose. I don't know that many people." For some reason, I was embarrassed to tell her what had happened at the bus stop that morning.

"You will get to know new people," Mimi told me confidently. "That I am sure."

"Thanks," I said and ran upstairs. On the way I heard the doorbell ring. It must have been Stacey. Good. She was right on time. The five of us could begin our meeting.

"Hi, you guys!" I called as I entered Claudia's room.

"Hi!" Claudia, Dawn, and Mary Anne were lying on the floor, looking through our club notebook. When Stacey came in behind me, the five of us scrambled for places to sit. Claudia dived for the bed, followed by Stacey. Dawn and Mary Anne remained on the floor, and I settled myself in the director's chair, put on my visor, and stuck a pencil behind one ear. I always get the director's chair.

I am the chairman.

I looked at the other members of the Babysitters Club: Claudia Kishi, Mary Anne Spier, Stacey McGill, and Dawn Schafer. All present. I guess I should introduce them. But first I should tell you how our club works. We hold meetings on Mondays, Wednesdays, and Fridays from five-thirty until six, and our clients know they can reach us at Claudia's house then. They call when they need sitters, and one of us signs up for the job. Simple. Our clients like the fact that they're pretty much guaranteed a sitter when they call, and we like all the jobs we get. Of course, we have an awful lot of clients now (we've been in business for a year), and sometimes we're so busy that none of us is able to take on a job. Then we call Logan Bruno. Logan is our associate member, sort of our safety. He doesn't come to meetings, but he likes to baby-sit. He's also Mary Anne's boyfriend.

The club officers are, our vice-chairman, Claudia; our secretary, Mary Anne; our treasurer, Stacey; and our alternate officer, Dawn. Claudia was chosen as vice-chairman since she has her own personal telephone and phone number. Because of that, we decided to hold our meetings in her room. Claudia works hard for the club, since she has to take a lot of job calls that come in while we're not having meetings. Here are the essentials about Claudia: Likes—art, mysteries, baby-sitting, boys. Dislikes—school. Looks—beautiful, Japanese, exotic. Dress—*very* trendy and cool, often outrageous. Personality—outgoing, sometimes feels inferior to Janine. (Who wouldn't?)

Mary Anne, our secretary, is my best friend. Before I moved to Watson's we lived next door to each other for years and years. We were babies, kids, and almost teenagers together. Right now, Mary Anne is changing. I think she's growing up a little faster than I am. And she has another best friend (Dawn). We're alike in a lot of ways and different in a lot of ways. For instance, my likes—sports, baby-sitting, TV. Mary Anne's likes—baby-sitting, movie stars, animals. My dislikes—you already know them. Mary Anne's dislikes—crowds of people, being the centre of attention. Looks—we're both small for our age, and we both have brown eyes and medium-length brown hair. Dress—I couldn't care less. Mary Anne is just beginning to care, but she needs a lot of help from Claudia and Stacey. My personality—outgoing, big mouth, friendly. Mary Anne's personality—cautious, sensitive, shy. (She has a boyfriend. I don't.) Mary Anne's club job is to keep our record book up to date. The record book is where we write down our clients' names, addresses, and phone numbers, list the money we earn (that's really Stacey's job), and most important, schedule our baby-sitting jobs.

Stacey McGill is sort of a newcomer to Stoneybrook. Until a year ago, she and her parents lived in New York City. They moved here just before we began school last September. Stacey is sophisticated and smart. Sometimes she seems years older than me. She and Claudia are best friends. Stacey's likes—boys, clothes, baby-sitting. Dislikes—doctors. (Stacey has diabetes and has to go to doctors quite often. She also dislikes the strict diet she has to stay on so as not to allow too much sugar in her body.) Looks—wild blonde hair, thin, pretty, older than her age. Dress—as trendy as Claudia, but a little less outrageous. Personality—outgoing, very grown-up, sensitive to other people. Stacey keeps track of the earnings of us baby-sitters, and is responsible for the subs we put in our club treasury.

Finally, there's Dawn, who's more of a newcomer to Stoneybrook than Stacey is. She moved here from California last January with her mother and younger brother after her parents got divorced. Dawn's job as alternate officer is to take over the duties of any other officer if someone gets sick or has to miss a meeting. Dawn's likes—health food, sunshine, baby-sitting, ghost stories. Dislikes—junk food, cold weather. Looks—the longest, palest, shiniest, silkiest blonde hair you can imagine. Dress—whatever she feels like. Dawn is an individual. Personality—confident, doesn't care what other people think of her.

And that's the five of us. Together we make a pretty good team.

I realized that my friends were looking at me, waiting for me to begin the meeting.

"The meeting will now come to order," I said, even though we already were in order. "Stacey, how much money is in the treasury?"

"Give me your weekly subs first," she replied. (Monday is Subs Day.)

Each of us handed Stacey a dollar.

"We've got nine dollars and eighteen cents," she reported.

"That's kind of low, isn't it?" I replied.

"Well, we pay Charlie to drive you to and from the meetings," said Stacey," and we just bought colouring books and sticker books for the Kid-Kits. We're okay as long as we don't buy anything for a while. We'll just let our subs pile up."

(Kid-Kits are boxes filled with games and books—our old ones, mostly—plus new colouring books, crayons, activity books, etc. that we sometimes take on baby-sitting jobs. The kids love them).

"Anything else to report?" I asked.

The club members shook their heads.

"Have you been keeping up with the notebook?"

The club members nodded their heads—but Claudia, Dawn, and Mary Anne looked a little guilty. I knew they'd just been reading the notebook before I came into the room. We're responsible for writing up every job we go on. We record the jobs in our club notebook and then we're supposed to read the notebook each week to see what happened when our friends were babysitting. It's not always very interesting, but it's usually helpful.

The telephone rang then with what was probably going to be the first job of the meeting.

Dawn answered it. "Hello. Babysitters Club."

(See how professional we sound?)

"Okay, Mrs Rodowsky. I'll call you right back." Dawn hung up the phone and turned to us. "Mrs Rodowsky needs a sitter for Jackie and his brothers next Tuesday afternoon from three-thirty till six."

"Let's see," said Mary Anne, who had already turned to the appointment pages of our record book. "Claudia, you're the only one free."

"Okay," said Claudia. "I think I can handle Jackie." (Jackie's a nice little kid, but he's accident-prone and always in trouble.)

Dawn called Mrs Rodowsky back to tell her that Claudia would be her sitter on Tuesday.

A bunch of other calls came in then but

the most interesting one—just before the meeting came to an end—was from Mr Papadakis. The Papadakises live not far from me in the new neighbourhood. They have three kids—Linny, who's eight and a friend of David Michael; Hannie, who's six and a friend of Karen; and Sari, who's just two. I knew the Papadakises a little through David Michael and Karen, but I'd never sat for them. Now Mr Papadakis was calling with a job.

"We saved your leaflet," he told me. "We need a sitter on Thursday afternoon and we know Linny and Hannie like you."

"You take the job! You take the job!" Mary Anne said excitedly to me after I'd told Mr Papadakis I'd call him back. "You're free and it's good for you to sit in your new neighbourhood."

"Well . . . okay!" I said.

At that time, I had no idea what a sitting job in my new neighbourhood would really mean, and so—I was foolish enough to look forward to it.

3rd CHAPTER

Charlie picked me up promptly at six o'clock and we headed back to our house. (It had been a long time before I could think of *Watson's* house as *ours*.)

"I can't wait to see how Louie's doing," I said as Charlie pulled up to a stop sign.

"Didn't you see him this afternoon?" he asked.

"I didn't have time. I stayed at school to watch a hockey game. The late bus dropped me off just in time for you to pick me up and take me to Claudia's."

"Oh," said Charlie. "Well, I'm sure he's fine.

"I hope so," I replied.

But when we got home, Louie wasn't fine. He was resting in the living room on his orange blanket, and he didn't get up when he saw us. Usually, he's on his feet in a flash, wanting to play or to be let out.

"Hi, Louie!" I said. "Come here, boy."

Louie lifted his head off his paws, but didn't get up. I had to call him two more times before he stood up. He began to walk towards me. It was still hard to tell whether he was limping, but what nobody missed was when he walked smack into a table leg instead of my outstretched arms. David Michael and Mum had just entered the room, so they saw the whole thing, along with Charlie and me.

"Oh, Louie," murmured Mum, leaning over to pat his head. "What's wrong, boy?"

"He's not too sick," announced David Michael. "I just gave him his supper and he ate it in one gulp."

"Well," said Mum, "maybe he ought to have a check-up with Dr Smith tomorrow. I'll call her answering service tonight and try to make an appointment. Charlie, could you take him after school?"

"Sure," replied Charlie.

"I'll go with you," I said.

"Me, too," added David Michael.

So it was arranged. The next afternoon, Charlie drove David Michael and Louie and me to Dr Smith's office.

Louie does not like the vet. He never has. And he's pretty noisy about it. Somehow, he works out where we're going when we're only halfway there. Then the whining starts. He can be really pathetic. David

Michael is always prepared, though. He fishes doggie treats out of his pocket and feeds them to Louie one at a time.

In between bites, though, Louie whines. Charlie says it drives him crazy, but we made it to the vet without incident.

Dr Smith's waiting room wasn't very crowded, thank goodness. There were only two patients ahead of us—a dachshund with his front paw in a cast, and a cat in a basket who kept yowling unhappily. Louie was well-behaved. He lay on the floor with his head resting pitifully on Charlie's shoe and whined so softly you could hardly hear him.

When Dr Smith's assistant called for Louie Thomas, Charlie, David Michael and I rose as one. With a lot of prodding, Louie came too. Charlie and I hoisted him onto the metal table in the examining room.

"Hello, Thomases," Dr Smith greeted us as she entered the room.

"Hi," we replied.

We really like Dr Smith. She's an older woman with greying hair and glasses who's wonderful with animals. She talks to them in a soft, soothing voice. I've never heard her raise it, not even the time Louie panicked and knocked over a box of sterile bandages.

"Well, what's wrong with Louie today?" asked the vet.

David Michael spoke up. "We're not sure. Yesterday I thought he was limping, but it's hard to tell."

"He just lies around," I added. "And last night he walked right into a table when he was aiming for me."

"But his appetite is fine," said Charlie. "He always eats his meals."

"Well, let's have a look." Dr Smith examined Louie carefully. She poked him and stroked him, listened to his heart, looked in his eyes and ears, and watched him try to walk. She frowned as Louie lumbered stiffly into the door. Then she examined his eyes again and sort of massaged his legs.

When she had finished, she looked at us gravely.

"What is it?" I asked, suddenly feeling afraid. Awful thoughts began to run through my mind. The worst was, *Louie has cancer*.

But what Dr Smith said was, "Louie is getting old."

My brothers and I nodded.

"And just like some old people, his body is beginning to slow down. He's developing arthritis and his eyesight is poor."

Is that all? I thought. Arthritis and poor eyesight? It didn't sound too bad.

"Can dogs get contact lenses?" asked David Michael seriously.

Dr Smith smiled. "I'm afraid not, honey." I wondered why she still looked so solemn.

"What can we do for him?" asked Charlie.

"Well, he's probably in a fair amount of pain. I can give you some pills to ease it, but they won't cure the arthritis, and the arthritis is probably going to get worse. His eyes may, too."

Now I understood. Louie was in pain. There wasn't much we could do for him and he wasn't going to get better. It wasn't as if he had a cold or an injury. I looked down at him. He had settled onto the floor of the examining room. It must be scary, I thought, not to see well and to know that you're in a strange place. No wonder Louie had walked into the side of the door.

I realized that Dr Smith was talking again. "Please tell your mother to call me anytime if she has questions. We can strengthen the dosage of the pills if Louie seems to be worse, but I don't want to do that yet. I have a feeling Louie's got a tough road ahead of him."

David Michael was sitting on the floor, talking to Louie. I was glad he wasn't paying attention. I couldn't speak to the vet because a lump had formed in my throat. But Charlie took over.

"We'll tell Mum," he said. "Is there anything else we can do for Louie?"

"Stairs will be difficult," replied Dr Smith, "so keep his food and water on the level of the house where he spends the most time. Carry him up and down stairs if you can. But he *will* need a little exercise. Short, slow walks. Let him go at his own pace."

Charlie and I nodded.

"Can we leave now?" asked David Michael impatiently, and Dr Smith laughed.

"Had enough of the vet's surgery?" she asked.

"Louie has."

Dr Smith handed a packet of pills to Charlie and explained when to give them to Louie. Then we left. Charlie and I looked as if we were on our way to a funeral. But David Michael walked Louie jauntily to the car, singing a song that he made up as he went along.

"Oh, you're going home, Louie, and you're fi-i-i-ine," he said. "No shots, no stitches, no treatment. You don't even have to spend the ni-i-i-ight."

Charlie and I glanced at each other. Obviously David Michael didn't understand that Louie was in bad shape. All he knew was that the vet had sent him home with some pills. How sick could he be? Pills always made David Michael better.

I felt awful by the time we reached our house. "I think I'll take Louie for a walk," I told my brothers. "A slow one, like Dr Smith suggested." I was hoping it would calm me down.

Charlie must have guessed how I was

feeling because when David Michael said, "I'll come with you!" Charlie said, "Why don't you come with me instead, kiddo? We can give your new football a workout."

I flashed Charlie a grateful smile, and Louie and I started slowly down the drive to the shady street. I remembered the day us Thomases moved into Watson's house. The morning before, we had really spruced Louie up because we'd wanted him to look his best when he came to this neighbourhood, where (I was sure) all the dogs were pedigrees, and groomed at doggie parlours.

Well, that was several months ago. Since I hadn't met many of the people around here, I hadn't met many of their dogs, either. I had no idea what they were like. No question about it, though, Louie was not at his best as we plodded down the street. His head was hanging (was he trying to see the ground better?), he moved stiffly, his fur was all ruffled from the examination, and he smelled of the vet.

So wouldn't you just *know* that I'd run into that curly-haired blonde girl I'd seen at the bus stop the day before? She was flouncing down the street towards me, a lead in her hand. At the end of the lead was an absolutely gorgeous dog. It looked something like a heavy golden retriever with the markings of a Saint Bernard. And with the girl and the dog was a littler blonde, holding a spotless white Persian cat in her arms.

Our eyes met, the pavement was narrow, there was no way the girls and I could avoid each other.

They stopped a couple of yards away from me, and the big snob girl flipped her hair over her shoulder, and put her hand on her hip.

"What," she said, pointing to Louie, "is *that*?"

"*That*," I replied, "is a dog."

The girl made a face at me. "Really? It's hard to tell. He's so . . . scruffy."

"Yeah, he's *icky*!" cried the younger one.

"He's old," I said defensively. "And he has arthritis."

The older girl softened just a smidge. "What's his name?" she asked.

"Louie."

"Oh. This is Astrid. Astrid of Grenville. A pedigree Bernese mountain dog."

"And *this* is Priscilla. She's pedigree. She cost four hundred dollars," said the little kid.

"Hoo," I replied, trying to sound like British royalty. I had to admit, though, that next to Astrid and Priscilla, Louie looked like a scruffy old orphan dog.

"Well," said the older girl. "I guess you should know that I'm Shannon Louisa Kilbourne. I live over there." She pointed to a house that was across the street, next door to the Papadakises. "And this is

Amanda Delaney. She lives next door to me."

"But Priscilla and I have to go home now. So 'bye!" the little girl called gaily, and ran off.

"Well, I'm Kristy Thomas," I told Shannon. "You know where I live."

"In Mr Brewer's house," she answered, clearly implying that I was not good enough to be a Brewer, just lucky enough to live with one. "Phew," she went on, "your dog smells. Where's he been? In a swamp?"

"Personally," I replied, ignoring her question, "I would rather live in a swamp than across the street from you."

"Oh, yeah? Well, you're only proving what a jerk you are," retorted Shannon.

"And you're only proving what a snob you are."

"Jerk."

"Snob."

Shannon stuck her tongue out at me, I stuck mine out at her, and we walked on.

4th CHAPTER

Linny and Hannie Papadakis are neat little kids. They love to "play pretend" and to organize activities for the other neighbourhood kids. And their little sister, Sari, is very sweet. All of the kids have dark hair, deep brown eyes, olive skin, and really terrific smiles.

On the afternoon that I was to baby-sit for them, Linny and Hannie were waiting for me in the front yard.

"Hi!" called Hannie, jumping up as soon as she saw me coming.

"Hi, you guys," I said.

"Guess what we want to do today," Linny said. "We want to have a pet fashion show."

"Yeah, we want to dress up Myrtle and Noodle," Hannie added.

This is the great thing about the Papadakises. They have just as much money as anyone else around here, but you wouldn't know it, except for the mansion. They're very down-to-earth, and their pets are named Myrtle the Turtle and Noodle the Poodle, not Astrid of Grenville, like some pets I can think of. The children are allowed to choose their own clothes every morning, even though they sometimes end up wearing stripes with checks, and they go barefoot all summer long.

"Let me talk to your mum first," I told Linnie and Hannie, "and then we'll see about Myrtle and Noodle."

"Okay," said Hannie cheerfully. She took my hand and led me inside the Papadakises' house. "Mu-um!" she yelled. "Kristy's here!"

Mrs Papadakis came bustling through the hallway from the back of the house. "Hi, Kristy," she said. "Thanks for coming."

Linny, Hannie, and Sari look exactly like their mother. Mrs Papadakis wears her dark hair so that it frames her face. And when she smiles her terrific smile, the corners of her wide-set brown eyes crinkle just the way Hannie's were crinkled then.

"I should be back by five o'clock," she told me. "I've got a meeting at the children's school."

"Okay," I replied. "Are there emergency numbers somewhere?" (As a baby-sitter, I always ask this if I'm working for a family I'm not familiar with. You just never know what could happen.)

"Oh, yes," said Mrs Papadakis. "I almost forgot. They're on the memo board in the kitchen. Paediatrician, grandparents, and George's—I mean, Mr Papadakis'—office number."

"Great," I said. "Where's Sari?"

"Upstairs napping, but she should wake soon. And she'll want apple juice then. There's some in the fridge. But no snacks for the kids, okay?"

"Okay."

Mrs Papadakis kissed Linny and Hannie and rushed off.

"Now," I said briskly, "what's this about dress—"

"WAHH!"

I was interrupted by a cry from upstairs.

"Oh, Sari's awake," said Linny.

"I'll get her," I told him. "Why don't you guys go and play in the back garden?"

"Okay," they agreed.

"But stay there," I added. "Don't leave without telling me."

"Okay!" They were already halfway out of the door.

I ran upstairs and followed the sound of Sari's sobs to her bedroom. I opened the door slowly, knowing she would be confused to see me enter instead of her mother.

"Hi, Sari!" I said brightly.

The sobs increased.

I cheerfully pulled up the shade and

straightened the room, talking to Sari all the time. "Hi, I'm Kristy," I told her. "We're going to have fun playing this afternoon."

"No, no, no, no, no!" wailed Sari.

But by the time I'd changed her, tickled her, and talked to her teddy bear, we were old friends. We walked down the stairs hand in hand. I gave her some apple juice, and then we joined Hannie and Linny in the garden.

"Hi, Sari-Sari!" cried Hannie, running over to her sister.

"Kristy," Linny said, "we want to have a fashion show for Myrtle and Noodle."

"You're going to dress up a turtle?" I replied. "Don't you think that's going to be kind of hard? Besides, where are you going to find turtle-size clothes?"

"Well, that's one of our problems," said Linny. "The other one is that we can't find Noodle. And we do have clothes for him, he fits into Sari's old baby clothes."

"Really?" I said.

"Yeah. For my pet show last summer, he wore this little sundress and a bonnet and two pairs of socks."

I giggled. "Maybe Noodle was embarrassed and now he's hiding so you won't be able to do that to him again."

"Maybe . . ." said Linny doubtfully, not seeing anything funny about that.

My eyes drifted across the garden and over a low stone wall in search of Noodle.

They landed in the garden next door—on one of the girls I had noticed at the bus stop. She looked like a short version of Shannon. She was sitting in the sun filing her nails and listening to a tape recorder.

I nudged Linny. "Hey," I whispered, pointing to the girl. "Who's that?"

Linny looked across the yard. "That's Tiffany Kilbourne."

"Tiffany," I repeated. "She must be Shannon's sister."

"Yeah," said Linny. "She is. You know what? Sometimes Shannon baby-sits for us."

"She does?" I asked in surprise. "Do you like her?"

"Sure. She's great."

"You know," I said, "I don't know too many people around here. Tell me who your neighbours are."

"Okay." Linny plopped to the ground, and I joined him. Not far away, Hannie was playing "This Little Piggy" with Sari.

"Shannon and Tiffany have another sister, Maria. She's eight, like me. They all go to Stoneybrook Day School. But Hannie and I go to Stoneybrook Academy."

"Oh," I said. "Right. So does Karen. She and Hannie are in the same class."

"Yeah," agreed Linny with a smile. I could tell he was proud that I'd given him the responsibility of telling me about the neighbourhood.

"Next door to the Kilbournes," he went on, pointing to the yard two houses away, "are the Delaneys. And they are —"

"Awful," Hannie supplied. She'd stopped wiggling Sari's toes and was listening to Linny and me.

"Really?" I asked. I'd met Amanda. She hadn't seemed too bad. "How are they awful?"

"Well, there are two of them," said Linny.

"Amanda and Max," Hannie added, making a horrible face.

"They're our ages." Linny pointed to himself and Hannie. "Amanda's eight and Max is six."

"But we never, ever play with them," said Hannie. "Because they are mean and nasty and spoiled. And bossy. Mostly bossy."

"Wow," I exclaimed. I'd never heard Hannie get so worked up. I was about to ask them some more about the Delaneys when Shannon Kilbourne came out of her house and joined Tiffany in the garden. I know she'd seen me, but she pretended she hadn't. At first. After a few minutes, though, she began to stare at me.

How rude.

"Come on, you guys. Let's go inside," I said. "Maybe Noodle's there. We'd better find him."

Since Linny and Hannie are endlessly

agreeable, they followed me into the house. I carried Sari on my hip.

"Noooo-dle!" Hannie called.

"Noooo-dle!" Linny called.

"Noooo-noo!" Sari called.

We hadn't got further than the living room when the phone rang. "I'll get it," I said. "You guys keep looking for Noodle."

I ran into the kitchen and picked up the phone. "Hello, Papadakis residence."

"Hello? Is that you, Kristy?"

The voice was vaguely familiar, but I couldn't quite place it. "Yes. This is Kristy . . . Who's this?"

"It's Shannon Kilbourne next door. Listen, there's smoke coming out of the upstairs windows at the Papadakises'. The house is on fire!"

I felt my stomach turn to ice. My knees buckled. This was the one thing I feared most when I was baby-sitting. A fire. But I had to stay calm. Don't panic, I told myself.

"Call the fire department!" I yelled at Shannon. Then I slammed down the phone and raced into the living room. I was hoping desperately that I would find all three kids together where I had left them.

But the only one there was Sari, sucking on one of her fingers. I scooped her up. From the other end of the house, I could hear Linny and Hannie calling for Noodle. I raced through the living room, a hallway, the library, and onto the sunporch. Thank goodness. There they were.

"Hannie, Linny," I said breathlessly, "I want you to pay very close attention to me. The house is on fire. We have to get out. There's no time to try to take stuff with us. Is there a way off the sunporch?"

"No," replied Linny. "It's not a real porch."

"We have to get Myrtle and Noodle!" Hannie cried, already sounding panicked.

"We can't," I told her, pushing her and Linny ahead of me into the library. "Now go straight to the front door. But don't run. You might fall."

The kids obeyed. On the way to the door, though, we passed Myrtle's box and in one swift movement, Linny stooped down, picked up the turtle, and kept on going. I didn't say anything.

As soon as we were out the front door, I cried, "Now you can run! Go right to the pavement, but don't run into the street."

Hannie and Linny ran, their legs pumping up and down. Myrtle was clutched between Linny's hands. Halfway across the lawn I dared to look back at the house. That's funny, I thought. I couldn't see even a wisp of smoke. I stopped. I sniffed the air. I didn't smell smoke, either. The house looked fine.

"Linny! Hannie! Stay where you are!" I called to them. They were standing on the pavement. Hannie was crying.

I was trying to decide whether it would be safe to approach the house with Sari in my arms, when I heard loud laughter from the Kilbournes' house. Shannon was in her front garden, doubled over. "Fake out! Fake out! Made you look!" she screeched.

I put Sari down and marched over to her. "Are you saying there's no fire?" I asked.

Shannon was laughing too hard to answer me.

So I stuck my tongue out at her and stomped away. I felt like a fool.

I calmed Hannie and Linny down, and then we found Noodle (who'd been napping under a bed). By then, Mrs Papadakis was due home, so we never did hold the pet fashion show.

Of course, I had to tell Mrs P. what had happened, since the false alarm was all Hannie and Linny could talk about. Mrs P. became very angry, put her hands on her hips, and said, "I'll have to have a talk with Shannon before she sits again." But I didn't feel much better about the situation. All I wanted to do was get back at Shannon. The question was how?

The idea came to me early that evening, and I have absolutely no idea where it came from. One moment, I didn't know what to do about Shannon Louisa Kilbourne. The next moment, this great idea was in my head.

I got out a phone book, found the number

of a nappy service, and dialled it.

"Mr Stork's Nappies," said a pleasant-sounding man.

"Hello," I said. "I'm sorry to be calling so late, but this is sort of an emergency. My mum is sick, so we're going to need nappy service for my baby sister for about two weeks, starting tomorrow morning, if possible."

"Of course," replied the man. "Name please?"

"Shannon Kilbourne."

"Address?"

I gave the man the Kilbournes' address. When I went to bed that night, I was smiling.

And the next morning, I was delighted with what I saw from one of the guest bedrooms at the front of our house. It was the Mr Stork truck. It pulled into the Kilbournes' drive, and even from across the street I could hear bells jangling out "Rock-a-Bye, Baby." Then a man dressed as a stork dumped a huge package of nappies on the Kilbournes' front steps and drove off.

I was nearly hysterical.

Gotcha, Shannon! I thought.

5th CHAPTER

Thursday

I baby-sat for Myriah and Gabbie this afternoon, and we had a little trouble. See, Mrs. Perkins is getting ready for the new baby. She's fixing up the room that used to be David Michaels. (You should see it, you guys. David Michael would die. There are bunny rabbits and alphabet letters everywhere!) Mrs. Perkins is also sorting through Myriah and Gabbie's baby toys and baby clothes. Myriah and Gabbie are excited and theyve been helping out, but Gabbie is *so* excited that she doesn't understand why anyone *wouldn't* be. So when Jamie Newton came over to play, he started to tell Gabbie how *he* felt about *his* sister. Poor Gabbie just didn't understand at all....

Mary Anne loves to sit for the Perkinses now that she's got used to the fact that *they* live in *my* old house. Lucky for her that such a nice family moved in. Even luckier that a new baby is on the way. Mary Anne is really excited. I know she's helped Mrs Perkins paint the room and pick out curtain material—although the baby isn't due for several more months.

She's excited, and Myriah and Gabbie are, too. What the Perkins girls didn't realize was that not everybody would share their feelings.

As soon as Mrs Perkins left on that Thursday, Jamie Newton came over to play. Myriah took him by the hand and said, "Come and look at the baby's room. It is so, so beautiful. Mummy and Gabbie and I have been working very hard." She pulled Jamie up to the tiny room that used to belong to David Michael. Mary Anne and Gabbie followed.

"Oh, it looks great now!" Mary Anne exclaimed as they stood in the doorway. "You've finished painting it."

"And one curtain is up, but Mummy's still hemming the other one."

"I didn't help my mummy with Lucy's room," said Jamie.

"How come?" asked Gabbie.

Jamie shrugged. "Just because."

"Well, we're helping," said Gabbie.

"You've been working hard," said Mary

Anne, stepping inside the room.

"Look in the drawers," Myriah said to Mary Anne, "and you'll see what we did."

Mary Anne opened the drawers of the bureau to find piles of neatly folded sleepers and undershirts and jumpsuits.

"We washed everything that was in the box in the attic," Myriah told her. "And I folded all those clothes."

"Boy, I guess you're almost ready for this baby."

"Almost," agreed Myriah, "except for one important thing."

"What?" asked Mary Anne.

"We need a name for the baby. You want to hear the names Mummy and Daddy like? They like Sarah or Randi-with-an-'i' for a girl or John Eric or Randy-with-a-'y' for a boy. But they haven't decided."

"What do you like?" I asked.

"I like Laurie for a girl, but I can't think of any good boys' names."

"I want to name it Beth," spoke up Gabbie.

"Laurie and Beth are both very pretty names," said Mary Anne. She glanced at Jamie. He was scowling.

"You know what I wanted to name my baby? I wanted to name her Stupid-head."

"Stupid-head!" cried Gabbie. She looked crushed. "Nah-nah and a boo-boo. That is so, so mean."

"It is not," said Jamie. "I'm going home."

Gabbie marched out of the room. "I'm going to take a nap," she called crossly to Mary Anne.

"Wow," said Mary Anne to Myriah. "Gabbie sounds really mad."

"She must be upset about what Jamie said. We love our baby, even though it isn't here yet."

"I'm glad you feel that way," said Mary Anne.

"How can Jamie be so mean?"

"I don't think he's being mean. He was jealous when Lucy was born. He used to be the baby of the family. Then everything changed for him. I think he felt a little scared."

"Now Gabbie feels bad," said Myriah.

"I know," agreed Mary Anne.

Myriah looked thoughtful. "Let's do something nice to make her feel better."

"That's a good idea," said Mary Anne. "Like what?"

"I'm not sure."

Myriah and Mary Anne sat down on the floor of the baby's room.

"What are some things Gabbie likes to do?" Mary Anne asked.

"She likes to colour."

"What's something special that she can't do every day?"

"Go on rides at Disney World."

"Not that special. Something we could do this afternoon."

"I know!" said Myriah. "She likes tea parties. She likes to give tea parties for her dolls, but sometimes it's a big pain because she wants to get dressed up first, and dress her dolls and teddies, too."

"Well, let's have a tea party, then!" exclaimed Mary Anne. "I'll go downstairs and set it all up. We'll have juice and biscuits You and Gabbie get dressed up, and then dress up the dolls and animals . . . I don't think Gabbie's really taking a nap, do you?"

"No way," replied Myriah.

So Mary Anne ran downstairs and found Gabbie's tea set in the playroom. She set eight places around the kitchen table. Then she put a biscuit at every place, and filled the tiny teacups with orange juice. She folded napkins and even grabbed a vase of flowers from the living room and put them in the middle of the table.

"Myriah! Gabbie!" she called from the bottom of the stairs. "Tea time!"

"We're not ready yet!" Myriah called back.

Mary Anne ran upstairs to see what was going on. In Gabbie's room she found Myriah wearing a pink party dress with white tights and shiny shoes. But Gabbie had had a different idea about getting dressed up. She was wearing one of her mother's slips, a tie belonging to her father, a feather boa, a straw hat, sunglasses, and snow boots.

"How do I look?" she asked.

Mary Anne glanced at Myriah who shrugged.

"Lovely," Mary Anne told her.

"I'm all dressed up," she announced.

"I see. Are your dolls ready?" It was hard to tell. One of them was wearing sunglasses. Another was wearing a bathing cap.

"Yes," replied Gabbie, "but the bears aren't."

"Show us how to dress the bears" said Mary Anne. "Myriah and I will help you."

Gabbie instructed them to put under-shirts and socks on the three bears, and then they carried the dolls and bears down to the kitchen, and sat them around the table.

"This is beautiful," said Gabbie, looking at the tea party and trying to sound grown up.

"It is too, too diveen," added Myriah.

Mary Anne giggled.

She and the girls drank their tiny cups of juice and ate their biscuits. Then they drank the bears' and the dolls' juice and ate some of their biscuits, too.

"Did you like the party?" Mary Anne asked Gabbie when it was over.

Gabbie nodded. "I loved it. It was too, too diveen."

Mary Anne smiled. The crisis was over.

6th CHAPTER

Linny and Hannie were right. The Delaney children are awful. They are nasty and bossy and everything Hannie said they are. I know because I baby-sat for them. Mrs Delaney called the Babysitters Club, and of course my friends urged *me* to take the job since it's in my neighbourhood.

I arrived at the Delaneys' after school on a Friday. (What a way to start the weekend.) Their house is the opposite of the Papadakises' or Watson's (I mean, mine). Last year, one of my spelling words was "ostentatious." (I'm a good speller.) And that's what the Delaneys' house was. Ostentatious. It was showy and show-offy and ornate. Guess what was in their front hall — a fountain. No kidding. There was this golden fish standing on its tail, fins spread, with water spouting out of its mouth and running into a little pool surrounding it.

Guess what's in our front hall—two chairs and a mirror.

Guess what's in the Papadakises' front hall—two chairs and Myrtle's box.

In the Delaneys' gigantic back garden are two tennis courts. In their library and living room are gilt-framed portraits and Oriental rugs, and the kitchen looks like a space control centre with gadgets and buttons and appliances everywhere. I hope I never have to give the Delaney kids a meal. I wouldn't even be able to work out how to toast a slice of bread. (I think the Delaneys have a part-time cook, though.)

But I could have handled all this stuff okay. It was the children I couldn't take.

For starters, they weren't even interested in meeting me. Their mother answered the door, gave me instructions and phone numbers, and put on her coat, and still I hadn't seen the children.

"Where are Amanda and Max?" I finally asked.

"Oh, of course," said Mrs Delaney, sort of breathlessly. "I suppose I ought to introduce you."

She led me into a room that I guessed was the family room, but it sure didn't look like ours. Our family room is always on the messy side—a newspaper strewn around, Louie lounging on the couch, Watson's cat, Boo-Boo, asleep on the television set, maybe a colouring book or some homework left out.

This room was not only tidy, it was clean. *And* it was all white. White shag rug, white leather couch, even white lacquer tables and a white TV set. Priscilla (fluffy and white, of course) sleeping daintily in a white wicker cat basket, looking as if somebody, maybe the director of a play, had posed her just so, to be the perfect complement to the perfect room.

Posed on the couch were two perfect (looking) children. Amanda, the eight-year-old I'd met with Shannon, her shoes polished, her brown hair parted evenly and held in place with a big blue bow, sat primly on one side. She was wearing a blue corduroy jumper over a white blouse. Her jumper matched her hair ribbon exactly. Next to her was Max, the six-year-old, a blond-haired, blue-eyed angel of a boy, dressed in corduroy trousers, an unwrinkled shirt, and brogues.

"Children," said Mrs Delaney, "this is Kristy. She's going to baby-sit for you this afternoon. I'll be back in a couple of hours. You do what Kristy tells you, all right?"

Amanda and Max merely nodded, their eyes glued to the TV. Amanda didn't give any sign that she'd met me before.

Mrs Delaney left then, and I sat down in a white armchair.

"Don't sit there!" Amanda squawked,

and I leaped up.

"Why?" I asked.

"It's Daddy's chair."

This didn't make any sense to me, since Mr Delaney wasn't at home, but I moved over to the couch anyway. Neither Max nor Amanda made any room for me, so I squished into a corner.

"What are you watching?" I asked the kids.

No answer.

But when a commercial came on, Amanda said, "Get me a Coke, Kristy."

"What do you say?" I replied in a singsong voice. When you have a little brother, a little stepbrother, and a little stepsister, you find yourself repeating this all the time, as a reminder to say "please" and "thank you."

"I say, 'Get me a Coke,'" Amanda repeated dryly.

"Get me one, too," said Max.

My mouth dropped open. What was I supposed to do? I couldn't very well scold Amanda and Max during the first fifteen minutes of my job. So I got up, went into the kitchen, found the Coke in the maze of appliances, and poured some into two glasses.

When I handed Amanda her glass, I didn't expect her to say "thank you" (I was too smart for that), but I also didn't expect her to say, "Where's the ice?"

I rolled my eyes, took the glasses back in the kitchen, dropped three ice cubes in each glass, and gave the Cokes to Amanda and Max. Amanda accepted hers and began to drink, but Max looked from me to his glass and back, and said, "I hate ice. Take it out."

Now if David Michael had said that to me, I would have replied, "Take it out yourself." But the Delaneys were new clients of the Babysitters Club, and I didn't want any unhappy children on hand when their mother returned. So I went to the kitchen for the third time and fished Max's ice cubes out of his glass with a spoon. When I handed the Coke back to him, he and Amanda drank in silence until their show was over.

"Well," I said, "let's go outside and play. There's nothing good on TV anyway."

Amanda shrugged. She handed me her empty glass and said, "Can you put this back in the kitchen? We're not allowed to leave stuff in here."

Max handed me his glass, too.

"And put them in the dishwasher," Amanda called after me.

I did so, my teeth clenched. Then I turned on a smile (a stiff one), walked back into the family room, and switched off the TV. "Time to go outside," I announced. "Come on."

Amanda and Max reluctantly followed me to the front door. So did Priscilla.

"Priscilla's a beautiful cat," I said to the kids, hoping, maybe, to start a conversation.

"She cost four hundred dollars," replied Amanda.

"I know. You told me." (Boy, what snobs.)

"You know how much my dog Louie cost? Nothing. He was free."

"Oh, a mongrel," said Max knowingly. "Too bad."

I rolled my eyes.

Then I opened the front door and who should I find there, hand poised to ring the bell, but David Michael. Louie was at his side.

"Hi!" I cried, unusually glad to see him. "What are you doing here?"

"Who's that?" interrupted Amanda before David Michael could answer.

"This is my brother, David Michael," I told her. "David Michael, this is Amanda Delaney and this is Max. Do you know each other?"

"I've seen them around," my brother said, just as Amanda said, "No."

The snob kids and Priscilla and I joined David Michael and Louie outside. "What are you doing here?" I asked David Michael again.

"I just walked Louie over," he said.

"Is Louie your mongrel?" asked Max.

"Louie is our *collie*," David Michael replied indignantly.

"He's not very pretty."

David Michael was completely taken aback.

"He's nothing like Priscilla," added Amanda. "Now *she* is beautiful. Look what good care she takes of her coat. Your dog—"

"Yeah?" David Michael challenged her, finally finding his voice.

"Well, he's just not pretty."

"Boys," David Michael informed her, "are not *supposed* to be pretty. Besides, he's old and he has arthritis."

"Ew," said Amanda. "I hope that never happens to Priscilla."

"David Michael, is anything wrong?" I asked him.

"I don't think Louie feels well," he said, his voice trembling.

"Well, Dr Smith said he wouldn't. Remember?"

"I thought the pills were supposed to make him better."

"They're supposed to help take the pain away, but he still has arthritis," I pointed out.

At that moment, Louie lowered his head and sneezed loudly—*whoof*!

"Ew! Ew!" cried Amanda. "Disgusting. His sneeze got all over me! I'm going to wash my hands. You come with me, Kristy."

I looked at David Michael sympathetically. "I have to go inside. Why don't you take Louie home and let him rest? Maybe Mum could call Dr Smith tomorrow."

"All right," David Michael agreed reluctantly. He turned and walked down the steps. "Come on, Louie," he urged. "Just three steps. You can do it." Louie followed him with his stiff-legged gait. As I looked after them, I sighed.

In the Snobs' opulent bathroom, Amanda commanded me to find first some violet-scented soap, and then a certain hand towel.

"Are you disinfected now?" I couldn't resist asking her when she had finished washing her hands.

She gave me a dark look. "I don't know what that means. But at least your dog's germs are off me."

The phone rang then and Max said, "You get it, Kristy. It's in the kitchen."

(What? No phone in the bathroom?)

"Hello, Delaney residence," I said when I'd picked up the receiver. (Hello, Snob residence, I thought.)

"Kristy? Kristy? Is that you? This is Shannon."

My heart sank. She must have seen me when I crossed the Delaneys' garden. Had she worked out that I'd sent Mr Stork to her?

"I'm baby-sitting at the Papadakises'," she said nervously. "I've been here dozens of times and nothing like this has ever happened."

"What's wrong?"

"Sari's crying and I can't get her to stop. She seems to like you, so I thought—"

"I'll be right over," I said, and hung up the phone. I wasn't sure I could trust Shannon, but I couldn't ignore a crying child. Sari could be sick or in pain . . . "Amanda, Max, come on. We have to go to the Papadakises'. Now." Amid moans and groans, I rushed the kids out of the door, across the Kilbournes' lawn, and to the Papadakises' front steps. I rang the bell and Shannon answered it. One of the bus stop girls (the brown-haired one) was with her.

"Yes?" said Shannon coolly.

"Here I am," I said, trying to catch my breath. "Where's Sari?"

"Why do you want to know?"

"I'm here to help—" I paused, listening. The house was silent. Shannon and her friend were trying not to laugh. I'd been tricked again.

At that moment, Hannie and Linny appeared. "Hi, Kr—" they started to say to me. Then they stopped, seeing Amanda and Max.

Amanda and Max immediately began whispering and giggling. Hannie and Linny frowned. Amanda pointed to her head, then to Linny, and said "Cuckoo"—just loudly enough for everyone to hear.

"I am not cuckoo," cried Linny. "*You* are!"

"Okay, okay," I said. I grabbed Amanda and Max by the hands, and headed for home. I was so mad, I couldn't even think of anything to say (or do) to Shannon.

The last thing I heard as we left the Papadakises' yard was Shannon yelling after me, "And thanks a lot for pushing me out of my baby-sitting jobs!"

Uh-oh, I thought.

7th CHAPTER

Saturday

I babysat for my brother tonight, and something is going on. Something's wrong. He hasn't been himself at all lately, but this was worse than usual. He was cross and mean and rude all evening. Finally we had this big fight and I couldn't believe what he said. I was so upset, I had to wait for Mum to come home so I could tell her about it. And then she called Dad in California to tell him about it.

This seems like personal, family business, but I guess you club members should know about it in case you sit for Jeff, because he's like a different kid these days. Better to be prepared. So this is what's going on . . . .

Wow. Talk about a different kid. Our even-tempered, unflappable alternate officer was a different person herself. Dawn was really upset. Not only did she write about Jeff in the club notebook, but she called both Mary Anne and me to tell us what had happened.

Apparently, ever since school began, Jeff has been having some problems. Actually, Dawn isn't sure if the problems are due to school starting again, or to the fact that Jeff got two letters on the first day of school, one from their father, one from Jeff's best friend in California. She thinks it's the letters' fault, though.

Dawn says Jeff has been acting up in class, and once he even walked right out in the middle of a reading lesson. He's had to stay after school twice, and go to the headmaster once. And he hasn't been too pleasant at home.

Anyway, Dawn's mum had needed a sitter on Saturday evening so she could go out with this guy Trip she's been seeing quite often. Two of us were free that night, but of course we gave the job to Dawn since it was for her own brother.

The Trip-Man (that's what Dawn and Jeff call their mother's date) was going to pick Mrs Schafer up at six-thirty. They were going to some fancy party in Stamford. Their evening was formal and would involve dinner, dancing, and entertainment. Dawn thought her mother looked very glamorous as she slipped on a long black gown with lots of sequins on the top part.

"You smell nice, too, Mum," Dawn told her mother as she hung around Mrs Schafer's bedroom.

"It's my perfume, I guess. Want some?"

"No, thanks," said Dawn. "I like it better on you. You always smell like this when you go out. I like to smell the perfume and watch you get ready and dream about what you'll do on your date."

Mrs Schafer smiled. "I used to do the same thing when *my* parents were getting ready to—"

"*You* were lucky enough to have *two* parents! " yelled Jeff from his bedroom.

Mrs Schafer sighed. "He sounds as though he's in another one of his moods," she said to Dawn.

"I heard that," Jeff shouted. "And it's not a mood!"

Dawn rolled her eyes. "You're making me take care of *that* all evening?" she teased.

"I'll give you a big tip," her mother replied. "Come on. Let's go downstairs and I'll show you what's for dinner."

Mrs Schafer isn't much of a cook, but she tries hard to make interesting health food for Dawn and Jeff. The Schafers are really into eating healthy, and are semi-vegetarians. They get tired of yoghurt and salad and fruit, though, so Mrs Schafer makes casseroles from vegetables and brown rice or pasta. She waits until she has a free day or weekend and then she makes four or five casseroles and freezes them.

Mrs Schafer had just finished explaining to Dawn how to heat up an aubergine casserole when the doorbell rang. "That's Trip," she said. "You know where we'll be tonight. The number's on the fridge, and you can always call Granny and Pop-Pop if there's an emergency."

"I know," said Dawn. "Have fun, Mum. We'll be fine." She was pushing her mother towards the front door, all the while checking her over to make sure nothing was missing or out of place. (Mrs Schafer is completely absent-minded.)

"Good-bye, Jeff!" Mrs Schafer called upstairs. "Have fun with Dawn."

"'Bye," was the sullen reply.

Dawn and her mother shrugged. Then Mrs Schafer answered the bell and Dawn said hello to the Trip-Man. Finally Dawn closed the door behind her mum, and breathed a sigh of relief. She began to get dinner ready. She set the table, put out whole-wheat rolls, and poured glasses of iced herbal tea. All the time she knew she should be asking Jeff to help her (even if she *was* the baby-sitter), but it seemed better to leave him alone when he was in one of his moods.

When the casserole was ready, Dawn called Jeff to supper. He walked into the

Schafers' old-fashioned kitchen, saw the table, and said, "It's Saturday. And Mum's not here. Why aren't we eating in front of the TV?"

"Because we'll turn into couch potatoes, that's why," said Dawn, trying to be funny.

Jeff grumbled some answer that Dawn couldn't understand, filled his plate, then began to carry it into the family room. "I want to watch *Leave it to Beaver*, not sit in here," he said over his shoulder.

"Then put your dinner on a tray," Dawn told him. "Otherwise you'll spill." She took two trays out of a cabinet, but before she could hand one to him, he shrugged away, saying, "And I *won't spill*. I don't need a tray. *I am not a baby*."

"Well, I'm using one, and I'm older than you are," Dawn retorted. She couldn't help sounding just a little cross.

Jeff ignored her and settled himself in the family room, watching *Leave it to Beaver*. He balanced his plate on his knees and his glass on the arm of the couch. Dawn sat beside him.

Sure enough, about halfway through the program, Jeff knocked over his tea. As he dived to catch the glass before it hit the floor, the food slid off his plate, into his lap, and all over the couch.

"Oh, Jeff!" exclaimed Dawn, quickly setting her tray on the coffee table and getting to her feet.

Before she could say another word, Jeff was on his feet, too. "Don't say anything!" he yelled. "This wasn't my fault!"

"Oh, no? Well, whose fault was it?"

"You and Mum always treat me like a baby! I am not a baby! I'm in fifth grade!"

"Jeff," Dawn said, "you're the one who just knocked over his entire dinner."

Now maybe this wasn't the most tactful thing Dawn could have said, but it was true.

"If you'd treat me like a grown-up person I'd act like a grown-up person!" Jeff's voice rose. He was yelling. Not just talking loudly, but really shouting. "I don't need a baby-sitter! I'm too old for one. Mum treats me like a baby. You treat me like a baby. The only one who doesn't treat me like a baby is Dad."

"Whoa," said Dawn under her breath. Personally, she didn't think she and her mother babied Jeff at all. He was ten, the same age as the Pike triplets, whom the club members sit for all the time. In fact, Jeff was often on his own during the day, something Mrs Pike rarely allows for the triplets.

"Jeff," Dawn began. He was facing her angrily while tea seeped into the couch and aubergine casserole dripped down the front of his jeans.

"Shut up!" cried Jeff. "Just shut up! I hate it here. I miss California. I *hate* it with you and Mum! I wish I lived with Dad."

Jeff left the mess on the couch, ran

upstairs, and locked himself in his room. Dawn decided it would be better to leave him alone. Slowly, she cleaned up the couch. Then she tried to finish her own dinner, but it was cold, so she cleaned up the kitchen instead.

Dawn told Mary Anne she felt stunned. (She called Mary Anne that evening while she was waiting for her mother to come home.) She said Jeff might as well have hit her. That was how bad she felt. Mary Anne isn't allowed to talk on the phone for more than ten minutes at a time, so Dawn had to hang up much sooner than she wanted. Then she called me. She was really scared for Jeff. She'd seen him get angry plenty of times, but she'd *never* seen him act like this.

Mrs Schafer had said she'd probably be home around twelve-thirty or one o'clock. Dawn knew she had to wait up for her, but one o'clock seemed like centuries away, and Dawn was a nervous wreck. She tried to keep busy. She read a short ghost story, but when she had finished, realized she hadn't paid a bit of attention and would have to read it again sometime. Finally, she just parked herself in front of the TV and watched one show after another until the Trip-Man brought her mother home.

As soon as Dawn heard the car in the drive, she ran to the front hall and blinked the outside lights as a signal to her mother. Then she flung open the front door. Mrs

Schafer was already halfway up the path.

"Mum! Mum!" called Dawn.

"Honey, what on earth is wrong? Are you and Jeff all right?"

"I am, but Jeff isn't," Dawn replied as her mother stepped into the house.

Dawn told Mrs Schafer everything that had happened. "He said he wants to go back to California, Mum," she finished up. "And he sounds like he means it."

Mrs Schafer had turned slightly pale. "Oh, boy," she said. "Maybe that trip to California this summer wasn't a good idea. It must have made him homesick."

"Well, it made *me* homesick," Dawn admitted, "but I still wanted to come back to Connecticut—and you."

"Thanks, honey," said her mother, giving Dawn a little hug. "I guess you and Jeff are just different. Everybody always says a boy needs his father. I thought that was very old-fashioned, but maybe it's true."

"Mum, you're not going to send Jeff back to Dad, are you?" Dawn was horrified. "We wouldn't be a family then. We'd be split in half."

"Oh, Dawn. We'll always be a family. But don't worry. I couldn't just send Jeff back to your father, even if I wanted to. At least not right away. I have custody of him. Legal custody. But I do think I'd better talk to your father. And," Mrs Schafer added, "you'd better go to bed. It's one-thirty. You'll be a Zombie tomorrow."

Dawn went to bed reluctantly. She noticed that Jeff's light was out and wondered when he'd gone to bed. She hadn't seen him since he'd run upstairs during dinner.

In the next room, Mrs Schafer phoned Dawn's father. It was only ten-thirty in California. Not too late. Dawn pressed her ear against the wall and tried to overhear her mother's end of the conversation, but the words were muffled. She could tell that her mother was upset, though. Dawn sighed. Her family was just getting used to being divorced. She'd thought the bad times were over. Now, she wasn't so sure.

8th CHAPTER

"Come to order," I said listlessly. I said it so listlessly that nobody heard me and I had to repeat myself. It was pathetic. I tapped a pencil on the edge of Claudia's desk and wished I had a hammer.

It was a gloomy day, gloomy outside and gloomy inside. Nobody felt like having a meeting of the Babysitters Club. Dawn and I were depressed. Claudia was mad because she'd flunked a spelling test. Mary Anne was upset because her kitten, Tigger, had worms, and Stacey was upset because she had a doctor's appointment coming up and she hates doctor's appointments.

"We're *in* order," said Mary Anne. "Sort of."

"Any Club business?' I asked.

My friends shook their heads.

"Boy, what a lousy, stinky, rotten day," I commented.

"Yeah," agreed the others.

"Have I told you about the Snob family?" I asked. "Amanda and Max?"

"You mean the Delaneys?" said Mary Anne, frowning down at the client list in our record book.

"I mean the Snobs," I said pointedly. "You guys, those kids are terrors. They make Jenny Prezzioso look like Little Miss Muffet."

"You're kidding. What'd they do?" asked Claudia. (Claudia once unexpectedly sat for some terrors herself—Jamie Newton's cousins—and she hasn't got over the experience. Stories about other terrors are always of special interest to her.)

"They are spoiled rotten," I told her. "They're demanding, they're rude, and they're snobby. We're watching TV, right? And at the commercial Amanda says to me, 'Get me a Coke.' Just like that. 'Get me a Coke.' No please or anything. And so I say. 'What do you say?' You know, like I always say to David Michael and Karen and Andrew. And she gives me this look and says, 'I say, "Get me a Coke."' Can you believe her nerve? Then *Max* says, 'Get me one, too.' So I do, but Amanda says, 'Where's the ice?' and I get ice and then Max doesn't want it. Then later they order me to put the empty glasses in the dishwasher and to answer the phone. Which I would have done anyway. But you don't expect an eight-year-old and a six-year-old to order you around."

"Why did you let them?" asked Stacey.

"Because . . . I don't know. I mean, what would you have done? They're new clients. We have to be nice to them. We don't want Mrs Snob coming home and hearing the little Snobs saying, 'Oh, that Kristy is so mean. She makes us say please and thank you and get our own Cokes.' Besides, I can't force them to do anything they don't want to do."

Stacey laughed. "No, but there are ways to get around those kids. Believe me. You don't have to—"

Ring, ring.

Stacey interrupted herself to answer the phone. "Hello, Babysitters Club . . . Oh, hi, Mrs Delaney."

"Mrs *Delaney*?" I whispered. I made a gagging sound and pretended to choke. Stacey turned away so she wouldn't have to look at me.

"Next Tuesday?" she was saying. "Both kids. Okay . . . Okay . . . I'll call you right back." She hung up the phone and turned around. "Kristy, don't *do* that!" she exclaimed, giggling. "You almost made me laugh. And I almost called Mrs Delaney 'Mrs Snob'!"

We all laughed then and felt a little better. Claudia, the junk-food addict, found a bag of wine gums stashed inside her pillow case and passed them around to those of us who'll eat sweets (herself, Mary Anne, and me). Then she found some Treets and passed those around, too.

Mary Anne was looking at our appointment calendar. "Three of us are free on Tuesday," she reported.

I wrinkled up my nose. *I* certainly didn't want to sit for the Delaneys again.

"It's you, Stacey, and Dawn," Mary Anne went on.

I noticed that Dawn looked as unenthusiastic as I felt.

"Can I go?' asked Stacey.

"*Can* you?!" I replied. "Be my guest. You can be the Delaneys' permanent babysitter, for all I care."

"Great," replied Stacey. "Because I know just how to handle the Snobs."

Once again she was interrupted by the ringing phone. We took a couple of jobs then and called Mrs Delaney back, and when we had finished, we'd forgotten all about Stacey's plans, whatever they were.

"You know," I said, leaning back in the director's chair and yawning, "there might be another snob-related problem. Not with *the* Snobs, but with the snobby girls I told you about. Shannon and Tiffany and their friends."

"Is Shannon the one who was mean to Louie?" asked Mary Anne, who has a soft spot in her heart for animals.

"Yes," I replied. "And the thing is, I didn't know it at first, but I guess she baby-sits in the neighbourhood, too. I know she sits for the Papadakises anyway. And the other day she accused me of pushing her out of her sitting jobs."

"Oops," said Claudia.

"Right," I replied.

"Well, she can't be the only baby-sitter in the neighbourhood," Dawn countered. "I mean, look at us. You started this club so there would be enough sitters to go around."

"That's true," I said slowly.

We were sitting silently, the five of us mulling this problem over, when all of a sudden Dawn began to cry. The rest of us looked at each other with our eyebrows raised. Not only is Dawn not a crier, but, well, what was she crying about?

"Dawn?" Mary Anne ventured. She and Dawn were sitting on Claudia's bed, and Mary Anne scrunched over until she was right next to her. "Dawn, what's the matter?" she asked worriedly.

At first Dawn just shook her head. She couldn't talk. Then she opened the club notebook and pointed to the account she'd written of sitting for her brother.

"Oh, you're upset about Jeff?" asked Mary Anne.

Dawn nodded, sniffling.

Mary Anne and I filled Claudia and

Stacey in on the news, in case they hadn't got around to reading the notebook. Then, when Dawn had control of her voice, she added that her mother had had a long talk with her father, and that her father, for some reason, hadn't seemed crazy about the possibility of Jeff living with him.

"I don't know," Dawn said, (only, with her stuffed nose, it sounded like "I dote dough"). "I don't know which is worse, the thought that Jeff hates living with Mum and me and wants to leave us, or the thought that maybe Dad doesn't want him. And," she went on, "if Dad doesn't want *him*, I assume he wouldn't want *me*, either. Not that I'd like to move back to California. It's just that it's awful to think your father doesn't want you."

"Tell me about it," I said bitterly. My parents' divorce hadn't exactly been friendly, and my dad never writes or calls my brothers and me. I don't think he cares about us at all. "But Dawn, are you *sure* he doesn't want you and Jeff?" I asked. "Maybe he's just enjoying being a bachelor again. I mean, first he was a family man, then he probably got used to living with*out* you and Jeff and your mum, and now he's just, I don't know, unsettled by the thought of *another* change."

"You know," said Dawn, brightening, "maybe you're right. I mean, he didn't say, 'I don't want Jeff.' He said something about having to change his work hours, and needing to get a housekeeper. Stuff like that."

We all agreed that Mr Schafer was probably an okay dad who'd just been taken by surprise by the ten-thirty phone call. The meeting ended then, and I went home feeling subdued. I had problems, we all had problems. At the moment, Dawn's were the biggest. (They were certainly bigger than Tigger's worms.) Although I knew our problems would work out eventually, I realized that, as a group, we were kind of under the weather.

Charlie parked the car in the garage and we went inside. We found Watson home early, starting dinner. In the living room, Sam was helping David Michael with a tricky subtraction problem. Boo-Boo watched them from an armchair. Maybe because he's a cat, or maybe just because he's Boo-Boo, he always seems to watch people suspiciously, as if, right now, my brothers weren't doing maths, they were plotting ways to torture Boo-Boo.

"Louie!" I called. "Louie! Where are you, boy?"

"Woof!"

Louie's woof came from Watson's library. I wandered in that direction and found him curled up on an Oriental rug.

"Hey, David Michael!" I yelled. "Did you feed Louie?"

"I put his food out and called him to dinner but he wouldn't come," he replied.

"Okay!" I knelt next to Louie. "Don't you want supper?" I asked him.

Louie's head was resting on one of his front paws. In order to look at me, he raised his eyes, but he didn't move his head.

"Come on. It's supper time," I told him, trying to sound excited about it. "Time for doggie treats. Maybe David Michael will let you have a people cracker later. Remember how much you liked the one in the shape of the vet?"

"Mmm-mm," whimpered Louie.

"Come on, I know you're hungry. All you have to do is stand up and walk into the ktichen . . . Come *on*."

I stood up, urging Louie to get up, too. He staggered to his feet—and I mean *staggered*. He got his front legs up first and tried to raise his hindquarters, but his left front paw collapsed and he fell stiffly. Finally I picked him up around his middle and held him in place until all four legs were steady. Louie and I started toward the kitchen. But we hadn't even left the library when Louie jerked to a stop, squatted, and had an accident on one of Watson's Oriental carpets.

"Louie!" I scolded. "Mu-um! . . . Watson, is Mum home yet?"

"Kristy, what's wrong?" called Sam. He and David Michael came running.

"What's wrong? *That* is what's wrong." Louie was getting painfully to his feet, and I pointed to the mess on the carpet.

"Louie!" David Michael cried. "How could you do that? He's never done that," he said to Sam and me. "Never."

"Oh, he did it all the time when he was a puppy," replied Sam mildly. "I'll go get some paper towels."

Louie knew he'd done something wrong and he slunk out of the library with his tail between his legs.

"Bad, bad dog!" exclaimed David Michael, shaking his finger at Louie. "You're not a puppy now." But then he bent down to hug him. "Louie, I'm sorry," he said. "I didn't mean that. I don't think you could help yourself. Could he, Kristy?"

I shook my head. "No, he couldn't."

David Michael looked at me from around Louie's furry neck. "He's really sick, isn't he?" he asked.

I nodded. Then I turned away before my brother could see me cry.

9th CHAPTER

Tuesday

Okay, so I sat for the Snobs today, and no big deal. You just have to know how to handle them. You have to know a little psychology. And I happen to. Know psychology, that is. I read this magazine article called "Getting what you want: Dealing with Difficult People the Easy Way." It's kind of hard to explain what you're supposed to do, so I'll just give you some examples of how I dealt with the Snobs. And you'll see that they can be tamed. Plus, I found that once you have tamed them, they're pretty nice little kids.

By the way, my parents have a book called The Taming of the Shrew. I think it might be a play. Now I could write a play called The Taming of the Snobs!...

Well, we were all pretty impressed with Stacey and her psychology. Especially since her job at the Snobs' started out as badly as mine had, maybe even worse. This time, when Mrs McGill had dropped Stacey off at the Delaneys', Mrs Delaney took Stacey upstairs to the little Snobs' playroom. Amanda and Max, looking gorgeous and immaculate, of course, were standing in the middle of the messiest room Stacey had ever seen. It was even messier than the way the Barretts' house used to look when Dawn first began baby-sitting for the impossible three. There were toys everywhere, and not just big toys, but Tinker Toys, Matchbox cars, and Legos, all mixed in with stuffed animals, board games, dolls, dressing-up clothes, you name it. It was toy soup. And Mrs Delaney asked Stacey, Amanda, and Max to clean it up before they did anything else.

'Well,' said Stacey when Mrs Delaney had left, "let's get this room in shape. Then we can go outside."

"If you want to go outside, then clean it yourself," said Amanda. "We like it messy." She stood back, folded her arms, and glared at Stacey. Max imitated her.

Stacey was prepared for something like this. She pretended to gaze around the room. Then she said seriously, "You know, you're right. I like a really messy room. In fact, I don't think this room is messy enough. Look at this. A whole set of Lincoln Logs. They're not even on the floor." Stacey poured the Lincoln Logs into the toy soup.

"Hey!" cried Amanda. "What do you think you're doing?"

"Yeah! What are you doing?" added Max.

"You said you like a messy room," Stacey replied. "Well, I do, too." She picked up a stack of cards and let them start floating to the floor card by card.

"Stop messing up our room!" shouted Amanda. She held her arms stiffly at her sides and stamped her foot.

"Why?" demanded Stacey, pausing long enough to let the remainder of the paper settle into the toy soup. Then she began scattering puzzle pieces.

"Because," said Max. "That's why."

"I thought you liked a good mess," Stacey went on.

"We do," Amanda began, then hesitated. "But not . . . not this good a mess. Cut it out!"

"I'm just trying to help you guys out," Stacey told her.

"No! I mean . . . we want it clean." Amanda scrambled around, picking up the paper.

"Whoops! You forgot these doll clothes," said Stacey. She dumped out a box of Barbie dresses. Max grabbed them up and shoved them back in the box. "CUT IT OUT!" he screeched.

Before Stacey knew it, the Snobs were cleaning up the room. After a while, Stacey pitched in, but neither Amanda nor Max said a word about it. They just kept glancing at her warily.

When the room was as neat as a pin, the Snobs stood in the doorway to admire their work. Stacey thought they looked pretty proud of themselves, but she knew better than to praise them. After all, they'd been tricked, and they probably knew it.

"Boy, am I thirsty," said Max. "Get me some milk, Stacey."

"Milk?" repeated Stacey. "Okay. And I guess while I'm at it, I'll get some orange juice, some fruit punch, maybe some iced tea—"

"No, no," Max interrupted her. "Um, that's okay. I'll just get it myself."

"Yeah, we'll get the milk ourselves," added Amanda.

"I'll join you," said Stacey, and followed them downstairs.

Max got a carton of milk out of the Snobs' space-age fridge. Stacey watched Amanda take two glasses out of a cabinet, think better of it, and remove a third for Stacey.

Then Max held the carton out to Stacey. "Pour," he commanded, and Stacey knew he was testing her.

"Okay," said Stacey. But instead of

taking the milk carton from Max, she opened a cupboard and began removing glasses and setting them on the table.

"*Now* what are you doing?" asked Amanda.

"Well, Max just said, 'pour.' He didn't say how much he wanted. I thought I'd better be prepared."

"Oh, never mind." Amanda took the carton crossly from Max and filled two glasses with milk. She hesitated. Then, "Do you want some?" she asked Stacey.

"Yes, please. Half a glass will be fine."

Amanda poured half a glass for Stacey and pushed it across the table to her. The three of them sat down and drank in silence. It wasn't long before Max knocked into his glass, sloshing milk over the sides.

He stared at the puddle on the table. "Wipe it up, Stacey," he commanded.

"Could you finish spilling it first, please?"

"Huh?" said Amanda and Max at the same time.

"Finish spilling it first. You've only spilled some of it. I don't want to have to stand up and get the sponge now if I'm just going to have to get it again in a few minutes. And by the way, since you like me to clean things up for you so much, you ought to know that I'll be happy to give you a bath later, I'm sure you'll want me to clean *you* up, as well as everything else."

"That just shows how much you know," said Max, pouting. "I don't want you to give me a bath. I don't want you to clean up *any*thing for me. I'll clean up my own messes. So there."

"Suit yourself," Stacey replied as Max mopped up the milk.

Max not only wiped up the mess, he brushed a few crumbs from the table, carried the sponge and the crumbs back to the sink, dropped the crumbs down the drain, and rinsed the sponge out before returning to the table.

"Thank you," said Stacey.

"You're welcome," replied Max.

"Stacey? What would happen if I asked you to get us some biscuits?" ventured Amanda.

"Well, if you said, 'Stacey, could you please get out the biscuits,' I would probably do it, especially if I thought you were going to thank me when I put them on the table. But if you just said, 'Stacey, get us the biscuits,' then I would give you every kind of biscuit I could find, because I wouldn't be sure what you meant, and I wouldn't want to have to jump up and get anything *else* for a person who never says please or thank you."

Amanda nodded thoughtfully.

"Aside from which," added Stacey, "I would feel very, very sorry that you are eight years old and unable to get biscuits yourself."

Amanda nodded again. Stacey thought she saw Max hide a smile. Then he said, "*I* can clean up myself."

"I know," replied Stacey. "I'm glad to see that." She smiled at Max, then turned to Amanda. "*Do* you want some biscuits?"

"No," said Amanda. "I just wanted to find out what would happen if I asked for them."

Stacey certainly hadn't expected *that* from the Snobs, but Amanda didn't seem to be acting snide or rude. In fact, she looked quite serious.

"You know," said Stacey, "you guys have worked really hard this afternoon. I think we should have some fun now."

"Like what?" asked Amanda.

"Do you know how to play hopscotch?" asked Stacey.

"Hopscotch is boring," said Amanda.

"It's for *girls*," added Max witheringly.

"Would you relax? I just asked if you knew how to play. I didn't ask if you wanted to play. Now. *Do* you know how to play hopscotch?"

"Yes."

"Yes."

"Do you have any chalk?"

"Yes."

"Yes."

"Do your parents let you draw on the drive with chalk?"

"Yes."

"Yes."

"Good," said Stacey. "Because I'm going to teach you how to play Snail, and it helps to know how to play hopscotch first."

"Snail?" replied Amanda, intrigued. "What's that?"

"It's a very great game," Stacey replied, "and I guarantee that if you show it to your friends, they will all want to play Snail with you. Now let's put our glasses in the dishwasher and go."

Without so much as a complaint, Amanda and Max marched their glasses to the sink rinsed them out, and put them in the dishwasher. Stacey did the same with her glass. Then Max found a box of chalk and he and Stacey and Amanda went outdoors to the drive where they found Priscilla sitting primly in a patch of shade.

Priscilla and the Snobs watched as Stacey drew a gigantic spiral on the drive. Then she blocked the spiral off in boxes about a foot long, like this:

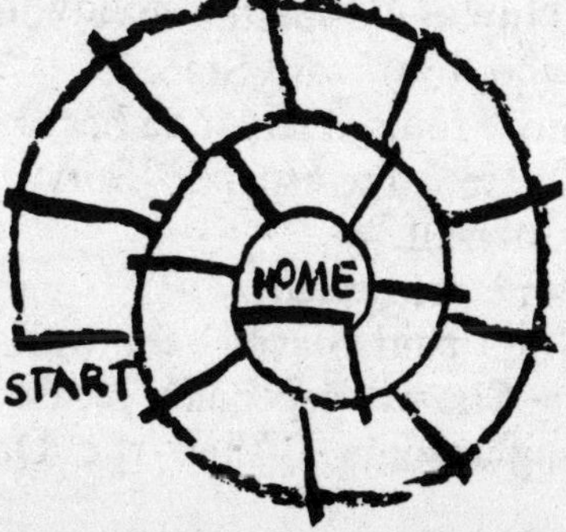

"Okay," said Stacey, "the object of Snail is to hop from the outside to the centre of the snail shell, one foot in each square. If you make it all the way to Home without stepping on any lines, you get to choose one square for yourself. You write your initial on it. Later, when you hop to one of your own squares, you can land in it with two feet and rest there. But everyone else has to jump *over* it. When so many squares are taken that we can't play anymore, the person with the most squares is the winner. Understand?"

The Snobs nodded. They were actually smiling. They even let Stacey go first so she could demonstrate.

Stacey and the Delaneys played Snail until Mrs Delaney came home. Stacey said she actually had fun—and she thinks Amanda and Max did, too. They giggled and shrieked, groaned when they missed, cheered when they earned new squares. The only sign of the old Delaneys was when Amanda ordered Stacey to get her a piece of chalk. "Maybe I'd better take your next turn for you, too," said Stacey.

"No, no," replied Amanda hastily, but a giggle threatened to escape. "Sorry. I'll get the chalk myself."

The game continued.

Mrs Snob paid Stacey very well for the afternoon. She was especially pleased to see the tidy playroom. When the Delaneys dropped Stacey off at her house, she called good-bye to Amanda and Max, who answered cheerfully, but as the door was closing behind her, Stacey heard Amanda say, "Mum, no kidding, she was the *weirdest* baby-sitter we've ever had."

Apparently, Mrs Snob didn't mind. She called the Babysitters Club again very soon.

And I got the job.

10th CHAPTER

I read Stacey's entry in our club diary, and while I had to admit that she'd certainly handled the Snobs well, I also had to admit that I didn't *quite* understand what her method had been.

"I don't get it," I said to Stacey at lunch one day. "What were you doing? Just freaking them out by giving them unexpected answers?"

"Not exactly," replied Stacey. "I started out by going along with everything they said—but taking an extra step. Like when Amanda told me she liked a messy playroom, I not only agreed with her, I added to the mess."

"I wonder why that made her clean it up?" I said slowly.

"Well, actually," Stacey answered, "I think two things were going on then. First of all, the Snobs like to be contrary, which I was counting on—that was the psychology part—but second, I think I did sort of freak them out. I was like Mary Poppins gone crazy, and they just wanted some normality. So cleaning up the playroom seemed a lot more normal than letting me do what I was doing."

I nodded.

"But later," said Stacey, "something else happened which I hadn't planned on at all. I realized that Max thought I was accusing him of being a baby. You know, by hinting that he wasn't able to mop up his spill or do other things by himself. Then I used that against both him and Amanda and it seemed pretty effective. No kid likes to think that anyone else thinks he or she is a baby."

"Pretty smart, Stace," I said. "I hope I can remember all this tomorrow."

I was going to sit at the Snobs' the next day, and I intended to be prepared for anything and anyone—fires, emergencies, Shannon, and especially the Snobs' behaviour.

As I crossed the street to the Delaneys' the next afternoon, I kept repeating to myself, "go along with everything they say, and take it one step further." It sounded easy enough, but I knew I'd have to think quickly.

Mrs Delaney left as soon as I arrived, and I found myself facing the Snobs again.

Well, not exactly facing them, since Amanda was up in her room and Max was out in the garage, but you know what I mean.

Amanda was in her room because she had been assigned to re-work some maths problems that her teacher thought she could do a better job on. As soon as she saw me in her doorway, she said, "Kristy, come here. Do this problem for me. I hate fractions."

"Sure," I replied. "It's unfortunate that I'm so bad at fractions, though. I mean, I like them and everything, but I always make mistakes. Oh, well. Here. Give me your book." I held out my hand.

"That's okay," said Amanda, hugging her maths book to her chest. "I'll do it myself. No problem."

"No problem!" I cried. "Hey, that's a pretty good pun. *Problem*? As in the maths problem? Get it?"

Amanda managed a smile.

"Come downstairs when you've finished," I told her. "Maybe we could play Snail. Stacey taught me the game, and she said she taught you, too."

I went to the garage to see what Max was up to. I found him swinging back and forth on a rope that had been tied to a beam in the eaves. He was singing, "Oh, I've never, never, never in my long-legged life seen a long-legged sailor with his long-legged wife!"

I giggled. "Where'd you learn that song?" I asked him. "It's funny."

"Our music teacher taught it to us today," he replied, slowing down. "He taught us another song, too. About a cat. But I don't understand something. What kind of cat is a hysle cat?"

I frowned. "I don't know. Why don't you sing me the song? Maybe we can work it out."

Max sang three verses of the song. Each time he came to the chorus, he would sing, "My hysle cat, my hysle cat," and touch his head the way his music teacher had shown the class.

In the middle of the fourth verse, I began to laugh. "Max!" I exclaimed. "This isn't a song about a cat. It's a song about a hat. Try saying, 'My high silk hat' instead of, 'My hysle cat.'"

"What? . . . Oh!" Suddenly Max understood. He began to laugh, too. Then he jumped off the swing and ran around the garage singing, "My hysle cat! My high silk hat!"

"What are you guys doing?" a voice demanded.

Amanda was standing in the doorway to the garage.

"Oh, sorry," I said. "Are we being too loud?"

"No," replied Amanda crossly. "I've finished with my homework. Now Max and

I want a snack. Right, Max?"

"Right," he replied, even though I'm sure he had been thinking about hats and cats, not snacks, before his sister showed up.

"Fix us a snack, Kristy," Amanda demanded.

"Okay," I said. "But from your tone of voice, I can tell you're very hungry, so I think I'll fix you dinner instead. Your mum won't mind if I use the kitchen, will she? Now let's see," I rushed on. "My specialities are monkeys' liver, braised goat's tongue, and rabbit brains. You know Mrs Porter across the street?"

"Morbidda Destiny?" whispered Max. (My stepsister, Karen, has all the kids around here thinking that lonely old Mrs Porter is a witch whose real name is Morbidda Destiny.)

"Right. I get all my herbs and spices from her," I told the Snobs.

Both Max and Amanda were staring at me incredulously. Suddenly Amanda's face broke into a smile. "That's a joke, right?" she said.

"Yeah," I agreed. "It's a joke."

"You're funny," Amanda said. "Come on. Let's play Snail."

"I thought you wanted a snack."

"Nah. We've already had one."

"Monkey's liver!" cried Max, giggling. "Hey, did you ever hear that yucky song? It goes, 'Great big globs of greasy, grimy—' "

"Max!" Amanda shrieked. "Don't sing that! It makes me sick . . . I'll race you to the chalk."

Amanda and Max and I were halfway through our game of Snail, and the Snobs had run indoors for drinks of water, when a white van drove up the Delaneys' drive. Large red letters on the sides spelled PIZZA EXPRESS. The driver jumped out and approached me with a flat white box.

"You Kristy Thomas?" he asked. "Here's your pizza."

"My pizza?"

"Yeah. You and your friend called about half an hour ago. The gigglers?"

It took a second for this to sink in. Then, in a flash, I realized what had happened. "Oh," I said, with a little laugh. "You want Kristy *Thomas*. Right. Well, I'm—just the baby-sitter. Genevieve. Kristy is next door. With her, um giggly friend. You'll recognize her right away. She's got long, wavy blonde hair. She wants the pizza over there. Really," I added when the delivery man looked at me sceptically.

"You're sure about this?" he said as he climbed back into the van.

"Positive," I replied, glad the Snobs hadn't heard me telling lies.

I watched the truck back down the drive, turn into the street, and head for the Kilbournes'. I ran to the front of the Delaneys' house for a better view, and hid behind a shrub just in time to see Shannon and Tiffany answer their door, argue with the poor pizza guy, and then crossly shove some money into his hand as he gave them the pizza.

The next thing I knew, Shannon and Tiffany were marching angrily over to the Delaneys', followed by Astrid of Grenville.

"Uh-oh," I said. I dashed around the corner of the house and into the garage, where I bumped into Amanda and Max. "Indoors," I hissed, and pushed them inside before they could say a word. As soon as the door was shut behind us, we heard a *ding-dong*.

"I'll get it!" cried Max.

"No don't—" I started to say, but it was too late.

Max was racing to the front door. He threw it open. Shannon, Tiffany, and Astrid were standing on the Delaneys' steps. Shannon was holding a wobbly PIZZA EXPRESS box. Grease stains were appearing on the sides.

"You owe me money," was the first thing Shannon said.

"Who, me?" I asked innocently.

"Yes, you. The delivery man said someone named *Genevieve* sent him over to our house with a pizza for Kristy Thomas, and then he described *me*."

"So why do I owe you money?" I asked. "My name isn't Genevieve."

"*Why*?" Shannon spluttered. "You know very well why. You told him *your* name was Genevieve and *my* name was . . ."

"But you started this whole thing. *You* ordered the pizza. *I* just out-smarted you," I said maddeningly.

Shannon narrowed her eyes. "*You* horned in on my baby-sitting territory. My sister and I used to be the only sitters around here." She opened the box and began to ease a gooey slice away from the rest of the pie. "How'd you like pizza in your face?"

"No! Don't throw it!" shrieked Amanda. "Mummy and Daddy just had the hall painted. And the fish fountain cost two thousand dollars!"

Shannon hesitated long enough for me to say, "You throw that at me and I'll throw it back at Astrid. You'll have a pepperoni mountain dog."

Shannon dropped the slice back into the box. She pressed her lips together. Was she crying? No, a giggle escaped. Then Tiffany stifled a laugh. Then Amanda and Max and I let out giggles of relief.

"A pepperoni mountain dog!" exclaimed Shannon.

We all laughed more loudly.

"Why don't you guys come in?" I said.

So the Kilbournes, including Astrid of Grenville, came inside. The five of us sat around the kitchen table and picked at the pizza. Astrid ate all the pieces of pepperoni.

Shannon asked me about the Babysitters Club and I told her a little about it. She seemed impressed.

When Max demanded, "Get me a napkin, Shannie," all she had to do was raise an eyebrow at him and he got it himself. Then *I* was impressed. Before the Kilbournes left, I offered to pay for half of the pizza. Shannon grinned. I felt as if, maybe, we were on the way to being friends.

11th CHAPTER

Saturday

Chicken pocks! The only way your going to apreciat what I wright here is if you rember how it felt to have the chicken packs. I do sort of. I was seven when I had them and it was not plesent. I itched and had a feever and my Mom said Don't scratch but it was the only thing I wanted to do. So keep that in mind.

Ok so malory pike and I sat for her brothers and sisters. The triplets and Margoe and claire were all ~~rec~~ ~~recov~~ getting over the chicken pax. They were not felling very good. What a night we had. Orders, orders, oders. I felt like there maid. ...

I know this sounds mean, but I'm glad it was Claudia, not I, who had to sit for the Chicken Pox Brigade. There are eight Pike kids, including the triplets, and five of them were sick. I think I'd rather have sat for the Snobs than for kids with chicken pox. (Well, the Snobs don't seem so bad any more.) Anyway, I did feel sorry for Claudia and Mallory. (Mallory, the oldest Pike, often helps us as a sort of junior baby-sitter when one of us has a job with her family.) They really earned their money that night. They weren't in any danger of catching the chicken pox themselves since they'd both had it, but there were five itchy, unhappy children to take care of, plus Nicky and Vanessa, who seemed unusually cranky.

Mr and Mrs Pike had decided to go out to dinner and a movie simply to escape from the chicken pox for a while. They'd been nursing sick kids all week. Now the five patients were just well enough to be bored. They weren't running fevers, but they were still uncomfortable and had to stay in bed. Mr and Mrs Pike needed a break.

"I've set some trays out," Mrs Pike told Claudia before she and Mr Pike left. "I'm afraid you'll have to give the triplets, Margo, and Claire their dinners in bed. Either you or Mallory can eat upstairs with them. The other one can eat downstairs with Nicky and Vanessa."

"Do we have to keep Nicky and Vanessa away from the kids upstairs?" Claudia asked. "I mean, so they don't catch the chicken pox?"

"Oh, no. Don't worry about that," Mrs Pike replied. "They've been exposed all week. Now, try not to let the sick kids scratch. They're pretty good about it, except for Margo, who scratches every time she thinks we're not looking. Poor thing, she's got a worse case than the others. If any of them complains of a headache, you can give them one children's aspirin. The aspirin is in the medicine cabinet on the very top shelf. Otherwise, just try to keep the kids happy. The portable TV is in the boys' room right now. At seven o'clock, it's the girls' turn to watch it. Mallory can help you with anything else. And the phone numbers are in their usual spot. Okay?"

"Okay," replied Claudia, who was beginning to feel a little apprehensive. Eight Pike kids were one thing; five cases of chicken pox were another.

As soon as Mr and Mrs Pike left, Claudia heard a strange little sound, sort of a tinkling noise. "What's that?" she asked Mallory.

She and Mallory were setting up dinner trays for the sick kids.

"What's what?" replied Mallory.

Tinkle-tinkle.

"That," said Claudia.

"Uh-oh! It's the triplets. Mum gave them a bell to ring when they need something. She gave Margo and Claire a triangle."

Ding-ding.

"That wouldn't be the triangle, would it?" asked Claudia.

"Yup," said Mallory, rolling her eyes.

"Well, let's go."

Claudia and Mallory dashed upstairs. Mallory looked in on her brothers while Claudia went to the girls' room. "Hi, you two," she greeted Claire and Margo.

Claire, who is five, put a pitiful expression on her face. "Hi," she said soberly.

"What's the matter?" Claudia asked, concerned.

"We're sick," Claire told her.

"I know. It's too bad."

It really was too bad. Claudia told me that the girls looked pathetic. Their faces and hands—any part of them that wasn't covered by their nightgowns—were a sea of spots. Some of Margo's looked awfully red, and Claudia suspected that she'd been scratching them.

"We itch," added Margo, who's seven. "Mummy gave us a bath and she put starch in the water to take away the itching, but now it's back again." Her hand drifted toward a spot on her neck, and she touched it so carefully that Claudia couldn't tell whether she was scratching.

"I'm really sorry," said Claudia sympathetically, "but we're going to have fun tonight, and that will take your minds off the itching. In a little while, I'm going to bring your supper upstairs. First I'll eat dinner with you, and then I'll have dessert in the triplets' room—but I'll bring the TV in here. How does that sound?"

"Good," replied Margo and Claire together.

"And now," said Claudia, holding an imaginary microphone to her lips, "for your entertainment pleasure . . . ta-dah! The Kid-Kit!"

Claudia had brought her Kid-Kit to the Pikes' and left it outside the doorway to the girls' room. She carried it in with a flourish and set it on the table between their beds.

"Yea!" cried Claire.

"You guys can play with this stuff until I bring the TV in. Then you can swap, and give the Kid-Kit to the boys, okay?"

"Okay," said Margo, forgetting to scratch as she pawed through the box.

Meanwhile, Mallory had returned to the kitchen and was setting the trays and the table. Further downstairs, in the playroom, eight-year-old Nicky and nine-year-old Vanessa were playing—supposedly. But as Claudia joined Mallory again, she heard Vanessa shriek, "Stop that! You stop that, Nicholas Pike! . . .STOP IT!"

"Whoa," exclaimed Claudia. "I'll go and

see what that's all about. You finish the trays, okay, Mallory?" She ran downstairs without waiting for a reply. "Hey! What are you two doing?" she cried.

Nicky and Vanessa were sitting on the floor surrounded by Lego. An entire town of Lego buildings had sprung up between them. Claudia couldn't see anything broken or wrong.

"Vanessa?" she asked.

"Nicky gave me the Bizzer Sign!" Vanessa sounded practically hysterical.

"She gave it to me first," grumbled Nicky. "She started it. Honest." He drew a hand wearily across his eyes.

"Did not!" said Vanessa.

"Did, too!"

"Okay, okay," Claudia cut in. Claudia has no patience for the Bizzer sign, which is a hand signal the Pike kids invented purely to annoy each other. "Look, it's almost time for supper. Come on upstairs. You're going to eat in the kitchen with Mallory. A nice, *quiet* meal," she added.

"I'm not hungry," Vanessa whined.

"Me, neither," said Nicky.

"Not even for cream cheese and jam sandwiches?"

"Well, maybe . . ." Vanessa conceded.

Mallory, Nicky, and Vanessa did eat a quiet, almost sombre, meal in the kitchen. Upstairs, Claudia tried to eat with the chicken pox crew, but she hardly had time.

No sooner had she settled onto the end of Claire's bed with her tray than she heard *tinkle-tinkle*.

"Coming!" she called, and ran into the triplets' room. "What is it?" she asked the three spotty faces.

"Could we have Coke instead of milk?" asked Adam. "Please? It feels so nice and cold."

"Sure," Claudia replied, feeling unduly sorry for them.

She was racing back upstairs with the Coke when *ding-ding* sounded from the girls' room. "Coming!" she called. She handed out the Cokes rather hastily and dashed back to Claire and Margo.

"Claudia, there's a speck in my cream cheese," said Margo. "I think it's a bug. If I eat it, I'll throw up."

Claudia examined the speck. "Just a crumb," she pronounced, but to be on the safe side, she picked it out of the cream cheese.

"Could I have some more milk, please?" Claire asked then.

Tinkle-tinkle. The boys were ready for second helpings of fruit salad, and Byron, who loves to eat, wanted dessert, too.

Claudia brought all the food upstairs, then realized it was seven o'clock and time to switch the TV for the Kid-Kit. She did so, wolfed down part of her sandwich, then began carrying the trays to the kitchen so she could help Mallory clean up.

The bell and the triangle were quiet for a full five minutes before Jordan asked for an aspirin for his headache. It was during the next lull that Claudia peered down into the rec room to see what Vanessa and Nicky were up to. She saw them both sitting in front of the TV, their shirts pulled up, examining their tummies and chests. "What are you doing?" she called.

"Counting," Nicky called back.

"Counting what?"

"Our spots."

"Uh-oh," said Claudia, and she dashed downstairs to find that, just as she'd feared, poor Mr and Mrs Pike had two new chicken pox patients.

"Bedtime, you guys," she announced, and neither one objected.

12th CHAPTER

Louie was in bad shape. Everyone could see it. Even David Michael. He didn't understand it, but he could see it.

"He's falling apart,' Mum said one Saturday as she and Louie returned home from a trip to the vet. "He's simply old. Nothing is working well anymore."

It was true. Louie had lots of accidents now, so we had to keep him in the kitchen and the family room, where there were no Oriental rugs. His arthritis was worse, and we could tell he was in a lot of pain. He didn't move unless he had to, and when he did, it was a big effort. Now, instead of calling Louie for dinner, David Michael took dinner to him.

"After all," said my brother, "when I'm sick, Mum brings me my meals on a tray, so I'm kind of doing the same thing for Louie."

Even though he didn't feel well, Louie tried to be the same good old collie as always. For instance, he usually tried to get to his feet and over to the back door so somebody could let him out before he had an accident. It's just that often he didn't make it. He was too slow. One day, the day before Mum took him back to Dr Smith, he staggered to his feet as David Michael was approaching him with his dinner.

"You need to go out, Louie?" my brother asked. "Okay, hold on a sec." David Michael set the bowl down. He went off in search of his mac since it had begun to rain, and returned to the kitchen in time to see Louie's hindquarters disappear through the open basement doorway.

"Louie!" David Michael cried. "No! Wait!"

Ever since Dr Smith had told us about Louie's eyesight, we'd tried to keep the door to the basement closed, but now and then one of us would forget. It just hadn't become a habit yet. Which was too bad, because a steep flight of fourteen stone steps led from that doorway into the dark cellar below.

David Michael grabbed for the banister with one hand and Louie's collar with the other, even though Louie had already stumbled down the first couple of steps. Thank goodness Louie moves slowly, otherwise he probably would have fallen headlong to the bottom of the stairs. As it was, he and David Michael fell several more steps together and David Michael banged his face on the banister and wound up with a black eye.

It was that accident that prompted Mum to take Louie to Dr Smith the next day. And it was at that visit that Dr Smith said Louie was deteriorating rapidly (translated into normal language, that meant "getting worse fast"), and suggested injections. I hadn't gone with Mum to the vet and didn't ask what the injections were for. I didn't really want to understand. All I did know was that Dr Smith said she could try a last resort with Louie—she would give him special injections two times *every day*.

Needless to say, this was not easy to fit into our schedule, although of course we agreed that it must be done, since no schedule was more important than Louie. We finally worked out a plan where Mum left the house early and drove Louie to Dr Smith's for his first injection of the day, while Watson took care of breakfast and seeing us Thomas kids off to school. Then Mum dropped Louie back at the house and arrived at her office fifteen minutes later than usual. On Monday and Wednesday afternoons, Charlie sped home from school, picked Louie up, drove him to Dr Smith's for his *second* injection, sped home, dropped Louie off, picked me up, and drove me to my Babysitters Club meeting. On Tuesday and Thursday, when Charlie was busy, Watson skipped lunch, and used his "lunch hour" in the middle of the afternoon to take Louie to Dr Smith. The new schedule was hectic, Mum and Watson and Charlie were harried by it, and worst of all, by Friday, after almost a week of injections, Dr Smith admitted to Charlie that they weren't helping Louie much—and that the two car trips every day were too much for him.

Charlie was upset by the news, and so was I, when he told me about it as we settled Louie into the kitchen. In fact, I was so worried that I actually called Claudia to tell her I wouldn't be able to make our Friday club meeting. Dawn, as our alternate officer, would have to take over my duties as chairman.

It was good thing I didn't go. If I had, I wouldn't have been around for all the commotion that was about to happen. Even though in a big family, especially a step-family, you learn to expect commotion, I wasn't prepared for what was to follow. Things started when Watson and his ex-wife somehow got their signals crossed and the first Mrs Brewer dropped Karen and Andrew off earlier than usual for their weekend with us, thinking that Watson was home. He wasn't, but it was okay since Charlie and David Michael and I were.

Karen ran inside, full of energy, with

Andrew at her heels. "Hi, everybody!" she called. "Here we are!" She dropped her knapsack and a bag in the front hall by the staircase. Andrew dropped his things on Karen's.

"What's for dinner?" asked Karen. "Where's Boo-Boo? Have you seen Morbidda Destiny? How's Louie?"

Karen usually leaves the rest of us in shock with her talk and excitement and enthusiasm. For the next half hour we were one step behind her as she and Andrew settled into the routine at their dad's house. First Karen ran to one of the windows that faces Mrs Porter's house next door.

"Eeee!" she screeched. "I can see her! I can see her in her kitchen. She's mixing something in a pot. You know what I think?"

(By this time the rest of us, including quiet Andrew, had gathered behind Karen and were peering at Mrs Porter.)

"I think she's mixing a wicked witch's brew! She's stirring up a brew that's going to grow fur all over Andrew or—"

"Dope," said Charlie fondly, clapping a hand over Karen's mouth. He smiled at her and shook his head. "You know she can't do stuff like that. She's probably making soup."

"Kristy?" asked Andrew, turning a worried face to me.

"Oh, Andrew," I said, kneeling down,

"you're not going to grow fur. Don't give it a second thought."

By this time, Karen was already gone. She'd run into Watson's study and found Boo-Boo asleep in a leather armchair. (I swear, that cat always picks the most uncomfortable spots for his naps.) And she summoned us from the window with another shriek.

"He's growing fangs! Boo-Boo is growing fangs!" Karen was crying as we caught up with her. "It's Morbidda Destiny again."

I was positive, no matter what Karen said, and no matter what doubts I have about our next-door neighbour, that Boo-Boo was not growing fangs. I tiptoed to the leather chair while everyone else looked on in silence. Despite Karen's shrieking a moment earlier, Boo-Boo was still sound asleep. He was sprawled on his back , and was, in fact, *so* sound asleep, that his mouth was slightly open. I saw why Karen thought he had fangs.

Smiling, I tiptoed back to her. "Those aren't fangs," I said, with a laugh. "They're just his ordinary old teeth. They're called incisors or something. I suppose you never noticed them before. Look, even humans have them." I opened my mouth and showed her my four pointy teeth.

"Whew," breathed Karen. "I was worried . . . I wonder if Louie has those teeth, too." And she was off again.

Her third screech came from the kitchen.

"What now?" asked Charlie wearily. We were getting tired of Karen's games. But her third screech was followed by a fourth, and both sounded truly terrified.

"Oh, boy," I said under my breath.

Charlie, David Michael, Andrew, and I ran to the kitchen. The four of us skidded to a halt behind Karen. For a moment, no one spoke. We just stared at Louie. I couldn't believe what he was doing.

David Michael began to cry. I turned him away from Louie and hugged him to me.

Charlie drew in his breath and app-roached Louie, while I tried to turn Karen and Andrew around and hug my brother at the same time.

Luckily, Mum and Watson both arrived home just then. I hoped one of them would know what to do.

Louie seemed to have lost complete control of his hind legs. He was pulling himself around the ktichen with his front legs, dragging the back ones as if they were paralyzed. And he was, as you might imagine, in a panic. He crawled into a leg of the kitchen table, and then into the cooker.

"Lou-ie!" David Michael howled.

"Charlie, take David Michael out of the kitchen," my mother ordered.

"Please take Karen and Andrew, too," added Watson.

Charlie did as he was told, but nobody

had asked me to do anything, so I just stood by the doorway and watched.

Mum ran for the phone and dialled Dr Smith while Watson tried to calm Louie down. He succeeded somewhat, and I relaxed a little and tried to work out what the phone conversation was about, but all Mum would say was "Mm-hmm," and, "Yes, that's right," and, "I see," and finally. "Okay, thank you." When she got off the phone, she turned to me. "Kristy, tell the others we'll have a family meeting as soon as Sam comes home."

That family meeting is something I wish I could forget, but know I'll never be able to. The eight of us—Mum, Watson, Charlie, Sam, David Michael, Andrew, Karen and I—gathered in the living room.

Mum said bluntly, "Kids, I'm sorry to have to tell you this, but Louie is very, very sick now. And he's not going to get better."

Charlie and Sam and I lowered our heads. But David Michael, Andrew, and Karen looked at Mum with wide, surprised eyes.

"What about the shots? And the pills?" asked my little brother.

"They're not working," Mum told him. "You can see that, can't you, honey?"

David Michael nodded, his eyes filling with tears.

"So what do we do now?" asked Sam.

Mum glanced at Watson and I could see that *her* eyes were watery, too. Watson took her hand reassuringly. "Dr Smith suggested that we have Louie put down tomorrow," he said gently.

I expected my brothers to get angry, to yell that *nobody* would *ever* do that to Louie. But they all began to cry instead. David Michael cried noisily. Sam and Charlie tried to hide the fact that they were crying, but I know they were. Then a lump that had been filling up my throat all afternoon, dissolved, and I began to cry, too, which made Andrew and Karen burst into tears. It didn't matter. Even Watson was crying.

After a few moments, David Michael announced, "I'm going to sleep with Louie tonight." We knew he meant sleep in the family room with him, and I'm sure he thought someone was going to try to stop him, but no one said a word.

So Louie and David Michael spent the night together. Just as Louie had often joined one of us in bed, to keep us company, David Michael kept Louie company during his last night with us.

13th CHAPTER

Mum said it wasn't necessary for all of us to go to Dr Smith's the next day, and I worried that we would argue about who stayed and who went. Sam and Charlie looked relieved, though, and said they wouldn't mind staying home. (I think they were afraid they'd cry at the vet's, and that people would see them.) Watson then asked if my brothers would watch Karen and Andrew. He'd decided they were too young to go. Sam and Charlie agreed right away. And that's how Mum and Watson, David Michael, and I became the four who accompanied Louie to the vet.

David Michael had spent an uncomfortable night with Louie. He'd insisted on sleeping next to him, on the floor. He wouldn't even consider the couch. Louie whined a lot that night, according to Mum, who (although David Michael didn't know it) spent most of the night reading in the kitchen, keeping her ears open for problems in the family room. But towards dawn, both Louie and my brother fell asleep. They stayed asleep until nine o'clock when Mum reluctantly woke David Michael. She wanted to get the trip to Dr Smith's over with as soon as possible.

At breakfast that morning nobody ate much. And we were silent. Nobody even asked for a reprieve for Louie. He was just in too much pain. We knew that giving Louie an extra day or two would be one of the cruellest things we could do to him.

At ten-thirty, David Michael and I wrapped Louie in his blanket and Watson placed him on the back-seat of our estate. Karen and Andrew looked on in awe.

"Do you want to say good-bye?" Watson asked them.

Karen stepped forward solemnly, ducked into the car, lifted Louie's ear, and whispered into it, "Good-bye, Louie." Then she fled to the house in tears.

But Andrew called gaily, " 'Bye, Louie!" and I realized that he was too little to understand what was happening. Or maybe he was able to see the good that we were doing Louie easier than the rest of us were.

Charlie and Sam asked to say good-bye in private. When they returned to the house to watch Andrew and Karen, the rest of us reluctantly climbed into the car. I squashed up in the very back part of the car so that David Michael could sit next to Louie.

Nobody spoke during the drive to the vet's, but David Michael held one of Louie's paws the whole way. And Louie, our noisy vet-hater, didn't so much as whimper, even though he must have known he was going to Dr Smith's. After all, he'd been there ten times in the past five days.

When we reached the vet's, Watson parked the car. Then he lifted Louie out and handed him to Mum. Watson had decided to let us Thomases take Louie inside by ourselves. He hadn't known Louie the way we had.

We walked slowly to the door to the veterinary offices, and David Michael held it open for Mum, while I reached into my pocket, pulled out a pair of sunglasses, and put them on so nobody would see my red eyes.

Five other people were in the waiting room, but the receptionist called to us right away. "Dr Smith is seeing a patient now," she said, "but as soon as she's finished, you can go in."

My mother nodded. Then she turned to me. "Kristy, I want you and David Michael to say good-bye out here. I'm the only one who needs to go inside. Do you understand?"

"Yes," I whispered. I began stroking Louie's muzzle.

"How do they put him to sleep?" asked David Michael tearfully.

"They just give him an injection," replied my mother. "That's all. It'll make him go to sleep and he won't wake up."

Mum had sat down on a couch in the waiting room with Louie stretched across her lap. Several people looked at us sympathetically. One elderly woman began to sniffle and dab at her eyes with a tissue.

"Will you hold him while he gets the injection?" asked David Michael. "I want you to hold him."

"Yes, I promise," said Mum. "That's why I'm going in. To be with him."

I looked down at Louie's liquid brown eyes. When he moved them, his "eyebrows" moved, too. He was paying attention to everything in the waiting room.

"Do you think he knows what's going to happen?" I asked softly.

"No," said Mum. "I'm sure he doesn't."

How can we do this to him? I asked myself. We are going to kill him. We were saying, "Okay, Louie, you must die now," and not giving him any choice about it. We were going to send him into a room and let someone give him an injection so that he would never wake up. But then I remembered what he had looked like the night before, and how much pain he was in, and knew we were doing the right thing.

The receptionist called Mum's name

then, and she stood up. David Michael and I gave Louie last pats and kisses, and then Mum disappeared down the little hallway. When she came back a few minutes later, her arms were empty.

Karen said the funeral was her idea, but I think it was Watson's. Anyway, later that day, right after lunch, Karen found David Michael and me sitting glumly in front of the TV set. We didn't even know what we were watching.

"I think we should have a funeral for Louie," Karen announced.

"A funeral?" I repeated.

"Yes. To remember him by."

I glanced at David Michael, who seemed to have perked up.

"We could make a gravestone," he said. "Even though we can't really bury him."

"And we can sing a song and say some nice things about him," added Karen. "We'll hold it at three o'clock. I'll go and tell everyone."

Right away, we began making plans. All six of us kids gathered on the back porch.

"What kind of marker should we make for his grave?" I asked. "I don't think we have any stone."

"A wooden cross," said Karen decisively. "There are some scraps of wood in the shed."

"We can take care of that," said Sam,

speaking for himself and Charlie. I could tell they were just humouring us. They felt bad about Louie, but they felt too old to be planning pet funerals, and wanted to go off on their own.

"Put 'Louie Thomas, R.I.P.' on the cross," instructed Karen.

"What's 'R.I.P.'?" asked David Michael.

"It means 'rest in peace.'"

"Shouldn't we write that out?" I asked. "Initials are tacky. It's like writing 'Xmas' instead of 'Christmas.'"

"No!" cried Karen, who's been wanting to have her own way a lot lately. "Put 'R.I.P.' That's how it always is in books and on TV."

Karen and I had a big discussion about the matter. Sam finally came to the rescue by suggesting that he and Charlie write 'Rest In Peace' with huge initial letters so the R, the I, and the P would really show up. Then they left David Michael, Karen, Andrew, and me to plan the rest of the service.

"We should sing a hymn," said David Michael.

But none of us knew any hymns by heart, except for Christmas carols.

"How about singing a song about a dog?" I suggested.

"I know one," said Andrew, and he began to sing, "There was a farmer, had a dog, and Bingo was his name-o. B-I-N-G-O—"

"We can't sing that at a funeral!" David Michael exclaimed.

"Old MacDonald?" said Andrew. "On his farm he could have a dog."

"*No.*"

"Let's just sing a sad song," said Karen.

"No, a happy one," I said. "Louie wouldn't want us all to be sad."

"But funerals are *supposed* to be sad," she insisted.

We talked and talked. Finally we reached a few decisions. Instead of singing a song, we voted to play "Brother Louie" on the tape deck. Then we decided that we would each say one nice thing about Louie, instead of having someone give a boring eulogy. Saying nice things was Andrew's idea. His nursery-school teacher had just read his class a book called *The Tenth Good Thing About Barney*, in which a family remembers their pet, Barney, after he dies. (I thought it was very lucky that Andrew had heard that story just before Louie died.)

At ten minutes to three, us six Thomas/Brewer kids called Mum and Watson, and our family walked out to the back garden and stood by a forsythia bush Louie had liked to sleep near. Sam was holding the cross he and Charlie had made, Charlie was holding a shovel, and David Michael was holding Louie's lead and food dishes. We were going to bury them under the cross. That was, we'd decided, almost like burying Louie himself.

"Okay," I said. "Charlie, why don't you dig the grave? Then we can say the nice things about Louie."

"No!" cried Karen. "Not everyone's here."

"Yes, we are," I told her. "Eight people. We're all here."

Just then I heard someone say, "Are we late?"

I turned around. Filing into our yard were Shannon and Tiffany, Hannie and Linny, and Amanda and Max. They were followed by two of Shannon's snobby friends. They gathered behind our family.

I looked at Karen in horror.

"I invited them," she said simply.

I shook my head. I didn't want Shannon at Louie's funeral. She'd made fun of him. Besides, what would she think about a dog funeral? But there was nothing to do except go ahead with it.

Charlie, red with embarrassment at the sight of our guests, finished digging the grave. David Michael stepped forward and placed the lead and the dishes in it. Then Sam covered them up and pushed the cross into the earth.

"Now," said David Michael, "we each say one nice thing. I'll go last."

Karen, of course, volunteered to go first,

and said. "Louie had good manners."

"He slept on my feet to keep them warm," said Andrew.

I dared to turn around and peek at the rest of the audience. To my surprise, not a single person was laughing. And Shannon was wiping tears away.

"Louie was a good football player," said Charlie.

"He had a sense of humour," I said.

"He was good company," said Sam.

"He was an adorable puppy," said Mum.

"He was nice to Boo-Boo," said Watson.

David Michael let out a sigh. "He was my best friend," he said.

After a moment of silence, David Michael pushed a button on the tape deck, and "Brother Louie" came on. We all thought of our good old collie while "Louie, Louie, Louie" was sung.

When the song was over, I felt both happy and sad. A hand touched my arm. It was Shannon. "I'm really sorry about Louie," she said seriously. "If anything happened to Astrid, I don't know what I'd do." Then she turned away, and Louie's mourners began to leave.

14th CHAPTER

It was on Monday, two days after Louie's funeral, that I sat for the Snobs again. I didn't really think the Delaneys were so bad any more, but the name had stuck.

"Tell us again what happened to Louie," said Max.

He and Amanda and I were playing Snail in the driveway, but the Snobs kept stopping to ask questions about Louie. They weren't being rude; they were just curious. They'd probably never known anyone or anything that had died.

"Louie was sick," I said for the fourth or fifth time. "He was really old and he didn't feel well any more. He hurt a lot . . . Your turn, Amanda."

Amanda hopped to the centre of the snail shell, expertly avoiding Max's and my squares. She selected a square for herself and drew an "A" in it. "How did Louie fall down the stairs?" she wanted to know.

"He couldn't see them. He just walked right down."

I stood at the edge of the shell and hopped around and around to the centre. Amanda handed me the chalk.

"And David Michael banged his eye?" said Max.

"Yup," I replied, choosing another square.

"Did he cry?'

"A little. His eye turned black and blue."

"Priscilla has never been sick," said Amanda. "I think it's because she cost four hundred dollars."

"Well, I doubt that," I told her, "but I'm glad she's so healthy."

"If Priscilla dies," said Max, "let's give her a funeral."

Amanda scrunched up her face in thought.

"Okay," she replied. "We could make a cross for her. And we could play music from *The Aristocats*."

"And I," said Max, "would say, 'Priscilla had a beautiful tail.'"

"And I'd say, 'Priscilla cost four hundred dollars,'" added Amanda.

I rolled my eyes.

Amanda was taking her turn again, when Shannon Kilbourne rounded a corner of the Delaneys' house and walked over to us. She was cradling something in her arms.

"Hi," I said uncertainly. I didn't dislike Shannon any more, I just never knew what to expect from her.

"Hi," she replied cheerfully. "This is for you." She held out the thing she'd brought over.

"Oh!" I squealed. I couldn't believe it. The "thing" was a puppy! A very tiny puppy, probably only a few weeks old.

"What do you mean he's for me?' I exclaimed. "Where'd you get him? Where'd he come from?"

"*He's* a *she*," replied Shannon, "and she's one of Astrid's."

"One of Astrid's? You mean one of Astrid of Grenville's *puppies*? But I thought Astrid was a boy."

Shannon grinned. "No!" she cried. "Astrid is a girl's name. It's Scandinavian or something. It means divine strength."

I just couldn't believe it. Why was Shannon giving me a puppy? None of this made sense.

"I don't know why I assumed Astrid was a boy, but I did. How come you never told me she had puppies?" I asked.

"I don't know. You never asked. The subject never came up. Anyway, we—I mean, Tiffany and Maria and my parents and I—want you to have this puppy. It's a pedigree. We're selling the others. But we really want your family to have this one. You know . . . because of Louie . . ."

Shannon's voice trailed off.

"Thank you," I said softly. I looked down at the fat little puppy that was nestled in my arms. She was a ball of brown and white fluff. When I leaned over to nuzzle her, she licked my nose.

"I'm afraid you can't have her yet," said Shannon. "She's only six weeks old. We want the puppies to stay with Astrid until they're eight weeks. But then she's all yours. If it's okay with Mr Br—with your parents."

"Well, I'll have to check with them, but I'm sure it'll be all right. They loved having Louie around. The one I'm worried about is David Michael. I don't know what he'll think about getting a 'replacement' for Louie. Or at least, getting a replacement so soon."

"Well, why don't you find out?" asked Shannon. "Is he home? Tell him to come over here and meet the puppy."

"I better phone my mum first," I said.

"Shannie, Shannie!" cried Amanda, jumping up and down. "Can we please play with the puppy?"

"Please, please, puh-*lease*?" added Max.

It was the first time I'd heard the Snobs say please on their own. I wasn't sure whether they were really being polite, or whether they just wanted to ensure that they'd be allowed to play with the puppy. Either way, it sounded nice.

"You can play with the puppy," Shannon replied, "but we have to take her inside. There are lots of germs outside, and she hasn't had her injections yet."

"Oh," said Amanda. "Well, is she going to wet or anything? We have to be careful. The fountain in the hallway cost two thousand dollars. And the rugs in the living room are genuine Oriental, and *they* cost—"

"Amanda," I interrupted her, "don't worry about it. We'll keep the puppy in the kitchen, and we'll put newspapers on the floor first."

Shannon, the Snobs, the puppy and I went into the Delaneys' house through the back door (to avoid the two thousand-dollar fountain). While I sat in the kitchen chair with the puppy in my lap, Shannon and the Snobs covered the floor with newspapers. Then I put the puppy down and let her frisk around. She pretended to act fearless and would stalk enemy chair legs and cupboard doors, but when Priscilla appeared, the puppy jumped a mile. Priscilla, startled, jumped a mile, too. She fled to the top of the fridge while the puppy fled to a corner.

Amanda and Max giggled hysterically.

"Here," said Shannon. "Throw the rubber toy to her, Max."

Shannon had produced a chewed-up rubber toy, and Max tossed it across the room. The puppy ran after it on fat legs, skidding on the paper.

"Well, what do you think of her?" Shannon asked me.

"I think she's adorable," I replied, "but I'd better get on the phone."

I dialled my mother at her office. "Mum!" I exclaimed. "You'll never guess what! Shannon Kilbourne—you know, from across the street? Well, her dog had puppies, little baby Bernese mountain dogs, and she brought one over to the Delaneys', that's where I'm baby-sitting, and said we can have her—it's a she—because of Louie. But we can't have her for two weeks." I hadn't given my mum a chance to say a word, because I'd suddenly realized how much I didn't want her to say "no." I'd realized what a thoroughly nice thing Shannon was doing, and that it could only mean she wanted to be friends. "Could we please have the puppy, Mum?" I asked, slowing down and trying to sound more grown up. "I think it would be good for David Michael. And if he doesn't like the idea, we'll still have two weeks to convince him. In two—"

"Kristy," my mother finally interrupted me, "we can have the dog."

"We *can*?" I squeaked.

"Yes. Watson and I had already decided to get another dog as soon as we thought David Michael was ready. We were even thinking about buying one of the

Kilbournes' puppies, so I know this will be okay with Watson. I'll call the Kilbournes tonight to thank them."

"*You* knew Astrid was a girl, too?" was all I could exclaim. "You knew about the puppies?"

Of course, Mum had no idea why I said that, and she was in a rush to get back to work, so we ended the conversation. Boy, I thought when I'd hung up the phone, I must really be out of it. I decided this was my punishment for thinking that all my neighbours were snobs, and not bothering to get to know them.

"Mum said yes!" I announced to Shannon.

"Great," she replied. "Now call your brother."

I did, but I didn't tell him why I was calling. I just asked him to come over to the Delaneys'.

While we waited for David Michael, Amanda and Max played with the puppy. "You know," I said to Shannon as we watched the kids, "I'm really sorry about taking your baby-sitting jobs away from you. I baby-sat so much in my old neighbourhood that it didn't occur to me *not* to sit when I moved here. It's just part of my life. I didn't think about the people here who might already be sitters."

"Oh, that's okay," replied Shannon. "There are more than enough jobs to go around. Tiffany and I are the only ones of our friends who really like to baby-sit, and we can't possibly do it all ourselves. I don't think I was mad at you as much as I was . . ." (Shannon blushed)" . . . jealous."

"Jealous of *me*?"

"Yeah. Because your club is such a good idea."

"But you and Tiffany kind of implied that our club is babyish."

"Yeah, we did. But we didn't mean it."

The doorbell rang then and I let David Michael in. When he saw the puppy on the kitchen floor a whole range of expressions crossed his face. First he looked surprised, then pleased, then sad (thinking of Louie, I guess), and then wary.

"Whose is that?" he asked. He looked from Shannon to the Snobs.

"Actually, she's ours," I answered. "If you want her." I told him about the Kilbournes' offer.

"I don't want her," David Michael said rudely, and I felt like shaking him. "She isn't Louie." But before I could do anything, David Michael knelt down on the floor, in spite of himself.

The puppy pranced over to him and stood with her front feet on my brother's knees. David Michael smiled.

Shannon and I looked at each other and smiled, too.

The puppy stretched up, David Michael

leaned over, and they touched noses.

"Ooh," said David Michael, "she has a soft nozzle."

"Muzzle," I corrected him.

"If we keep her," said my brother, "she won't be Louie. Louie was special."

"No,' I agreed. "Louie was one-of-a-kind. This puppy is a girl, and she'll look different and act different. She's not a new Louie."

"Good," said David Michael.

"So do you want her?" asked Shannon.

"Yes," replied my brother.

"And what do you say?" I prompted him.

"I say, let's name her Shannon."

So we did.

15th CHAPTER

"Help! Kristy! Save me! The ghost of Ben Brewer is after me!"

Karen ran shrieking through the second-floor hallway and burst into my room in a panic. "Kristy! Kristy!"

"Ahem, Karen,' I replied.

Karen was only fooling around. She knew as well as I did that there probably wasn't any ghost in our attic. And if there was (because we just weren't *sure*) he certainly wasn't going to chase little girls around in broad daylight.

It was Saturday afternoon, two weeks to the day since Louie's funeral. Karen and Andrew were spending another weekend with us, and Shannon the puppy was almost ours. The members of the Babysitters Club were gathered in my room. We'd just had a meeting the day before, of course, but every now and then we like to get together and *not* conduct business. Besides, my friends enjoy visiting the mansion.

Karen plopped down on the floor between Mary Anne and Dawn. "You know who old Ben Brewer is, don't you?" she asked them.

"Your great-grandfather?" Mary Anne ventured. (Ghost stories make her nervous.)

"Right. Before he became a ghost, anyway. He was a—what's the word, Kristy?"

"Herpitologist?" I suggested.

"*No*!" cried Karen, laughing. "The word that means he stayed in the house all alone for years. He never went out and no one ever went in."

"He was a recluse," I said, "according to Brewer family history."

"And he ate fried dandelions," Karen added. Stacey snorted.

"Well, he *did*," Karen insisted, turning to Stacey indignantly. "Anyway, he's a ghost now and he haunts our attic."

"Only the attic?" asked Claudia.

"Yes, thank goodness," I replied.

"But every now and then he leaves it," said Karen. "Just for a few minutes. He likes to chase me through the halls. He says otherwise he never gets any exercise."

"You mean any e-x-o-r-c-i-s-e?" spelled Mary Anne, but Karen wasn't old enough to get the joke. The rest of us laughed, though.

"You do know that's not true, don't you, Karen?" I asked.

"Yes," she admitted. "But it's fun to pretend. Sometimes I'm *sure* he's behind me." (I shivered.) "But it's not pretend about the attic. He really haunts it."

"We have an honest-to-goodness secret passage in our house," spoke up Dawn.

"You do?" Karen's eyes widened.

"I've been in it," I announced.

"You *have*?" Karen's eyes became the size of soup tureens.

Crash, bang, THUMP.

"What was that?" exclaimed Stacey.

"My brothers," I replied. "I think."

"Yup, that's right," said Karen. "They're playing football."

"In the house?" I asked.

"Yes. Andrew is the football."

I rolled my eyes. Mum and Watson were out for the afternoon. I wasn't baby-sitting, since Sam and Charlie were home, but I felt I should be on top of things. There were ten kids in the house, plus Boo-Boo.

"This house," I informed my friends, "is actually a *mad*house. Can you imagine what it'll be like when Shannon arrives?"

At that moment, Charlie charged into my room with Andrew in his arms and threw him on the bed. "Touchdown!" he shouted.

Andrew squealed and giggled. He sounded a little *too* wild, which was unlike him. "Do a cannonball!" he shrieked. He tucked himself into a ball and Charlie picked him up again and ran him down the hall chanting, "Ba-boom-ba-boom-ba-boom." We heard a soft thud as my brother tossed him onto another bed.

"Hey, you guys! Perk up!" I shouted to them.

My friends laughed.

Karen ran after Charlie shouting, "My turn! My turn!"

"When do you get Shannon?" Mary Anne wanted to know.

"In two or three days," I replied.

"You know, Kristy," Claudia began, "I hate to say this, but—"

"Then don't," I interrupted.

"Don't what?"

"Say it."

Claudia made a face at me. "*But*," she continued, "you complained an awful lot about Shannon Kilbourne and the other snobby girls around here, and now Shannon's giving you a puppy. That's a pretty nice thing to do."

"I know," I said in a small voice as I traced the pattern of the bedspread with my finger. "She's not as bad as I thought she was. In fact, she's sort of all right."

"Well, what happened?" asked Dawn.

I shook my head. "I'm not sure. But we did have a talk the day Shannon brought Shannon to meet me."

"What kind of talk?" asked Claudia. She

was lying on her back on the floor and began blowing a gigantic pink bubble with a wad of bubble-gum.

"You know, if that pops, it's going to cover your face and goo up your hair," Stacey pointed out after a few seconds.

Claudia ignored her and kept on blowing.

"We had a very pleasant talk," I replied. "We talked about baby-sitting. I said I hadn't realized that I might be stepping on someone else's territory when I started sitting around here. it was just *natural* for me to sit."

"What did Shannon say?" asked Mary Anne. "Did she understand?"

"Oh, yes. Believe it or not, she said she was *jealous*."

"You're kidding," said Dawn and Stacey at the same time.

"Nope. She said she wasn't really mad, because she and Tiffany—that's her sister — are the only ones who are interested in sitting, and there are more than enough jobs for them in this neighbourhood. But she's jealous of our club."

"I wonder," said Mary Anne slowly, "if she'd want to be another associate member of the club. Like Logan is. We can always use extra people to call on when we're too busy."

"Yeah," I agreed. "And that way she could be part of the club without actually joining it."

"Why shouldn't we ask her to *join*?" wondered Stacey. "It wasn't too long ago that we were so busy we wanted new members. Of course, we'd have to meet her first."

I looked at the rest of my friends. Except for Claudia, they were shrugging and nodding, as if to say. "Why not?" Claudia was still blowing her bubble. Very, very slowly, it was becoming an award-winning size.

"I'll call Shannon," I said. And did. Shannon's mother informed me that Shannon just happened to be on her way over, bringing Shannon to visit David Michael.

"That's perfect," I told the club members, after I'd hung up. "Shannon the puppy can play with David Michael. Shannon the baby-sitter can meet you guys."

This seemed like an ideal plan—except that Shannon the baby-sitter entered my room just as three things happened: Claudia's bubble popped (and, as predicted, covered her face and gooed up her hair), Stacey spilled a Coke and Charlie cannon-balled Andrew onto my bed.

Shannon looked around as if she'd just entered the loony bin.

"Hi!" I called nervously. I passed tissues to Stacey while Charlie and Andrew crashed out of the room. I closed the door after them.

Claudia sat up, picking pink shreds out of her eyelashes.

"Um, meet the Babysitters Club,' I said. "The normal ones are Dawn and Mary Anne. The sticky ones are Claudia and Stacey. This is Shannon Kilbourne, everyone."

There was nothing to do but laugh. So we did.

"Are you having a club meeting?" asked Shannon when we'd calmed down.

"Not really," I said. "We hold our meetings during the week. On Mondays, Wednesdays, and Fridays from five-thirty until six." I added. (I might as well fill her in on the workings of the club.)

"You meet that often?' she replied, sounding impressed. "Gosh. I could never do that."

I exchanged a look with Stacey. "How come?" I asked.

"Oh, tons of reasons. Homework. After-school stuff. I'm usually pretty busy. I could never be so, you know, committed to something. This club must mean a lot to you."

"Oh, it does," I assured her.

"You're sure you couldn't commit to the club?" Stacey asked.

"Yeah," answered Shannon, puzzled. "How come?"

"Well," I said, "we'd been wondering if you'd like to join. Lots of times we get more jobs than we can handle. And clients like to get baby-sitters who live in their own neighbourhood so they don't have to pick them up and take them home. I'm the only club member who lives around here. We thought you'd be a good addition to the Babysitters Club."

Shannon looked both pained and thoughtful. "I'd really *like* to join," she said, "but I just don't see how."

"Well," Mary Anne jumped in, wanting to make her feel better, "listen, don't worry. You could be an associate member of the club. We already have one and we could use another. That would be perfect for you because associate members don't have to attend meetings. We just call them and offer them any jobs we can't take. You earn some extra money, maybe find some new kids to sit for, and we keep our clients satisfied by always being able to provide them with sitters."

We looked expectantly at Shannon. "What do you think?" I asked her.

"I think it sounds fabulous," she replied. "I accept."

"Yea!" I cried. "Shannon is our new associate member of the Babysitters Club."

"You asked a *dog* to join your club?" spoke up an amazed voice.

My friends and I turned to see David Michael standing in the doorway, holding Shannon the puppy awkwardly, her hind legs dangling.

"No, silly!" I exclaimed. "The other Shannon. Shannon the human."

"Oh," he replied, and set Shannon on the floor. The puppy frisked into my room and David Michael followed her, smiling happily.

I knew David Michael would never forget our Louie. None of us would, because Louie had left a sort of legacy. He'd brought Shannon and me together so we could be friends instead of enemies, and that in turn had brought a new puppy for our family, but especially for David Michael. So, I thought. Endings could sometimes be beginnings. They were sad, but sometimes they brought happiness.

That's what Louie had shown us, and that's just one of the things we would remember about him.

The Babysitters Club

CLAUDIA AND THE NEW GIRL

1st CHAPTER

I'd been watching this fly for ages. First it had landed on the back of Austin Bentley's head and crawled around on his hair for a full minute. Then it had flown to Dorianne Wallingford's right shoe, but had had to move when Dorianne used her shoe to scratch the back of her left leg. It tried Pete Black's pencil, but Pete flicked the pencil immediately and sent the fly on its way again.

I wondered whether the fly was a boy or a girl. I wondered whether flies have families. I wondered whether flies have family reunions and decided they didn't, because family reunions are almost always picnics, and at a flies' picnic, how could you tell the guest flies from the ordinary, uninvited flies who just want to land on the food for a while? Then I wondered what it would be like to look out through those gigantic fly eyes, and whether flies would say "eyesight" or "flysight."

I wondered whether the fly found the English class as thoroughly boring as I did. I'll say this about Mrs Hall, our teacher, she at least *tries* to make the class interesting. For instance, most of the other English classes in our year have to read *The Yearling* and *A Tree Grows in Brooklyn.* Mrs Hall is doing something different with us—this big project on books that have won the Newbery Award. This gives us a wide selection of books (some of them are an awful lot shorter than *The Yearling*), but the thing is I just don't like reading. Except for Nancy Drew mysteries. They're fun. And I'm a pretty good sleuth.

Mrs Hall was talking about *From the Mixed-up Files of Mrs Basil E. Frankweiler* and *The Westing Game.* Okay, I'll admit it. I hadn't got around to reading either of them, even though there is a character in *Mixed-up Files* with my name—Claudia. In fact, the only Newbery Award-winner I had read so far was this one called *Sarah, Plain and Tall.* That was because it was only fifty-eight pages long.

"Claudia?" said Mrs Hall.

"Yes?" (Was she just trying to get my attention or had she asked me a question?)

"Can you help us out here?" (I think she'd asked a question.) I could feel the blood rising to my face. I looked down at my notebook in which I'd been doodling pictures of some of the kids I baby-sit for. "Um, with what?" I replied.

Mrs Hall sighed. "Claudia Kishi." (This was not a good sign. Mrs Hall hardly ever uses our last names.) "Would you *please* pay attention?"

I nodded. "Yes," I managed to reply.

Mrs Hall shook her head sadly. I wanted to add, "Sorry for ruining your day," because that's just what she looked like—a person whose day had been ruined. By *me*! I felt kind of powerful, although I wasn't proud of it. Imagine being able to ruin a grown-up's entire day single-handledly.

Mrs Hall took my boredom pretty hard. "Class, please close your books and take out a fresh piece of paper. I want to give you a spelling test."

The class groaned. A few kids directed murderous glances at me, as if this whole thing were my fault. Well, I bet I hadn't been the only one watching that fly and doodling in my notebook.

"The words," Mrs Hall went on, "will be taken from chapters seven and eight of *Mixed-up Files*, which you should have read last night."

"Should have" is right, I thought.

"The first word," Mrs. Hall said, "is 'pharaoh.' "

I waited for her to use it in a sentence (not

that it would do me any good). Mrs Hall always uses spelling words in sentences, and she pronounces the sentences very carefully, with lots of emphasis.

"The *children* are *stu*dying a *fa*mous E*gyp*tian *pha-raoh*."

Ah-ha! I thought. Mrs Hall was giving us a hidden clue. She used "famous" and "pharaoh" in the same sentence. They must begin with the same letter. Now, I'm a terrible speller, but I do know that "famous" begins with an "f." Very slowly, I printed "f-a-r-o" on my paper. Then, thoughtfully, I erased the "o" and added another "r." At the last moment, I tacked a "w" onto the end. That looked pretty good. Farrow. I was proud of myself for thinking to add one of those killer silent letters to the word. Who invented them, anyway? They're such a waste.

" 'Institute,' " Mrs Hall went on.

I barely heard her. Outside the window, our cheerleaders were practicing for our upcoming game against Stamford Junior High. They were really good. I wished I could do the splits. Then I remembered what I was supposed to be doing, and scribbled "instatute" on my paper. Not a moment too soon.

" 'Quarterly.' "

Before Mrs Hall could use "quarterly" in one of her emphatic sentences, the door to our classroom opened. Every single head, including Mrs Hall's, swivelled towards it. When we saw Ms Downey, the school secretary, standing there, we grew really interested. The secretary only comes to a classroom for something major, otherwise the head sends a student messenger.

Mrs Hall crossed the room to Ms Downey, and the two of them put their heads together and whispered for a moment. I hate it when grown-ups do that. Then they pulled apart, and Ms Downey stepped back and showed someone else into the room. Mrs Hall greeted her warmly. "Hello, Ashley," she said, smiling. "We're happy to have you."

Then Ms Downey handed Mrs Hall some papers and left.

I was breathless. A new girl. We had a new girl in our class! I always think new kids, especially the ones who transfer in the middle of the school year—the middle of the *day*, for heaven's sake—are pretty interesting.

But this one (what had Mrs Hall called her?) was more interesting than most. It was her clothes that first attracted my attention. They reminded me of something. What was it? Oh, yes. On television not long ago, I'd seen this film called *Woodstock*. It was about a gigantic outdoor rock concert that took place ages ago, in the sixties, and all the young people who attended it were what my parents call hippies. You know—they wore tons of beaded or silver jewellery and funny long skirts or bell-bottom jeans. The men pierced their ears and wore their hair in ponytails and the women looked like gypsies. (Only my mum said they were "bohemian." I think it means the same thing.)

Well, this girl, this Ashford or whatever her name was, looked like a hippie. She was wearing a very pretty pink flowered skirt that was full and so long it touched the tops of her shoes—which I soon realized were not shoes, but sort of hiking boots. Her blouse, loose and lacy, was embroidered with pink flowers, and both her wrists were loaded with silver bangles. Her hair, which was almost as long as my friend Dawn's and was dirty blonde, was pulled into a fat plait (which, I might add, was not held in place with a rubber band or anything; it just sort of trailed to an end). But the amazing thing was that because her hair was pulled back, you could see her ears. And she had *three pierced earrings* in *each* ear. They were all silver and all dangly, but none matched.

Wow. Was she lucky. My parents would never let me have *six* holes.

Boy, would I have something to tell the other members of the Babysitters Club that afternoon.

The girl, looking fragile and delicate, faced my classmates and me.

"Class," said Mrs Hall, "this is Ashley

Wyeth. She's just moved to Stoneybrook and will be joining us for English. I hope you'll make her feel at home."

Mrs Hall directed Ashley to the one empty desk in the room, which happened to be right next to mine. My heart leapt. Someone new, someone different. English class had suddenly become much more interesting.

The spelling test continued and I tried to pay attention, but my eyes kept drifting to Ashley Wyeth. Not to her paper. She probably hadn't read *From the Mixed-up Files of Mrs Basil E. Frankweiler*, and anyway I wouldn't cheat. No, I was just looking at Ashley. I couldn't get over the way she was dressed . . . or her six earrings.

Then there was the matter of her last name. Wyeth. I wondered if that was Wyeth as in Andrew Wyeth, the famous painter. I may not be a wonderful student, but I'm a pretty good artist, and I hoped that maybe I could grow up to be as good an artist as Andrew Wyeth. Even half as good would be okay with me.

On my fourth peek at Ashley, just after I'd spelled out m-e-d-i-c-l-e, I caught her peeking back at me. We both looked quickly at our papers. Then I looked a fifth time. Ashely was looking, too. I smiled at her. But she didn't smile back.

When the spelling test was over, we passed our papers forward and Mrs Hall collected them in a tidy pile.

"Ashley," she said, after she'd stuck the papers in a folder on her desk, "we're discussing two books right now—*The Westing Game* and *From the Mixed-up Files of Mrs Basil E. Frankweiler*. Have you read either of them?"

"Yes, I have," replied Ashley.

"Which one, dear?"

"Both of them."

Mrs Hall raised her eyebrows.

"We studied the Newbery Award-winners in my old school last year," she said seriously.

"Mm-hmm." Mrs Hall looked slightly disappointed. "And have you read *The Yearling*? Or *A Tree Grows in Brooklyn*?" I could tell she was thinking of transferring Ashley to one of the other English classes.

Ashley nodded. "I read them over the summer. But I don't mind doing the Newbery books again. I mean, we didn't read *all* of them. There are too many. Maybe I could do a special project on some of the older ones. The ones from the nineteen-thirties, if that's okay."

Mrs Hall looked impressed. I was pretty impressed myself. What kind of kid got away with suggesting work to a teacher?

When class was over, Ashley and I looked at each other again. Then Ashley said quietly, "Um, hi. Do you know where room two-sixteen is?" It sounded as if it were killing her to have to talk to me. She certainly wasn't the friendliest person I'd ever met.

"Sure," I answered. "It's on the way to my maths class. I'll take you."

"Oh, okay. . . . Thanks."

Ashley and I edged into the crowded hallway and headed for a staircase.

"My name's Claudia," I told her. "Claudia Kishi. Um, I was wondering. I know this sounds funny, but are you related to Andrew Wyeth?"

"No," replied Ashley. She paused, as if deciding whether to say anything else. Then she added, "I wish I were, though."

So she knew who I meant!

"So do I," I told her.

"Do you like his work?" asked Ashley. She glanced at me, then quickly looked away.

"*Like* it? I love it! I take all kinds of art classes. I want to be a painter some day. Or a sculptress. Or maybe a potter."

"You do?" said Ashley. "So do I. I mean, I want to be a sculptress."

She was going to say something more then, but the bell rang and we had to duck into our classrooms. Before I did, though, I glanced once more at Ashley's retreating figure. I knew that somebody very . . . different had walked into my life.

2nd CHAPTER

I didn't see Ashley again that day, but no wonder. There were only two periods left, and I had a remedial maths class (that's maths for kids who find it difficult) and a help session in the Resource Room. No way a smart kid like Ashley would have either remedial maths or time in the Resource Room.

I was a little disappointed at not seeing Ashley again, but I had a meeting of the Babysitters Club to go that afternoon, and I always look forward to meetings. Remember I mentioned my friend Dawn? Dawn Schafer is the one whose hair is longer and blonder than Ashley's. Well, she's in the club, too, and so are my other friends, Kristy Thomas, Mary Anne Spier, and Stacey McGill. The club is really fun. We meet three times a week, and people here in Stoneybrook, Connecticut, call us when they need baby-sitters. We get lots of jobs and I earn lots of money, which is important, because I need it to buy art supplies and make-up and jewellery and stuff.

As you can probably see, the club is really a little business. It's a year old now, and we run it very professionally. Here's how it works: we meet in my room on Monday, Wednesday and Friday afternoons, from five-thirty until six. (We use my room because I have my own private phone and phone number. For that reason, I get to be vice-chairman of the club.) Our clients know they can call us at our meeting times. Then they tell us when they need sitters and one of us signs up for each job. With five of us here, our clients almost always find a sitter with just one phone call, and they really like that. You're probably wondering what happens if two or three of us are able to take the same job. Who gets it? Well, luckily, we're busy enough for that not to happen very often. When it does, we're pretty nice about saying things like, "Well, I've got two other jobs that week. You take it, Stacey," or, "David Michael is your little brother, Kristy. You take the job."

Mary Anne, our club secretary, keeps track of all our jobs in the appointment pages of our club record book. In fact, she's responsible for the whole record book (except for the account of how much money we earn). The record book is where we note the addresses and phone numbers of our clients, information on the kids, our job appointments, and other commitments, like art classes.

Stacey's our treasurer, so she keeps track of the money we earn, as well as the money in our treasury, which comes from the subs we pay each week. Our subs money goes for the club expenses. For instance, we pay Kristy's big brother Charlie to drive her to and from each meeting. This is only fair, since Kristy, our chairman, started the club but had to move out of our neighbourhood over the summer. We also use the treasury money to buy colouring books and stuff for the Kid-Kits. (Kid-Kits are something Kristy thought up. They're cardboard boxes filled with our old books, games, and toys, plus activity books and crayons and other things we buy, which we sometimes take with us when we go on a baby-sitting job. Whenever one of us brings a Kid-Kit, we're a huge hit.)

Here are some other things you should know about the club: Dawn is our alternate officer, which means she's like a substitute teacher. She can take over the job of any other member who has to miss a meeting. We also have two associate members, Logan Bruno and Shannon Kilbourne. They're sitters we can call on in a pinch if a job comes in that none of us can take. (Luckily, that doesn't happen very often.) Last thing—besides the club record book, we keep a notebook. Kristy insists on this. In the notebook, we write up every single job we go on, and then we're responsible for reading the other entries about once a week. That way, we know what went on when our friends were sitting, which is often very helpful. (But—do you want my honest opinion? Reading that notebook every week can be a total bore.)

When school was over on the day I met Ashley Wyeth, I ran right home and did what was left of my homework (I had done a lot of it in the Resource Room), and then I took a look at *Mixed-up Files*. It really was time I read it, especially if Mrs Hall was going to give us "tests" on it every now and then.

I read until 5.15. The story wasn't bad. After all, there was a girl named Claudia in it. Furthermore, this Claudia felt that she was a victim of injustice. When I looked up "injustice" and found out what it meant, I was pretty interested. I often think things in my life are unjust, particularly where school or my genius sister Janine is concerned.

At 5.15, I went downstairs to find my grandmother Mimi and wait for the members of the Babysitters Club to come over.

Mimi was in the kitchen, starting supper. She had a stroke last summer but is much better now except for two things. She can only use her left hand (she used to be right-handed), and she still has a little trouble with her speech—but not much, considering that Japanese, not English, is her native language. Anyway, she likes to feel useful, so she insists on starting supper every weekday afternoon while my parents are at work, and doing whatever housework she can manage.

"Ah. Hello, my Claudia," Mimi greeted me when I entered the kitchen. "You have been study hard?"

"I guess so," I replied. "I'm reading this book. Some of the words are pretty big, but I like it. It's funny."

"How about having special tea?" asked Mimi.

"Oh, I can't. I mean, I don't have time. We have a club meeting. Everyone'll be here in about ten minutes."

"Ah. Yes. I see." (That's what Mimi always says these days when she wants to say something *else*, but the right words won't come.)

"Mimi," I began, pulling a cutting board towards me and starting to peel carrots for the salad, "there's a new girl at school. She's in my English class. Her name is Ashley Wyeth, and she likes art just like I do. We only talked for a couple of minutes today, but I think maybe we're going to be friends. Isn't that funny?"

"It happens that way sometimes. Happen when I meet your grandfather. In one second I know . . . knew . . . we would fall in love, be married, have children."

"Really?" I said. I was awed. What a second that must have been. I guess you *need* those seconds to make up for all the dull ones when you're just watching flies land on people's heads.

The doorbell rang then and I ran to answer it. It was probably Kristy. She often arrives either early or late since she's at the mercy of Charlie's schedule.

Sure enough, it was Kristy. She let herself in even before I'd answered the door.

"Hi, Claudia!" she cried. She looked like she was in a really good mood, but I wished for the thirty-nine thousandth time that she'd do something about her clothes and hair. Kristy is really cute, but she never bothers to make herself look special. All autumn she's been wearing the same kind of outfit—jeans, a turtleneck, a sweater, and trainers. And she hasn't been doing a thing to her long (well, longish) brown hair except brushing it. Here's an example of one of the big differences between Kristy and me. I was wearing a very short pink cotton dress, white tights, and black ballet slippers. I had swept all of my hair way over to one side, where it was held in place with a piece of pink cloth that matched the dress. Only one ear showed, and in it I had put my big palm tree earring. (Kristy was not wearing any jewellery.)

We are so different, it is amazing.

Dawn, Mary Anne, and Stacey arrived a few minutes later. Actually, as you might guess, we are *all* different—but some of us are more different than others. Stacey is kind of like me. She wears trendy clothes and is always getting her hair styled or permed or something, but she's not as outrageous as I can be. I did notice that day, though, that she had painted her fingernails yellow and then put black polka dots all over them.

Mary Anne, who is quiet and shy, dresses more like Kristy (who's a loudmouth). But Mary Anne is beginning to pay some attention to what she wears. Dawn falls in between Stacey and me, and Kristy and Mary Anne. She's just an individual. She's originally from California and tends to dress casually, but with flair.

The five of us went upstairs to my room and closed the door. I found a bag of sweets in my stash of junk food and passed it around, while Kristy took her seat in my director's chair and Mary Anne opened the record book so she'd be ready with our appointment calendar when the first call came in.

While we ate the sweets and waited for the phone to ring, I said, "Did any of you see that new girl? Ashley Wyeth?"

The others shook their heads. But nobody made any snide comments about new girls. That's because Stacey and Dawn were both new girls themselves not long ago. (Stacey's from New York City. She moved to Stoneybrook about a year ago, which was about six months before Dawn moved here from California.)

Ring, ring! We all leapt for the phone. That usually happens with the first call of the meeting. Kristy got it, though.

"Hello, Babysitters Club," she said in her most adult voice. "Hi, Mrs Rodowsky. . . . Thursday? That's short notice, but I'll check and call you right back, okay? 'Bye."

"Mrs Rodowsky?" I said, groaning, as Kristy hung up the phone. The Rodowskys have three boys, and one of them, Jackie, is completely accident-prone. The only thing that ever happens when you sit at the Rodowskys' is that Jackie falls off things, on things, or into things. Sometimes he gets caught in things or breaks things or loses things. He's a nice little kid, but *sheesh*.

Mary Anne began to giggle. "Hey, guess what, Claud?" she said. "You're the only one who's free that day."

"Oh, no!" I clapped my hand to my forehead as Kristy picked up the phone to call Mrs Rodowsky back. But I didn't mind as much as I let on. I've sat for Jackie and his brothers a few times now, and Jackie's beginning to grow on me.

The meeting continued. Calls came in, we got jobs. It was an average meeting. Pretty uneventful.

I loved every second of it.

The Babysitters Club is very important to me. It's almost as important to me as art is. I don't know what I'd do without the club—or my friends.

3rd CHAPTER

All that night and all the next morning on my way to school, I looked forward to seeing Ashley Wyeth again. Would she be in any of my other classes? What was her morning schedule? But I didn't see her until the English class, not even at lunchtime, although she must have been in the lunch hall since everyone in my year eats at the same time.

In English, I smiled at her and she smiled back, but when the bell rang at the end of class, Mrs Hall asked to see me privately, so I missed walking upstairs with Ashley. (By the way, I wasn't in any trouble. Mrs Hall just wanted to assign me some grammar stuff to work on in the Resource Room.) I couldn't believe I had completely missed Ashley. Oh, well. Maybe the next day.

That afternoon, I went to one of my art classes. I'm taking two kinds of classes right now. One is this general art class where we work in all different media. (That means we get to sculpt, draw, sketch, and paint in acrylics, watercolours, and oils.) We're working on sculpture now. I like it, but it's hard. I'm better at painting and drawing. At the weekends I take a pottery class. Pottery is my new love. Over the summer my family went to this mountain resort where you could swim, ride horses, go on hikes, and take art classes. (It was sort of like camp, except it was for adults, too.) Anyway, I went to some pottery classes and *loved* throwing pots, so Mum and Dad signed me up for a Saturday class in Stoneybrook.

Since the Stoneybrook Arts Centre isn't far from Stoneybrook Middle School, I got to my class a little early that day. I was the second person there. (I'd even beaten the teacher.) I set up the piece I was working on in class and was about to make a little change in one part when someone tapped me on the shoulder.

I turned around.

"Ashley!" I exclaimed.

There she was. She was wearing a puffy white blouse, a blue-denim jacket, a long blue-denim skirt, and those hiking boots again. Beaded bracelets circled both wrists, and she'd tied a strip of faded denim around her head, like an Indian headband. Since her hair was loose that day, I couldn't get a good look at her ears. I wanted to see if she was wearing six earrings again.

"Hi, Claudia," she said, fixing her serious gaze on me. "I can't believe you're in this class."

"You're joining it?" I cried, even though it was obvious that she was.

Ashley nodded. "I took lots of art classes in Chicago. This was the only one we could find here, though. Is it a good class?"

"It's great. You should see all the stuff we're doing."

"What's the teacher like?"

"Ms Baehr? She's nice. Really, you know, encouraging."

"Where did she study?" Ashley wanted to know. "Has she exhibited any of her work?"

"Huh?" I replied brightly.

"What's her background? Is she qualified?"

I could feel my cheeks burning. Of course Ms Baehr was qualified. She was the teacher. If she weren't qualified, she couldn't teach . . . could she? "I—I don't know," I stammered, but Ashley was already off on another subject. She eyed my sculpture, which was of a hand. Just a hand. If you think it's easy to sculpt (or draw) a realistic hand, try it sometime.

"Hey, Claudia, that's terrific," said Ashley. "It's beautiful." She walked all around the hand, looking at it from different angles.

"Thanks," I said. "It's just an exercise piece, though. I'm practicing on it, learning things."

"Well, it's still terrific. What else have you done?"

I noticed that Ashley was carrying a portfolio under one arm. "Do you want to see my portfolio?" I asked her shyly. I always feel like I'm boasting when I offer to let someone look through my portfolio, even though I'm not sure my work is all that good. Lots of people say it is, but I usually think, What do they know?

"Sure," replied Ashley.

"Well . . . okay," I said uncertainly. Our portfolios are stored on shelves that line the back wall of the room. I retrieved mine, laid it on the worktable next to my sculpture, and opened it for Ashley.

Very slowly, Ashley looked at every sketch and drawing that I'd saved in the portfolio. She turned them over one by one and studied each before going to the next. I stood across from her, watching her face for a reaction. I felt as nervous as if I were waiting for a teacher to tell me whether I'd passed an exam.

When Ashley had finished, she closed the portfolio and regarded me gravely with china-blue eyes. "You are really talented," she said. "I hope you know that."

I let out a sigh of relief. "Oh, thanks," I replied. "I'm glad you liked everything." Since art is one of the few things I think I'm any good at, I just die if people *don't* like my work. I hesitated. "Could I look at your portfolio?" I asked her. "Would you mind?"

"Oh, no. I wouldn't mind." Ashley slid her portfolio across the table to me.

I opened it, wondering what kind of artist Ashley was. You can tell a lot from a person's portfolio. I always look at the subjects that the person has chosen to draw or paint, and the pieces that she's decided to save in the portfolio. That kind of thing. It's psychological, I guess.

Ashley's first drawing nearly made me gasp. It drove all thoughts of psychology right out of my head. I had never seen a more realistic portrait in my life. It looked like a photograph.

I'm sure my eyes were bugging out in a really undignified way.

"Whoa," I whispered. "Amazing."

Ashley waved her hand at it. "That's not really anything," she said. "It's old. But this *next* one . . ."

I turned to the next piece in the portfolio. It was a watercolour. I wasn't sure what it was a watercolour *of*, but I knew it was very, very good.

"*That* is innovation," Ashley told me.

I glanced at her to see if she was kidding,

but she looked as grave and serious as always.

The rest of Ashley's portfolio was as amazing as the beginning. When I finally closed the folder, my heart was pounding. "How long have you been taking art lessons?" I asked.

"Oh, ages," Ashley replied. "Since I was four or five."

"Wow. Where did you take lessons? Anywhere speical?"

"Do you know the Keyes Art Society? It's in Chicago. That's where I used to live."

"You studied at *Keyes*?!" I could barely contain my excitement.

Ashley nodded.

"Wow. But how'd you get in? Only a few kids are chosen to study there." Keyes was famous among art students. I once asked my parents if I could try to get in for the summer session, but they said it was too far away and *much* too expensive.

"I was just chosen," Ashley said modestly. "When I was eight." She looked uncertainly around our little room in the Stoneybrook Arts Center. "I hope this school is good. And I hope Ms Baehr is as good as Mr Simmons. Mr Simmons was my old teacher."

"Oh, I'm sure it's all . . . fine," I lied. "Wow, did you really like my portfolio?"

"Are you kidding? It's fantastic. If you

lived in Chicago you could go to Keyes."

"Wow. . ." I felt as if the floor were melting away under my feet. A person who had gone to *Keyes* thought *my* work was good. I hoped I was impressing Ashley as much as she was impressing me.

A bunch of kids had arrived by then and I introduced Ashley to them. I thought it was a good way for her to get to know some other kids in Stoneybrook. But Ashley didn't seem very interested in the other students. I noticed that she always looked at the kid's sculpture (not at the actual kid) while I was making introductions. Then she'd just kind of nod, and we'd go on to the next person. The only person she looked at for a moment was Fiona McRae, the second best student in the class. (I'm the first. At least, I was the first until Ashley arrived.) Ashley looked appreciatively from Fiona's sculpture of a stag to Fiona and back to the stag before we moved on. Then I showed Ashley where our supplies were stored, and *then*, just as Ashley was sitting down next to me, Ms Baehr entered the room.

Ashley got to her feet, looking both nervous and hopeful, and I introduced her to our teacher.

Ms Baehr was apparently expecting Ashley and seemed just as impressed that Ashley had studied at Keyes as I had been. She looked through Ashley's portfolio, raising her eyebrows, murmuring to herself.

I knew I should feel jealous, but I didn't. After all, Ashley had studied at Keyes and she'd said *I* was really talented. She ought to know. Furthermore, she'd chosen me (out of all the kids in the class) to be her friend. She'd barely looked at the other kids, and the only people she'd talked to were Ms Baehr and me.

I was so wound up, I thought I couldn't stand another ounce of excitement.

And just as I was thinking that, Ms Baehr finished talking to Ashley, went to the front of the room, and said, "I have an announcement to make. A new art gallery will be opening in Stoneybrook, and in honour of the opening, the owners have planned a sculpture contest for the students at the Arts Centre. I'd like all of you to think about entering. You can start a new piece for the show or finish one of the pieces you're working on now. Even if you don't win, your entry will be exhibited at the gallery the week it opens. I think it would be a good experience for all of you."

Ashley turned to me excitedly. "A show!" she whispered. "Oh, we *have* to enter!"

"Is there a prize?" Fiona McRae wanted to know.

"First prize is two hundred and fifty dollars," replied Ms Baehr.

Wow! What I could buy with two

hundred and fifty dollars! It was mind-boggling.

"When's the show? I mean, what's the deadline for entering?" asked John Steiner.

"Four weeks from today."

Only four weeks. My face fell. I could kiss the prize money good-bye. No way could I have something good enough to enter in a month. My hand was a practice piece, not a show piece. At home, I was working on two sculptures—one of Mimi (my favourite subject) and one of Mary Anne's kitten, Tigger. The Mimi sculpture was too personal to enter, and Tigger wasn't the right kind of thing for a show. No, if I were going to enter, I'd have to start from scratch. And a month wasn't enough time to start *and* finish a piece, take my pottery course, keep up in school, and baby-sit.

"I can't enter," I told Ashley later, when class had begun.

Ashley looked up from the lump of clay before her. "Why not?"

I explained my reasons.

"You have to enter," said Ashley. "It would be a sin not to. You shouldn't waste your talent. I could help you," she went on. "I bet I could teach you lots of things. Show you ways to branch out. And I only spend time on people with talent."

"I can't enter," I said simply.

"Well, I'm going to. If it's all I do for the next four weeks, I'm going to create a piece worth entering. And I think you should, too. Remember. I'll help you."

"We-ell," I said. "I'll see."

Ashley smiled. "I thought you'd change your mind," she said.

4th CHAPTER

"Oh, no! Look out!" I cried.

THUD! Crunch, cruunch.

"Oops," said Jackie Rodowsky.

I buried my face in my hands. I was hoping that maybe when I opened my eyes the Rice Krispies would have disappeared from the kitchen floor. But no, when I took my hands away, the floor was still covered with a crunchy carpet of cereal, and Jackie was still sitting in the middle of the mess with the overturned box in his hands.

It was Thursday, and my ordeal with the Rodowskys had only just begun. After his mother had left, the very first words out of Jackie's mouth had been, "I'm hungry. Let's make a snack." The next thing I knew I was up to my ankles in Rice Krispies.

I glanced at the kitchen table, where nine-year-old Shea and four-year-old Archie were sitting. (Can you imagine naming a helpless little baby Archibald?) Shea and Archie were never any trouble. Well, not usually. They might *look* exactly like Jackie, but that red-haired, freckle-faced seven-year-old was the only walking disaster in the Rodowsky house.

"Well, let's clean up," I said with a sigh. I meant for Jackie and me to clean up, but Shea and Archie leaped out of their chairs, disappeared for a moment, and returned with a dustpan and brush, and a mini vacuum cleaner. They know everything there is to know about cleaning. Life with Jackie has done that to them.

Archie held the dustpan, Shea swept the cereal into it, and I followed them around vacuuming up Rice Krispie dust.

Jackie watched from the sidelines. "What can I do?" he asked.

"Stand still," I replied.

But for Jackie, that was much, much easier said than done.

I concentrated on making sure that Shea and Archie and I left no traces of cereal on the floor. Then I helpfully added "Rice Krispies" to Mrs Rodowsky's grocery list, which was fastened to the fridge with a magnet.

I was just finishing when I heard Shea speak the dreaded words: "Where's Jackie?"

"Uh-oh," I said. "Shea, you and Archie look upstairs. I'll look down here and in the play room."

The boys tore upstairs while I dashed into the living room and then the dining room. No Jackie and no signs of him, either—everything was intact and unstained. I leaned down into the play room. "Jackie?" I called.

No answer.

Then I heard Shea's voice. "Um, Claudia? Can you come here?"

I ran upstairs and found Shea and Archie standing outside the bathroom. The door to the bathroom was closed.

"Is Jackie in there?" I asked.

"Yes," answered Shea. "And the door's locked."

"Hey, Jackie!" I yelled. "Unlock the door! You know how to do that, don't you?"

"Yeah!" he replied. "Only I can't."

"How come?"

"I'm stuck in the bath."

"How can you be stuck in the bath?"

"My hand's down the drain. I can't get it out."

Archie tugged at the hem of my shirt. "He was trying to get his Blasto-Plane out. It gurgled right down the drain last night."

"Oh, for heaven's sake," I said, clapping my hand to my forehead. "All right. Shea, where's the key to the bathroom?"

Shea shrugged.

"You don't *know*?" I exclaimed. Us babysitters think to ask parents a lot of questions, such as whether any of the children has food allergies and where the first-aid kit is, but I'd never bothered to ask about the key to the bathroom.

Shea looked at me, teary-eyed. "I'm sorry," he said.

"Oh, Shea. No, *I'm* sorry. I didn't mean to sound angry. It's just that I don't know how to help Jackie."

"I do," said Shea, brightening.

"You do?"

"Yeah. It's simple. Go in through the window."

"But Shea, we're upstairs," I reminded him.

"I know. All you do is get on the kennel roof, then get on the toolshed roof, then get on the porch roof and you can open the bathroom window from there. Want me to do it?"

"No, thanks. I'd better be the one," I said grimly. "I hope the bathroom window isn't locked, too."

Five minutes later, I was standing on top of the kennel. Archie and Bo (the dog) were watching me. Shea was inside so he could talk to Jackie. As I struggled to hoist myself onto the toolshed, I thanked my lucky stars I was wearing jeans, and decided to wear jeans to the Rodowskys' from then on.

"Yea!" cried Archie as I walked unsteadily across the toolshed roof and began the last leg of my trip.

When at last I was standing by the

bathroom window, I prayed silently, Please let it be open.

It was. "Thank you," I said as I crawled into the bathroom.

"For what?" asked Jackie.

"I didn't mean you," I told him.

I unlocked the bathroom door. Shea was still standing patiently on the landing. Now what? I thought, eyeing Jackie with his hand down the drain. All at once I had an idea. It was a good idea, and it also made me appreciate the Babysitters Club Notebook a whole lot more than I ever had. I'd just remembered reading about how Mary Anne and Logan Bruno had once got Jackie's hand out of a mayonnaise jar.

"Shea," I said, "could you run into the kitchen and get some margarine? Oh, and also call Archie inside."

"Sure," replied Shea. In a moment he returned with Archie and a tub of margarine.

I rubbed a healthy, greasy amount around Jackie's hand and the edge of the drain. "Now pull your hand up very slowly," I instructed him.

He did, and after adding a few more glops of margarine, his hand was free.

"Whew," I said.

"Whew," said Jackie.

"Whew," said Shea and Archie.

"Why don't we go outside?" I suggested. Somehow, the Rodowskys' garden seemed much safer than the inside of their house.

"Okay," agreed the boys. So as soon as we'd cleaned the margarine off Jackie, we went into the front garden. The front garden was closer to the street, but there wasn't much room to play in the back garden, what with Bo's kennel and the toolshed.

"What do you want to play?" I asked the boys. They couldn't agree on anything, so I said, "Do you know Red Light, Green Light?"

Three red heads shook slowly from side to side.

"Okay, it's easy," I told them. "You guys stand here." I lined them up on one side of the garden. Then I ran to the other side. "I'm the policeman. When I turn around and close my eyes, I'll say, 'Green light.' Then you start sneaking up on me. But don't go too fast. Because when I say, 'Red light,' I'm going to turn around again and open my eyes. And anyone I see moving has to go back to the beginning. The first one to sneak all the way over here and touch me is the winner and gets to be the new policeman. Got it?"

"Got it," said Shea.

"Got it," said Jackie.

"Got what?" asked Archie.

"Never mind," I said. "Let's start the game and see what happens. If you don't understand the rules, stop and tell me, okay?"

Archie nodded.

"Now remember," I went on. "I'm the policeman, so you have to do what I say." I turned my back and closed my eyes. "Green light!" I shouted.

I heard rustlings as the boys snuck toward me.

"Red light!" I spun towards them as I opened my eyes. Shea and Archie, both about a third of the way across the garden, were standing stock-still in running position, as if they'd been on a videotape and someone had pushed the pause button on the video. But Jackie, who was slightly ahead of them, was still moving. When he tried to freeze, he lost his balance and fell over. "Okay, back to start," I told him.

Grumbling, Jackie took his time returning to the opposite side of the garden. When he was ready, I closed my eyes and called, "Green light!" again. Almost immediately, I felt a tap on my shoulder. "Winner!" I announced in surprise. Who had reached me so quickly? I opened my eyes.

Ashley Wyeth was at my side.

"Ashley!" I exclaimed.

The three Rodowsky boys, who didn't know whether to stop or go, all lost their balance and toppled to the ground.

I giggled, but Ashley was looking at me strangely.

"What are you doing?" she asked.

"Baby-sitting," I replied. "We're playing Red Light, Green Light. What are *you* doing? I mean, what are you doing *here*?"

"I live next door." Ashley pointed to the house to the right of the Rodowskys'.

The Rodowsky boys had recovered their balance and abandoned the game. They crowded around Ashley. I guess they'd never seen anyone wearing a long petticoat and work-boots. Not anyone from the twentieth century, anyway.

"Why do you have to baby-sit?" Ashley asked me.

(The boys looked somewhat hurt.)

"I don't *have* to," I replied. "This is my job. I love sitting." I told her about the Babysitters Club and how it works and the kids we sit for.

"What do you do in your spare time?" I asked Ashley.

"I paint. Or sculpt," she replied.

"I mean, what do you and your friends do? Well, what did you guys do in Chicago?"

"Just . . . just my artwork. That's really all that's important to me. I had one friend, another girl from Keyes. Sometimes we painted together. The only way to develop your talent is to devote time to it, you know."

I listened to Ashley with interest. She must know what she was talking about, being from Keyes and all. Maybe, I thought, I should set aside one afternoon a week just for my art. No distractions, no interruptions. I bet Ashley did that—and more.

"The baby-sitting club must take up a lot of your time," said Ashley.

"It does," I answered proudly. "The club's doing really well."

"But when do you have time for your sculpting?"

"Whenever I make time," I replied. Was Ashley saying I wasn't serious enough about my art?

Ashley frowned slightly at Archie, who had wrapped his arms around my legs and was blowing raspberries on my jeans. Suddenly I felt embarrassed and sort of . . . babyish. I unwound Archie and stepped away from him.

"I," I said, "spend plenty of time on my art. In fact, I've decided I have enough time to enter something in the sculpture show."

Ashley smiled. "Good," she said. Then she started to walk away.

"Hey, don't you want to stay for a while?" I asked her.

"Well, I do. I mean, I'd like to talk. But—" (she paused, eyeing the Rodowskys as if they were ants at a picnic) "—not right now."

And then she left.

I thought about Ashley for most of the

rest of the afternoon. She seemed so grown-up. She was serious and she set goals for herself and then went right ahead and worked towards them. That was how I wanted to be—serious and grown-up, just like Ashley. As I rode my bike home from the Rodowskys' that day, I decided two things: I would let Ashley help with my sculpture, since she had offered. And I would not let her see me play any more stupid outdoor games when I sat at the Rodowskys'.

5th CHAPTER

One of the very nicest things about the Babysitters Club, is how it made good friends out of the five members. A year ago, we were all split up. Mary Anne and Kristy, because they were a little immature and were already best friends anyway, always stuck together. And when Stacey moved to town, she and I were so much alike (and so different from Kristy and Mary Anne) that we became best friends immediately. The four of us hardly ever hung around together, except at meetings. We even ate lunch with different groups of friends. Then Dawn moved to Stoneybrook. She became Mary Anne's friend first, but once she joined the club, she was sort of friends with all of us and would go back and forth between our crowds in the lunch hall.

This year is different, though. Right off the bat, the five of us club members started eating together and going places together and generally being a group (even though we've got non-club friends). It's just expected that when that bell rings before lunch period, we'll all run to the lunch hall and the first one down there will save our favourite table.

So when Ashley Wyeth caught up with me in the hallway on my way to the lunch hall, the day after I'd sat at the Rodowskys' and said, "Let's eat lunch together, Claudia," I wasn't sure how to answer her. I didn't want to desert my friends.

Finally I said, "Do you want to sit with my friends and me? The members of the Babysitters Club always eat together."

Ashley thought that over. Then she said, "Let's sit by ourselves. You don't *always* sit with them, do you? Besides, what are you going to talk about? Baby-sitting?"

"Not necessarily," I replied. "We talk about lots of things, like boys and school dances and . . . and . . . stuff."

"Well, we need to discuss art," said Ashley.

"You and me?"

"Who else around here knows as much about sculpture as we do?"

I felt extremely flattered.

"We have an art show to enter," Ashley reminded me. "We have to figure out what the subjects of our sculptures are going to be. I'd like to help you, if you want help."

Did I want help from a person who'd studied at Keyes? I thought. Of course I did. "Oh, thanks. That'd be great," I told her. "But don't you mean *who* the subjects will be?"

Ashley smiled and shook her head.

Mystified, I pushed open the double doors at the back of the lunch hall.

Ashley headed towards a table by the windows that overlooked the playing fields, but I pulled her in the opposite direction. "I have to talk to my friends for a sec first," I told her. Then I paused. "Are you *sure* you don't want to sit with them?"

"I just don't think we'd get anything accomplished," Ashley replied. "Time is valuable—if you want to become a great artist."

"I guess so."

My heart began to pound. How would the club members react when one of us "defected"? It wasn't as though I was sick or had to do work in the Resource Room or something.

I led Ashley over to the Babysitters Club's table, where Kristy and Mary Anne were just settling down with trays. They'd bought the hot lunch, and as usual, Kristy was making comments about it. "*I* know what this looks like!" she was exclaiming, indicating the pizza. "It looks like . . . remember that squirrel that got run over?"

Next to me, Ashley was turning green, so

I said hastily, "Hi, you guys."

"Oh, hi!" said Mary Anne. She pulled a chair out for me. "Dawn and Stacey are buying milk. How come you're late?"

"Well," I replied, stalling for time. "It's . . . Do you guys know Ashley Wyeth? She's the new g—, I mean, she's new here. And she's in my art class. And, um, we're going to eat together today because we have to discuss something, this project," I said in a rush, not even giving anyone a chance to say hello.

Ashley slipped her arm possessively through mine.

"Oh," replied Kristy, shifting her eyes from Ashley and me to her tray. "Okay."

Mary Anne looked away, too, but didn't say anything.

Neither did Ashley. Finally I just said, "Well, um, see you guys later."

"Yeah. See you," said Kristy.

As Ashley and I made our way across the lunch hall, I began to feel angry. Why, I thought, shouldn't I have a new friend? Was there some law that said I had to eat lunch with Kristy, Mary Anne, Dawn, and Stacey every day? No, of course not. They had no right to try to make me feel like I'd committed a crime or something.

"Hey," I said suddenly to Ashley as we set our books on an empty table. "Aren't we forgetting something?"

"What?" asked Ashley. She swept her

hair over her shoulders, and I could see her earrings. Sure enough, six altogether. Two gold balls and a hoop in one ear. A seashell, a real feather, and a dangly flamingo in the other. Pretty cool.

"We forgot our lunches," I said, grinning.

Ashley broke into a smile. "Oh, yeah."

We left our things on the table and went through the lunch line. I never bring my lunch to school, but I refuse to buy the revolt-o hot lunch. I usually eat a sandwich instead. Ashley bought a yoghurt and an apple. Health food. She and Dawn would probably get along well since Dawn only eats stuff like fruit and nuts and vegetables. It was too bad Ashley didn't seem to want to get to know my other friends.

When we returned to our table, Ashley said, "So, have you thought about what you want to sculpt?"

"No," I replied. This wasn't quite true. I had thought about it, but I'd been hoping Ashley would have some good ideas, since she was such an expert. "Do you have any ideas for your project?"

Ashley shook her head. "Well, I mean, there are plenty of possibilities. I just haven't narrowed them down. But I have a great idea. I read that there's a new exhibition opening at Kuller's Gallery."

Kuller's was the other gallery in Stoneybrook, the old one.

"I think it's a watercolour exhibition, but we ought to go and check it out. I always get really inspired when I'm at a show."

"But we need ideas for sculptures," I said, "not paintings."

"You never know what might strike you, though."

I paused just long enough for Ashley to jump back into the conversation with, "Oh, Claud, you *have* to go with me. Nobody else will appreciate the show the way you will."

I beamed. "Okay," I said. "I'll go. Just as long as I'm home by five-thirty. I've got a meeting of the Babysitters Club."

I didn't get home until 5.45. At five o'clock I'd started saying things to Ashley such as, "I'd better leave soon," and, "I'd really better go."

But every time I said something, Ashley would pull me over to another painting, saying, "Just look at this one, Claud. You have to look at this one." She was so intense. I think she barely heard what I was saying.

I must admit, I got much more out of a show with Ashley than I did by myself. She made me look at paintings in different ways and see things in them that I wouldn't have noticed by myself. And she listened, really *listened*, to anything I had to say about the watercolours.

So I had a hard time leaving. I was just enjoying appreciating the art. I knew my other friends would never get so much out of an exhibition. They didn't enjoy art the way Ashley and I did.

At a quarter to six, when I finally ran into my bedroom, I found the club meeting in progress.

"You guys started without me!" I exclaimed accusingly.

"Hello yourself," said Kristy. "Of course we started without you. The phone began ringing. What did you expect? That we'd tell everyone to call back later—after Claudia got here? We weren't sure you were coming at all. Where were you?"

"Ashley and I went to an exhibition at Kuller's."

At the mention of Ashley's name, my friends exchanged glances.

"Why didn't you call to say you were going to be late?" asked Kristy. "That's a club rule, you know."

"I was trying to get here," I said. "I ran the whole way home. I left the exhibition late. It was just . . . Ashley and I were having such a good time."

"*How* good a time?" spoke up Stacey, and I thought she looked a little pale. "As good a time as when you and I go to the mall?"

"Stace, I don't know," I said, forcing a laugh.

The phone rang, and we stopped our discussion to take a job. And then two more.

"What did I miss?" I finally dared to ask.

"I mean, at the beginning of the meeting."

"Three calls," replied Kristy. "On the appointment pages, it looked like you were free for a couple of them, but we couldn't be sure. Stacey and Mary Anne took them instead."

I nodded. That was fair. And anyway, it was a rule. If you were going to be late to a meeting and didn't tell anyone about it first, you lost privileges. Still, I didn't like the way being left out felt.

Or the way Stacey was looking at me.

6th CHAPTER

Uh-oh, you guys. I had some trouble with Jeff today and it affected my baby-sitting, so I guess you should know about it. I was sitting at the Perkinses', and Myriah and Gabbie were being as good as gold. In fact, they were entertaining themselves really well. They had a messy project going, but it was in the bathroom, and Mrs. Perkins said it was all right because it would be easy to clean up. The three of us--Myriah and Gabbie and I -- were having a great time. Chewbacca wasn't even bothering us. And then the phone rang....

What you need to know about Dawn's younger brother Jeff is that ever since school started this year, he's been having problems. He's been saying he misses his father. See, the reason Dawn moved to Stoneybrook last January was that her parents had just got a divorce, and Stoneybrook is where Mrs Schafer grew up. Her parents, Dawn's grandparents, still live here. So Mrs Schafer moved Dawn and Jeff back to her home town. Mr Schafer stayed in California.

At first, things seemed okay. I mean, Dawn didn't like the cold Connecticut winter, but she made friends and joined our club, and Jeff made friends, and Mrs Schafer found a job and even started dating. Then at the end of the summer, Dawn and Jeff flew back to California to visit their dad. Maybe Jeff got homesick or something. Who knows? Anyway, he's become a real handful. He's been saying he misses Mr Schafer and that he doesn't want to live with Dawn and their mum any more. And he's been getting into trouble at school. So that's what had been going on in Dawn's life at the time she took the job baby-sitting for Myriah and Gabbie Perkins.

When Dawn rang the Perkinses' bell it was answered by the gallumphing feet of Chewbacca, their big black Labrador retriever.

"Chewy! Chewy!" she could hear Mrs

Perkins saying. Then she heard a little scuffle. "Dawn?" Mrs Perkins called.

"Yeah, it's me," Dawn replied.

"Let yourself in, okay? I'm going to put Chewy in the back garden."

"Okay!" Dawn opened the front door and stood listening. Apart from the sounds of Mrs Perkins taking Chewbacca outside, she couldn't hear a thing. Where were Myriah and Gabbie? Usually they race to answer the door if one of us baby-sitters is coming over.

When Mrs Perkins returned, she put a finger to her lips and whispered, "I want to show you something. Follow me."

Dawn followed Mrs Perkins upstairs and into the girls' bathroom. Mrs Perkins gestured for her to peek inside.

Dawn did. Seated on the (closed) toilet, she saw Gabbie, who's almost three, holding a mirror and carefully applying a streak of green eye shadow in a long line from one eye, across her nose, to her other eye. She looked like a cave woman.

Myriah, who's six, was standing on a stool, leaning over the sink to the mirror on the medicine cabinet, and smearing on purplish lipstick.

Strewn around them—on the floor, on the back of the toilet, and all around the sink—were cotton balls, Q-tips, hair curlers, and dribs and drabs of leftover make-up, such as the ends of lipsticks, almost empty pots of blusher, and drying tubes of mascara. And seated carefully in a line on the floor were the girls' dolls and teddy bears.

Myriah glanced up and saw her mother and Dawn in the mirror. "Hi!" she called excitedly.

"Hi, Dawn Schafer!" added Gabbie, who calls almost everyone by both first and last name.

"We're having a beauty parlour!" exclaimed Myriah. She put down her lipstick and jumped off the stool. "These are our customers," she said, pointing to the dolls and bears.

"Our customers," echoed Gabbie.

"And now we're fixing ourselves up," said Myriah. "I'm doing my make-up first."

"Girls, I'm going to leave now," Mrs Perkins interrupted. She turned to Dawn. "I've got another checkup." (Mrs Perkins is expecting a baby.) "The obstetrician's number is on the fridge. I have some errands to run afterwards, so I probably won't be home until five o'clock. You know where everything is, right?"

Dawn nodded.

"Any questions?" asked Mrs Perkins.

"Well," said Dawn, looking around the messy bathroom, "is it *really* okay for the girls to play with all this stuff?"

"Oh, yes. Don't worry about it. I give

them the ends of all my make-up. Don't worry about cleaning up, either. We'll do that tonight or tomorrow. They've got a good game going."

Dawn grinned. Mrs Perkins is great. What a nice mummy. We know one mummy—Jenny Prezzioso's—who gets hysterical at the very thought of a mess or a little dirt.

After Mrs Perkins had left, Myriah introduced Dawn to some of the "customers" in the beauty parlour. First she held up a bear whose plastic snout was covered with lipstick and who was wearing a shower cap.

"This is Mrs Xerox," she said. "She's having her hair permed."

"I put her lipstick on," spoke up Gabbie. She had finished her own make-up job and looked at Dawn solemnly from garish eyes. Lipstick, red and pink, stretched from ear to ear. She held up the hand mirror again. "Don't I look pretty? I'm a lovely lady."

"And this," Myriah went on, holding up a baby doll, "is Mrs Refrigerator. She just needed an eye job. . . . Oh! I better do *my* eyes!" Myriah jumped up on the stool again and began collecting tubes of mascara and eyeliner.

The phone rang.

"Can I get it?" cried Gabbie. She leaped off the toilet, spilling a lapful of hair curlers.

"Better let me," said Dawn. "I'll be right

back. You guys keep . . . keep up the good work." She dashed into Mr and Mrs Perkins' bedroom and picked up the phone, which was ringing for the third time.

"Hello, Perkins residence," she said.

"Dawn?" asked a disgruntled voice.

"Yes. Jeff? Is that you?"

"Yeah."

"What's up? Are you at home?"

"Not exactly. I'm kind of at school. Using the teachers' phone. And I'm kind of in trouble."

"What do you mean, '*kind of* in trouble'?"

"Oh, all right. I *am* in trouble. And Ms Besser wanted me to call Mum. She won't let me go home until she talks to her. Only I called Mum's office and they said she went to a meeting somewhere in Stamford. So then I remembered you said you were sitting at the Perkinses' and I looked up their number. What should I do now, Dawn?"

"Okay," Dawn said, trying not to get upset, "let's start at the beginning. Why are you in trouble with Ms Besser?"

"I threw an eraser across the room. You know, a big blackboard eraser."

"Gosh, that doesn't sound *so* bad. I mean, you shouldn't have done it, but—are you sure that's all you did?"

"It was sort of the third time I threw it across the room. And it knocked over Simon

Beal's tile mosaic. And the mosaic broke. And one of the tiles cut Lynn Perone's leg. . . ." Jeff's voice was fading into nothingness.

"Oh, *Jeff*," was all Dawn could say. She paused, thinking. "You're *sure* you can't get in touch with Mum?"

"They said she isn't coming back to the office today. She's going to be in Stamford until five o'clock."

"Well," said Dawn slowly, "I guess I could come to school myself. Maybe I can talk to Ms Besser or something. I can't let you sit there all afternoon."

"Oh, that'd be great."

"All right. But Jeff, I want you to know I'm not happy about this. I'm baby-sitting. I'll have to bring Myriah and Gabbie with me."

"Okay," replied Jeff, but he didn't say he was sorry.

Dawn returned to the bathroom. "You guys," she said, "I'm really sorry, but we have to close up your beauty parlour for a while. We've got to go over to your school, Myriah."

"We *do*?" Myriah looked awed. At her age, going to school after hours is like sneaking into an amusement park when it's been closed for the night.

Dawn tried to explain why they had to go, while figuring out the fastest way to get the girls there.

"But let's not *close* the beauty parlour," said Myriah. "Let's take it with us."

"Whatever," replied Dawn, who just wanted to get going fast.

"Goody!" cried Myriah and Gabbie, scooping up make-up and curlers and supplies.

Dawn hustled the girls and their junk downstairs. She didn't have time to wash their faces. She just loaded them and their things into Myriah's red wagon and ran them over to the infant school in what must have been a wagon-pulling record.

When she reached the front door, she wasn't sure what to do with the wagon, so she pulled the girls right inside and down the hall to Jeff's classroom. She found him sitting sullenly at his desk, while Ms Besser worked quietly at hers.

"Um, excuse me," said Dawn.

Ms Besser and Jeff both looked up in surprise at the sight of Myriah and Gabbie in the wagon with their lipstick-smeared faces.

"I'm Dawn Schafer, Jeff's sister." Dawn explained why she had come instead of her mother.

"And *I*," spoke up Myriah, "am Miss Esmerelda. I run a beauty salon. This is my assistant," she added, climbing out of the wagon and pointing to Gabbie.

"I am Miss Gabbie," said Gabbie.

"Would you like a make-over?" Myriah

asked Ms Besser.

"Oh . . . not today, Miss, um—"

"Esmerelda," supplied Myriah. She turned to Jeff. "Would *you* like a make-over? From our travelling beauty parlour?"

"No way," replied Jeff, turning red.

"I would like a make-over," Gabbie told her sister.

"Oh, good," said Myriah, and got to work.

Ms Besser led Dawn into the hall. "I'm very concerned about your brother," she said. "He's gone beyond just being a nuisance or a disturbance in class. If Lynn's cut had been any worse, she would have needed stitches. I wanted to talk to your mother in person. I think we have a serious problem."

"I'm really sorry we can't reach her," said Dawn.

"So am I," Ms Besser replied.

"I can get her to call you tomorrow. Or even at home tonight. Maybe she could set up a meeting with you or something."

Ms Besser nodded. "At the very least. All right. Please do get her to call me tonight. I'll give you my home number." She paused. Then she added, "Thank you for taking the trouble to come over here. I can see that it wasn't very convenient for you. You seem quite responsible."

Dawn wasn't sure how to respond to that, so finally she just said "Thank you." A few minutes later she had left the school with her brother and the Perkins girls. Jeff immediately headed angrily for home. He had barely spoken to his sister. By the time Dawn and the travelling beauty parlour reached the Perkins house it was 5.15.

Mrs. Perkins met them at the front door. "Where *were* you?" she asked anxiously.

"I'm really sorry," said Dawn. "I should have left a note." She told Mrs Perkins what had happened, and apologized six or seven times. Luckily, Mrs Perkins was forgiving and understanding.

Later, as Dawn pedalled her bike home, she wondered how often she'd have to bail Jeff out of trouble. She flew over a little hump in the road just then, and as she did, pictured herself in a roller coaster, just beginning to pick up speed. Mum, she thought, I have a feeling you and I are in for a bumpy ride.

7th CHAPTER

"I am an artist and my craft is calling," said Ashley earnestly.

"Calling what?" I replied.

"Calling *me*. Like the call of the wild."

It was lunchtime, and Ashley and I were sitting by ourselves again. We had this conversation going, only (and this was so stupid) I didn't know what we were talking about. It's pretty pathetic to be one of the persons in a two-person conversation and not following the drift of things at all.

I glanced across the lunch hall at the Babysitters Club's table and sneaked a peak at Kristy, Stacey, Mary Anne, and Dawn. The usual lunchtime things seemed to be going on. Dawn was eating what looked like homemade fruit salad. Kristy was holding up a noodle from the hot lunch and saying something about it which was making Mary

Anne turn green. Stacey was rolling her eyes.

I smiled to myself. Kristy always gets disgusting at lunch and we always give her a hard time about it, but right now I was missing her disgusting comments.

I kind of hoped that one of my friends would look over at me and smile or wave, but none of them did.

I was sitting with Ashley because it was getting to the point where, if I didn't choose a subject for my sculpture and start working right away, I'd have to withdraw from the show. Here's what had led up to Ashley's saying, "I am an artist and my craft is calling":

"Ashley, we really better get to work on our sculptures." (That was me, of course, since what with baby-sitting and pottery and everything else I do, I'm more pressed for time than Ashley is.)

"Well, I've reached a decision," said Ashley.

"What?" I asked excitedly.

"I'm going to sculpt an inanimate object. I think maybe you should, too."

"You're going to sculpt what?" (Why is it that when I'm with Ashley, the word that gets the most use is "what"? But Ashley never seems to mind explaining things to me.)

"An inanimate object," Ashley repeated. "Something not alive."

"You want us to sculpt dead things?" I asked in horror. I was imagining ghouls and corpses and mummies.

"Oh, no. I just mean I want to sculpt objects that aren't living. Look at us. We're surrounded by inanimate objects—books, pencils, tables, chairs, trays. They're all inanimate."

"But," I said sceptically, "I've hardly ever seen sculptures of, um, un-alive things. Aren't most sculptures of people or animals? I mean, except for abstract sculptures. That's what Ms Baehr says sculpting is all about—capturing the spirit of something alive in something that doesn't move, like clay or stone. . . . I don't know, Ashley. Are you sure we want to go out on a limb like that? Why don't we stick to the more usual stuff?"

And that was when Ashley had said her craft was calling and I'd got some good mileage out of the word "what."

"Come into town with me after school today," she said finally. "We'll go right into the field. I'm sure we'll be inspired."

"What field?" I replied.

"I mean the real world."

"Oh. Well, all right." The "real world" sounded very exciting. Going into the field was probably something only true artists did. A smile spread across my face. We were going to be pioneers, sculpting pioneers. Ashley and I would try techniques other sculptors had never thought about. I looked across the table at Ashley's serious, eager face. "Great idea," I added. "It'll be exciting. Plus, then we can get to work right away. . . . Oh, but I have another club meeting this afternoon, so I have to be home by five-thirty."

"Sure. No problem," replied Ashley tightly.

Just as going to the watercolour exhibition with Ashley had been an eye-opening experience, so was simply walking around Stoneybrook with her. Maybe because she was new to town, or maybe because she was such a talented artist, Ashley noticed all sorts of things that had never seemed particularly noticeable to me before. And she saw things *in* them that I never saw. Well, never saw first. After Ashley pointed them out to me, I saw them.

As soon as we reached Stoneybrook's main street, Ashley grabbed my arm.

"What, what?" I cried, getting double use of the word.

"Look at that!" said Ashley, pointing.

"What?"

"*That.*"

"That fire hydrant?"

"Yes. Look at the way it's shaped. It's . . . almost noble. It's little and squat, but it's sitting up straight and square, like a jockey on a prizewinning steed."

"Wow," I said, letting out a breath I hadn't realized I was holding.

"That just might be my subject," said Ashley thoughtfully, nodding her head.

"For your *sculpt*ure?" I repeated incredulously. "But why would you sculpt it? What's so special about an old fire hydrant?"

"That it's little, but noble. I'd try to bring out those qualities when I sculpt it. I think that the secret of sculpting inanimate objects is making them look animated."

The word "what" was on the tip of my tongue, but I bit it back. When I thought about it, I understood what Ashley meant. I just couldn't see any way to *do* it.

"Come on, let's see what else there is."

Now, over the years I have scoured Stoneybrook in search of a new pair of shoes, in search of a certain kind of blue-jean jacket, in search of school supplies, and once in search of Mary Anne's reading glasses. But this was the first time I'd scoured the town exclaiming over hubcaps and bins and street lamps. I did sort of get into the spirit of things, though.

"Oh!" cried Ashley. "Look at that traffic light!" Ashley sounded more excited that afternoon than I'd ever heard her. It was amazing what art did to her.

"Yeah," I replied. And (I swear I don't know where this came from) I added, "Think of the power it holds. It *controls* the traffic. It can make people late. It can prevent accidents. It's a little box doing an awfully big job."

"Yeah!" said Ashley admiringly. She paused, then added thoughtfully, "Maybe that's your subject."

"Maybe," I replied uncertainly.

We walked on.

"Look at the sweet wrapper," said Ashley.

"Look at that squashed soda can," I said.

By the time we sat down in Renwick's for a snack, all I could say was, "Look at that straw!" and "Look at that dish rag!" Stuff like that. Until I checked my watch. Then I cried, "Look at the time!"

"What time is it?" asked Ashley.

"Ten past five. I'm going to be late for another meeting. I'm sorry, but I've got to leave."

"But Claudia, we haven't made any definite decisions. We have to go back and look at the fire hydrant and the traffic light again."

"I *have* to go to the meeting. The club is important to me. We started that club. We made it work. It's a business. And besides, the other club members are my friends."

Ashley blinked. "But I'm your friend, too . . . am I not?" she said, sounding like my genius sister, Janine. (I have this older sister who's a genius. Not just smart, like Ashley, but a true and honest genius. How is that I always end up hanging around people who know enough to say things like "am I not" instead of "aren't I"?)

"Yes," I replied slowly. "You're my friend."

Ashley gave me a tiny smile. I began to feel bad. Maybe I was really important to her. I wasn't sure. I was *pretty* sure I was her only friend, though. I had four good friends, but so far, Ashley only had me. Besides, this was art. What Ashley and I were doing was important—and it was something I could do only with Ashley, not with any of my other friends.

"You know," I said, "that meeting isn't urgent or anything. We really should go back and look at the fire hydrant and traffic light again. Why don't you wait for our food while I call Dawn and tell her I won't be able to make the meeting. I'll be right back."

I stood in the phone box by the front door of Renwick's and dialled Dawn's number, hoping fervently that she was at home and not out baby-sitting. I breathed a sigh of relief when she answered the phone herself.

"Hi," I said. "It's me, Claudia."

"Oh, hi," replied Dawn lightly, but there was a cautious edge to her voice.

"Listen," I told her, "I'm not going to be able to make the meeting today. Ashley and I *have* to choose subjects for our sculptures —you know, for the show. So can you be the

vice-chairman for me today?"
"Sure."
"And tell the others that I won't be coming."
"Sure."
An embarrassing pause followed.
Finally Dawn said, "Do you want us to sign you up for any jobs? I mean, are your art classes and things on the appointment pages so we know when you're busy?"
"I think so," I said. "Well, I'd better go before my money runs out. I'm in town in a phone box."
"Okay," said Dawn shortly. "Bye."
She hung up before I could answer her.
With a sigh, I returned to Ashley, who greeted me with a smile.

That evening I read, for the fifth time, the note Mary Anne, as club secretary, had left for me after the meeting which had been held in my room that afternoon: Claudia— you're sitting for Nina and Eleanor Marshall next Friday from 3.30–6.00 — M.A.S.

That was it. The entire note. No "Hi, Claud!" or "See you soon," or anything. I suppose my friends were mad at me. By the time I went to bed, I was sure of it. That was because, hidden under my pillow, I found a note from Kristy which said: Everyone at school thinks Ashley is weird. I just thought you should know — Kristy.

The worst thing about the day was that I hadn't even chosen a subject for my sculpture. Ashley had chosen the fire hydrant, but I just couldn't bring myself to sculpt a traffic light. Not even in order to become a sculpture pioneer. I had missed a meeting, wasted an afternoon, and was no closer to entering the art show than before.

8th CHAPTER

Some people around here are TRAITORS. And you know who you are. Ordinarily, this notebook is used to record our baby-sitting jobs, but it's also for club problems, and we have a little problem right now: The little problem is a certain person who keeps missing meetings. It's a good thing we have an alternate officer because Dawn sure has had to take over the duties of our vice-chairman a lot lately.

But I don't mind being vice-chairman you guys.

Okay, so Dawn doesn't mind, but we do mind having a V.C. who'd rather be an artist.

Yeah, our V.C. used to be very nice, but now she never shows up at meetings and she hangs around with a person who wears BELL-BOTTOM BLUE JEANS to school.

Kristy's notebook entry went on for so long that I got a pretty complete idea of what happened at the second club meeting that I couldn't attend. Plus, later—when we were friends again—Stacey filled me in on every little thing I'd missed.

But I'm getting ahead of myself. What made me miss another meeting was that Ashley convinced me to take a second inspirational walk in "the field" with her, looking for something to sculpt, since I couldn't bring myself to sculpt the traffic light. We ran late again, I had to call Dawn to ask her to take over my duties, and another meeting was held in my room without me.

The meeting started out with Dawn running into my room, arriving just after Kristy had, and announcing, "Well, I'm the vice-chairman again today."

"You are?" Kristy said. "How come?"

"Claudia just called. She and Ashley are doing something."

"*What*?" demanded Kristy.

"I don't know. It has to do with that sculpture show."

Kristy, mumbling and grumbling, began pawing around my bed, lifting up my pillow and cushions, and finally sliding off the bed headfirst and peering underneath it.

"What are you doing?" asked Dawn.

"Looking for Claudia's bubblegum. I know she's got some stashed somewhere."

Mary Anne entered my room then, followed by Stacey. "What are you doing?" she asked Kristy. (Everyone seemed to want to know.)

"Looking for Claudia's bubblegum."

"It's in her hollow book," said Stacey, pointing to the bookshelf. "Where's Claudia?"

"Three guesses," replied Kristy, biting off the words angrily. She pulled the hollow book from my shelf. (It's my best, most clever hiding place ever.) Then she reached in, pulled out two pieces of gum (one for her, one for Mary Anne—Dawn and Stacey won't touch the stuff), and began chewing.

"I only need one guess," said Stacey, "and it isn't a guess. It's a 'know.' She's with Ashley again."

"Right."

"Ha." Stacey flumped onto my bed. "Ashley was wearing *bell-bottoms* today. Everyone was talking about her."

"She's so weird," said Mary Anne. "She doesn't talk to anyone but Claudia. I think she's stuck-up."

Ring, ring.

My friends were slower than usual in answering the phone. Stacey picked it up after three rings and arranged a job sitting for Jamie and Lucy Newton. Then Dawn's mother called needing a sitter for Jeff one evening.

"How are things going with Jeff?" Mary

Anne asked Dawn after she'd finished talking with Mrs Schafer.

Dawn shrugged. "Okay, I guess. Mum had a meeting with his teacher and told her what's going on with Jeff at home. Then Ms Besser told her what Jeff was doing in school. Like, *not* working, *not* bothering to raise his hand. All these *nots*. They've decided that they're just going to try being very firm with him and not let him get away with a thing. And really praise him for the good things he does. That doesn't sound like much to me. I thought they were going to talk about bigger things, like whether Jeff should move back to California to be with Dad. But I suppose you start with something small and hope it will do the trick."

"Sure," said Mary Anne. "It's like giving a sick person a pill instead of going ahead and doing a huge operation."

The girls had to laugh at Mary Anne's comparison. The idea of Jeff on an operating table having his bad humour removed was pretty funny.

"But," Dawn went on thoughtfully a few moments later, "Mum and Dad have been talking a lot lately."

"About Jeff?" asked Stacey.

"Probably. The only reason I know is because I was in Mum's desk the other day looking for tape, and the phone bill was right on top of a pile of stuff. I didn't even have to snoop to see all the calls that have been made to Dad's number. It was a whole long list of them. All from the last few weeks, and most of them late at night. I guess they're talking at night because they don't want Jeff and me to know what they're discussing. Which means the subject must be Jeff. What else could be so important to both of them? They're sure not going to get remarried or anything."

"What do you think they're saying?" asked Mary Anne in a small voice.

Dawn shook her head. "I . . . I don't know. . . ."

The phone rang and Dawn leapt for it, as if she were glad for the chance to avoid Mary Anne's question. "Hello, Babysitters Club," she said. "Yes? . . . Yes. . . . Okay. . . . Okay. . . . Until eleven? Well, I'll check and get back to you. . . . Right. . . . 'Bye."

Mary Anne, always organized and ready, was waiting with the record book in her lap by the time Dawn hung up the phone. It was open to the appointment pages." "A night job?" she asked, her eyes shining. We all love baby-sitting late at night, even though sometimes we get scared.

"Yup," replied Dawn. "At the Papadakises'."

"When?" asked Mary Anne.

Dawn told her.

"Well, let's see. Kristy, you're free, and so's Claudia," said Mary Anne.

"Oh, give the job to Kristy," said Dawn

and Stacey together. The two of them were so busy being smug about the thought of not giving the job to *me*, that they didn't even bother to hook their baby fingers and say "jinx."

The thing is, the Papadakises live over in Kristy's neighbourhood, and we usually let Kristy take jobs that are near to her because it's so much more convenient for both her and our clients if nobody has to drive anywhere. But at that meeting, it was plain that my friends didn't want me to get the job. They were punishing me for not being at the meeting.

Mary Anne wrote Kristy's job on the appointment calendar, while Dawn called Mrs Papadakis back and told her that Kristy would be sitting. When she hung up, Mary Anne said, sounding guilty, "Do you think we should have offered that job to Claudia, too? We could have called Mrs Papadakis tomorrow."

"No way," said Stacey. "Why make a good client wait? Besides, Kristy usually sits for the people in her neighbourhood. We do that on purpose. Right, Kristy?"

"Right," she agreed.

For a moment, nobody spoke.

Then Stacey said, "Claudia probably wouldn't even have *time* to sit. She's so busy with Ashley."

"She hasn't eaten lunch with us for days," added Dawn.

"I don't think she likes me any more," said Stacey softly.

Mary Anne was looking sympathetically at Stacey. As Stacey's eyes filled with tears, so did Mary Anne's.

"*Darn* it," cried Stacey, mashing her fist into my pillow and smushing a packet of biscuits that were hidden underneath. "I *hate* crying."

"It's okay," whimpered Mary Anne, edging closer to Stacey. "We don't mind if you cry. We know Claudia's your best friend. You must feel . . . terrible . . ." Mary Anne's tears spilled down her cheeks before Stacey's did.

"Oh, this is just *fine*," exclaimed Kristy. "Claudia's not even here, and look what she's turned this meeting into. A cry-fest. Where are Claudia's cakes? I know they're here somewhere. I need a cake. I'm having a cake attack." Kristy was practically destroying my room in her search for junk food. It was so silly. Anyone with half a brain would know I keep the cakes in my sock drawer.

"Mary Anne, get a grip on yourself," said Stacey, who'd already stopped crying. "Think of pleasant things. Think of Tigger." (Tigger is Mary Anne's kitten.)

"Think of Shannon," said Kristy. (Shannon is the Thomas kids' new puppy.)

"Think of Logan," said Dawn. (Logan is Mary Anne's boyfriend. Believe it or not, she's the only club member who has a boyfriend).

"I'm trying," said Mary Anne, sniffling.

"Oh, bother," said Kristy. "Listen to us. Think lovely thoughts. Do you know who we sound like? We sound like Peter Pan, that's who. Peter *Pan*. We are baby-sitters, not magical, flying boys. Now, you guys."

"Yes?" said Dawn, Stacey, and Mary Anne.

"Dry your eyes, sit up straight, wait for the phone to ring, stop thinking like Peter Pan, and—*behave like baby-sitters*."

9th CHAPTER

I slammed my locker shut, heard a rustling sound inside, and immediately wrenched my locker open again. I knew what had happened. My poster of Max Morrison, the most gorgeous star in the history of television, had fallen off the inside of the door. This happens about once a day. At Stoneybrook Middle School you're not allowed to put things up in the lockers with tape, so we kids get around this by using bits of chewed-up gum. The only problem is, the gum loses its stickiness after a while.

I smacked the poster back onto the gum bits, reminding myself to chew up some new gum soon, and closed my locker again. Then I turned around and nearly ran into Ashley. She was wearing a long, all-the-way-to-her-ankles dress with three rows of ruffles at the bottom. A strip of black cloth was tied around her head. I couldn't see her earrings, but she looked . . . well, all right, I'll admit it. She looked a little bizarre.

"I'm glad I found you," said Ashlcy. "I had a great idea this morning—for your sculpture—and I wanted to tell you about it right away."

"Thank goodness," I said, "because I'm not too sure about an, um, inanimate object."

"I know—" Ashley began.

"Hi, Claudia."

"Hi, Claudia."

"Hi, Claudia."

"Hi, Claudia."

I turned around. There were the other members of the Babysitters Club. I was really glad they'd come to talk. They hardly ever do that when Ashley's around.

"Hi, you guys!" I replied. I waited for my friends to say hi to Ashley or for Ashley to say hi to my friends, but none of them spoke.

"Well . . ." I said nervously.

"We missed you at the meeting yesterday," said Kristy pointedly.

"I'm sorry. I had to think about—"

"We know, we know. Your sculpture," said Dawn.

Stacey eyed Ashley critically. "Nice dress," she commented.

Ashley flushed with embarrassment, but she didn't reply. We all knew Stacey was being sarcastic.

"Do you suppose you'll be able to clear time in your busy schedule to get to the next meeting?" Dawn asked me.

I looked at her in surprise. What kind of question was that from our even-tempered alternate officer?

"I plan to," was all I replied.

"I hope *you* approve of that," said Kristy to Ashley.

Ashley still looked awfully uncomfortable. "Claudia," she began uncertainly, and then seemed to gain some confidence. "Claudia is an artist—"

"Don't remind us," interrupted Kristy.

"She's an artist," Ashley went on, "and she needs to spend time on her work."

"What are you? Her tutor or something?" asked Stacey.

"I'm her mentor," replied Ashley, as serious as always.

Well, that put a stop to things for a moment or two because only Ashley knew what a mentor was. (I looked it up in the dictionary later. It means a wise and trusted teacher. I guess that's better than a plain old tutor.)

"If Claudia is going to develop her talents to the fullest—and I do think she can go a long way in the world of art—"

(I beamed again. I couldn't help it. You just don't shrug off compliments like that one.)

"—she has to devote as much time as

possible to her art," Ashley finished.

"But she does," insisted Mary Anne. "Plenty of time." And I thought, my friends really don't understand, do they?

Ashley shook her head. "Spending time on anything else, especially baby-sitting, is just a waste."

"Hey," said Kristy, turning angrily to me, "does this mean you're quitting the club? It would be nice if you'd let us know. We'd like to hold the meetings somewhere other than in your room, if you are. And of course we'll have to give our clients our new phone number, make up new fliers, all sorts of things."

"I'm not quitting the club!" I exclaimed.

"Could have fooled us," said Stacey.

"Yeah," spoke up Mary Anne, sounding unusually fierce.

"We could use a little warning if you are," said Kristy.

"I AM NOT QUITTING!" I cried.

"Good," said Kristy and Stacey.

"Good," I said.

"Good-*bye*," added Dawn and Mary Anne.

"Good-*bye*," I replied.

My four friends turned and walked off down the hall. I was left standing with Ashley. "Oh, who needs them anyway?" I said grumpily.

"Right," agreed Ashley. "Who needs friends when you have art?"

I tried to smile at Ashley, but it was difficult.

"Ew, ew! Get away from me! Get *away*!" shrieked Fiona McRae.

"Oooo-eeee-oooo. You'll never escape the Mud Monster from the deep." John Steiner, his hands dripping with watered-down clay, chased Fiona around the room.

This is the sort of thing that usually goes on at our art class if Ms Baehr arrives a few minutes late. John and Fiona weren't the only kids acting up. Seth Turbin was making fake eyeballs out of his clay, and Mari Drabek was trying to fashion a pair of glasses for the eyeballs.

I kept looking around and giggling—especially at the eyeballs and glasses—but Ashley sat stiffly in front of her fire hydrant sculpture. She worked busily, not even aware of the other kids. I wished I could be as focused as Ashley was.

"Good afternoon, class!" called Ms Baehr's voice.

We snapped to attention. John ran to the sink—as if that's where he'd been headed all along—to clean up his hands. Seth and Mari smashed their eyeballs and glasses flat. And everyone else flew into their seats. (Except for Ashley, who was already in her seat.)

"While you're working today," Ms Baehr said, ignoring all the confusion, "I want to find out how each of you is doing with your piece for the show. I'll walk around and talk to you privately. Feel free to interrupt me if you need help with anything."

Since Ashley and I were at the worktable in the front of the room, Ms Baehr approached us first. "Ashley?" she said. "You've definitely decided to go ahead with the fire hydrant?"

"Yes," replied Ashley. "And this is it. I mean, the beginning of it." She indicated the lumpy clay that was slowly gaining form in front of her.

Ms. Baehr looked at it for several seconds. Her face was expressionless. At last she said, "You do realize that this is an odd choice for a sculpture, don't you?"

Ashley frowned. "Well," she said slowly, "I think it's just different. I want to do something different."

"Wouldn't you like to finish up the eagle you started? It was lovely. It would be perfect for the show."

"No," said Ashley. "It's too . . . commonplace. I really want to make a statement with my work."

Ashley bit her lip and I knew she was afraid that Ms Baehr would tell her she couldn't work on the fire hydrant. But I kept wondering what kind of statement a fire hydrant would make. I could tell Ms Baehr was wondering the same thing. She usually keeps an open mind, though, so all she said was, "Very well."

Then she turned to me.

I was working on my hand sculpture again, and Ms Baehr said, "Beautiful, Claudia. That's coming along fine."

"What, this?" I replied. "This is just a practice piece. It's not for the show. I don't know what I'm going to enter."

"You'd better choose soon, Claud, and then get cracking," said Ms Baehr kindly. "But I like the hand. Why not enter it?"

"I—I want to make a statement, too," I said with a sidelong glance at Ashley.

Ashley smiled. I knew she was pleased that I was listening to her, my mentor.

But Ms Baehr sighed. "Okay, Claud." She straightened up and walked over to Fiona McRae's table.

"Hey, I'm proud of you!" Ashley said to me, speaking softly so Ms Baehr wouldn't hear.

"Really?" I replied, glowing.

"Yes. And—well, I never got to tell you the idea I had this morning. We got interrupted by your, um, friends. My idea is that if you don't want to sculpt an inanimate object, you could make a statement by sculpting a concept."

"What?" (There was that word again. Thank goodness someone had invented it.)

"You know, sculpt 'love' or 'peace' or 'brotherhood.' "

"I . . ." I had absolutely no idea how to do

that and no idea what to say to Ashley.

"Oh, don't worry. I don't mind if you use my idea. Really."

"Well, I . . . um, I don't know what to say. Um . . . I'm speechless."

Ashley laughed. "I think you should try it. Anyone who can see power in a traffic light ought to be able to come up with a great visual representation of a concept."

I cleared my throat. "Oh, right. How—how would *you* sculpt 'love'?"

"With gentle curves and tender feelings."

Well, that was no help.

"Hmm," I said. "I'll think about it." I turned back to my hand. What I *really* needed to think about was how to tell Ashley that I wasn't going to sculpt a non-living thing or an idea. I just couldn't do either one. The problem was how to tell her without looking so stupid.

"Hey, Claud?"

"Yeah?"

"Do you want to come over to my house sometime? I could show you some of the sculptures I'm working on at home. And also the studio my parents are having fixed up for me. It's on the top floor of our house, where the best light is. I'll be able to paint and draw and sculpt there. A whole room for my work."

"Gosh, that's great!" I exclaimed. "Sure I'll come. I'd love to see everything."

My doubts were replaced with excitement. Ashley, a great artist, liked me and valued me and trusted me. What else could you want in a friend?

10th CHAPTER

All right, so how many meetings do you plan to miss, Ms. Artist? How many shopping dates do you plan to skip out on? And what does "friend" mean to you, anyway? To me, it means somebody who keeps up her half of certain bargains, who keeps in touch with you -- calls you from time to time and eats lunch with you. And who doesn't LIE or BREAK DATES. It means somebody who doesn't forget her old friends just because someone new comes along, whether that someone is a girl, or a boy as gorgeous as Max Morrison.

I don't feel that you're my friend anymore. Or that you want me for yours.

Boy, does Stacey know how to bring tears to a person's eyes. Maybe if I'd read her entry sooner, things among us club members wouldn't have got as bad as they did. But not only had I been missing meetings, I hadn't kept up with our club notebook.

Furthermore, I had done something terrible to Stacey. I hadn't meant to, exactly. But it had happened. At the end of school one day, Stacey asked me to go to the mall with her. I told her I couldn't because I had to catch up on some English assignments. That was true. I was really (*really*) planning to go to the library. But on the way there I ran into Ashley, who invited me to her house. Since I needed to discuss my sculpture subject with her, I went. I forgot all about Stacey. I forgot so completely, in fact, that when I called Dawn to tell her I'd have to miss that afternoon's meeting, I also told her why.

That was my big mistake. (Well, one of them.)

Let me tell you, I didn't feel good about missing club meetings and spending so little time with my friends. But I felt great having a mentor who liked my work so much and thought I was smart and kept telling me how much artistic potential I had. When you're a C-student who has to go to the Resource Room, "potential" is a word you don't hear a lot, unless someone, usually a teacher or guidance counsellor or one of your parents, says, "It's really a shame. I don't see why her grades aren't better. She does have potential. . . ."

But I'm getting way off the subject. I wanted to tell you about the next meeting of the Babysitters Club—the next one I missed, that is. It started, as usual, with my friends coming over to my house and being greeted by Mimi. Mimi told them to go straight to my room, even though I wasn't there. She understands how important the club is, and she really likes my friends. It might have seemed funny to Kristy, Stacey, Dawn, and Mary Anne to be in my room without me, but it was okay with Mimi.

I had called Dawn around five o'clock that day. She had seemed quite cool, but, well, you'd think she'd enjoy the chance to be real officer instead of just sort of an officer-in-waiting . . . wouldn't you?

She didn't seem too thrilled, though and told me later that as she biked over to my house for the meeting, a mean little ryhme kept running through her head:

Traitor, traitor.
Claudia–we hate 'er!
Traitor, traitor.
So long, see you later!
Good-bye, Claudia.

Dawn and Kristy reached my house first, and as soon as Mimi ushered them inside, they ran to my room. Stacey arrived next. She stood in the doorway of my room, looked at Dawn sprawled on my bed and Kristy reading the notebook, and said, "Okay, where is she?"

"You mean Claudia?" replied Dawn.

"Who else?"

"She's at Ashley's."

"Ashley's?!" Stacey's face turned the colour of a pomegranate. "That big liar! Are you sure? She told me she couldn't go to the mall with me this afternoon because she had to study at the library."

"You're kidding," said Kristy.

"I'm dead serious," replied Stacey, who became so mad then that she couldn't even speak. That was when she took our notebook (grabbed it right out of Kristy's hands) and started writing all that stuff about friendship.

Mary Anne showed up at five-thirty on the dot. "Hi, you gu—" she started to say. Then she narrowed her eyes. "Is *she* missing again?" she asked.

"Ha," said Kristy. "Very good, Sherlock Holmes."

"Hey, don't snap at me," retorted Mary Anne, sticking up for herself for once. "*I* didn't skip another meeting. *I'm* here on time."

"Sorry," said Kristy contritely.

"You know what I feel like doing?" said Stacey, setting the diary aside. "I feel like raiding Claudia's junk food. It would serve her right if she came back and found we'd eaten everything."

"But you can't eat that stuff!" Dawn exclaimed.

"I can eat some of it," Stacey replied. "I can eat her crisps and her crackers—not too many, of course. And I know where they're hidden. Crisps in that old pyjama bag, crackers in the Monopoly box."

"I wouldn't mind eating up some of her stuff," said Kristy with a slow grin. "Let's see, she's got marshmallows in that shoe box and liquorice sticks under her mattress."

"*I'll* even help you eat that junk," said Dawn, making, for her, a supreme sacrifice.

"Well, I'll help, too," said Mary Anne. "And hey! After we've finished? We should take whatever's left and put it back in the wrong places!"

My friends began giggling but had to calm down when the phone rang three times with job calls. When the sitters were all lined up, Stacey began raiding my junk food. She tossed the liquorice sticks to Mary Anne, the marshmallows to Kristy, the crisps to Dawn, and took the crackers for herself. My friends ate for a while, then stopped to switch the food. Dawn actually wolfed down three marshmallows, but then made a big deal out of having to rinse her mouth out so she wouldn't get cavities.

When they couldn't eat any more, Stacey said, "Okay, now take what's left and put it away—where it doesn't belong."

Mary Anne stuffed the bag with the few remaining marshmallows in one of my trainers.

Kristy stuck the liquorice sticks into the back of a drawer.

Dawn hid the crackers in a purse I don't use anymore.

And Stacey saw my old black fedora on the shelf in my wardrobe and put the crisps underneath it.

Then my friends began laughing hysterically.

(That night, it took me almost an hour to find everything. Plus, a bag of sweets are missing, but no one will tell me if they had anything to do with that.)

The club members had to calm down, though, when Mrs Perkins called needing a sitter for Myriah and Gabbie, and Mrs Delaney called needing a sitter for Amanda and Max.

But as soon as that business was taken care of, Kristy said, "Let's short-sheet her bed!" They didn't even use my name any more. They just called me "she" or "her" and knew who they meant.

So Kristy and Mary Anne short-sheeted my bed. Was I ever mad that night when I discovered what they'd done! I was dead tired because I'd stayed up late trying to catch up on my homework and read *The Twenty-One Balloons* (another Newbery book). By the time I was ready to go to bed, I was so sleepy I could barely turn my duvet back. When I did, and I slid between the sheets, my legs only went halfway down. I kicked around. I couldn't imagine what was wrong. Finally I lifted up my duvet and looked. I couldn't believe it! Pinned to the sheet was a note that read: Ha, ha, Sleep tight!

It wasn't the only note I found. That was because while Kristy and Mary Anne had been working on my bed that afternoon, Stacey had said, "Hey, Dawn, let's hide some notes for Claudia to find."

"Notes? What kind of notes?"

"Mean ones."

Stacey ripped a sheet of paper out of the club notebook. Then she stopped to think, tapping a pencil against her mouth. Finally she wrote: Roses are red, violets are blue, traitors are jerks, and so are you.

"Now what?" asked Dawn.

"I think I'll put it under her pillow."

Dawn grinned. Then she tore a piece of paper out of the book and wrote down the rhyme she'd made up earlier. I found that note in my jewellery box.

It was Kristy's idea to hide a blank piece of paper under Lennie, my rag doll.

"What for?" asked Stacey.

"To drive her crazy. She'll wonder if we

used invisible ink, or maybe wrote something so mean we had to rub it out."

Stacey began giggling. But she had to get herself under control when the phone rang. A new client was calling. Stacey took down the information we needed and got the man a sitter for his twin girls. Then she said, very seriously, "You guys, why do you think Ashley Wyeth wants Claudia to be her friend so badly?"

"What do you mean?" asked Mary Anne, after a pause. "She just wants a friend, doesn't she? She's new here. She doesn't know anyone."

"I guess what I mean is, why *only* Claudia? Doesn't it seem that she wants just one friend and that friend is Claudia?"

"Yeah," said Dawn slowly. "I see what you mean, Stace. When I first moved here, I wanted friends—in general. It was great when you and I got to know each other, Mary Anne, but it wasn't like I wanted just one friend and once I had you I was happy. I was really glad when you introduced me to the rest of the club. I had a bunch of friends in California, and when we moved, I hoped I'd have a bunch in Connecticut, too."

"Exactly," said Stacey. "I felt the same way when I moved from New York. I met Claud first and we're still best friends . . . I think. But I was really happy to meet all of you, too. Plus Pete and Howie and Dori and everyone we ate lunch with last year. But

Ashley doesn't seem to want any friends except Claud."

"Yeah, she hardly ever speaks to us," added Dawn.

"She doesn't pay much attention to anyone but Claudia. She doesn't talk to other kids, either. If she didn't eat lunch with Claudia," said Stacey, "I'm sure she'd eat alone."

"Ashley's in my gym class," spoke up Mary Anne. "She's always alone. You know, I think all Ashley really cares about is art, and she's found a good artist in Claudia. Maybe Claudia is sort of a project for Ashley." Mary Anne paused, putting her hands in her lap and staring down at them. "Oh, I'm not explaining myself very well."

"You're explaining yourself fine," said Stacey. "What you just said is that Ashley likes Claud because she's an artist, not because she's Claud. And if that's true, I'm beginning to wonder just how good a friend Ashley Wyeth is."

11th CHAPTER

"Whoops," said Jackie Rodowsky.

You know how I'd be absolutely lost without the word "what"? Well, Jackie would be absolutely lost without "whoops," "oops," and "uh-oh."

I hadn't really been doing much baby-sitting lately. Since I kept missing meetings, I wasn't signed up for many jobs. But I'd been signed up for this afternoon with the Rodowsky boys for quite some time, and to tell you the truth, I'd really been looking forward to it. Jackie might be accident-prone, but whenever his mother comes home and finds something broken or a spill on the carpet or a plaster on Jackie's finger, she never minds. Well, of course she's concerned if Jackie hurts himself, but she never gives me, as the baby-sitter, any grief. I guess she's used to such things.

Besides, there's something about Jackie's

freckles and his shock of red hair and his great big grin with one tooth missing that always makes me want to grin, too. Even if Jackie's holding out a toy he's broken or is coming to tell me he's just accidentally poured glue over the telephone.

So I had looked forward to sitting for the Rodowskys that day. Nevertheless, I glanced up warily at the sound of Jackie's "whoops" that afternoon. I knew it meant trouble of some sort. I was in the kitchen rinsing off dishes from the boys' afternoon snack. As I shut off the water, I heard the vacuum cleaner being turned off.

"Jackie?" I called. "Archie? Shea?"

"Um, we're in the dining room," said Shea as the vacuum cleaner whined into silence. Shea sounded as if he were admitting to the Great Train Robbery.

I dashed into the dining room. There I found Jackie peering into the hose of the vacuum cleaner as Shea and Archie looked on guiltily. All three boys were barefoot. Their shoes were lined up under the dining room table.

"What's is going on?" I asked, trying not to sound too exasperated.

"We tried a speriment," said Jackie. "And guess what? You can vacuum up socks."

"*Socks*?!" I exclaimed. "Did you vaccum up *all* of your socks?"

"Six of 'em," said Archie. "Three pairs, six socks."

I groaned.

"We didn't mean to, exactly," spoke up Shea. "They were in a pile. We thought maybe the vacuum would just get one, but they all went. Whoosh, whoosh, whoosh, whoosh, whoosh, whoosh," he said, demonstrating with his hands.

"Shea, really. You're the oldest," I said, knowing that didn't mean a thing. (Why should it?)

"It was Jackie's idea," he countered.

"Well, what did you plan to do about your sock if it was vacuumed up?" I asked Jackie.

"See what happened to it," he replied simply.

This wasn't getting us anywhere. "All right," I said, sighing. "The next thing to do is find the socks."

"Goody!" cried Jackie, jumping up and down. "I wonder what they'll look like."

"Maybe the Vacuum Monster attacked them. Maybe they'll be all chewed up," suggested Archie.

I was just dying to ask Archie what he thought the Vacuum Monster was, but I didn't want to start anything. Instead, I lifted the cover of the vacuum, pulled out the dust bag at the back, and headed into the kitchen with it. The boys trailed behind me.

"What are you going to do?" asked Jackie.

"Cut it open and see what's inside," I replied.

"Awesome," said Shea.

I took a look. Nothing but a cloud of dust.

"Ew, disgusting," said Jackie, and sneezed.

I threw the bag away and returned to the vacuum cleaner. I noticed that the boys hadn't put an attachment on the end of the hose. Gingerly I reached into the hose as far as possible, which really wasn't very far, and withdrew my hand, a sock between my fingers. The sock was rumpled but otherwise fine.

The Rodowskys looked on in surprise.

"I wonder why the Vaccuum Monster didn't want it," said Archie.

"Some experiment," commented Shea.

It took more than fifteen minutes, but after poking, prodding, and digging around with a pair of toast tongs, I managed to remove all the socks from the hose.

"Will you guys promise me something?" I said as they put their socks and shoes back on.

What?" asked Jackie.

"That you won't use the vacuum again without asking me first."

"Promise," they replied.

"Thank you. Now let's do something fun."

"Let's watch *Sesame Street*," said Archie.

"Wouldn't you rather play a game?" I asked.

"Red Light, Green Light!" cried Jackie. "Please, Claudia?"

"Well . . ." I replied, remembering my vow not to play stupid games in the Rodowskys' front garden any more.

"Puh-*lease*?" added Archie. "That was fun. Can I be the policeman?"

I hadn't even answered the boys and already they were racing for the front door.

I followed them. Red Light, Green Light it would be. That was my responsibility as their baby-sitter.

Jackie threw the front door open. Standing on the step was Ashley, her hand poised to ring the bell.

Despite the fact that the boys had been somewhat awed by her the first time they met her, Jackie began jumping up and down. "Hi!" he cried. "We're going to play Red Light, Green Light again. You want to play?"

He pushed open the screen door and squeezed by Ashley, jumping down the steps (and narrowly missing the hedge that lined the front walk.)

Archie followed, calling, "But you can't be the policeman. I'm the policeman first. That's my job today!"

Shea was the last one out the door. Just before he leaped down all four stairs in a single bound, he turned and said, "Claudia's the best police officer, though. Right, Claudia?"

Luckily, he wasn't really expecting an answer.

I stepped onto the front porch, closing the doors behind me.

Ashley looked at me, an eyebrow raised.

"Red Light, Green Light again?" she asked.

I tried to laugh. "They love it," I replied.

Ashley frowned. "I just don't understand why you waste all your time on . . ." (she held her hand toward the Rodowskys, who were gearing up for the game)" . . .all this."

I paused. "All *what*?" I finally said, somewhat testily.

"This uselessness."

"They're children," I replied quietly. "They're important to me."

"Oh, you sound so sentimental," Ashley scoffed, looking at the ground.

"Sentimental doesn't sound so bad for an artist. Artists are very *feeling* people. They have to put their emotions into their work."

Ashley didn't respond and I realized this was the first time I'd ever tried to tell *her* something about art.

"Besides," I went on, as Ashley fidgeted with the ruffles on her peasant blouse, "who was the one who said she'd sculpt 'love' with gentle curves and tender feelings? That's pure mush if I ever heard it."

"Mush?!"

"Sentiment, soft stuff, you know."

Ashley's ice-blue eyes turned icier. "This is the thanks I get for--"

"For what, Ashley? What did you do that you expect thanks for? What did you do that you wouldn't have done just because you're my friend?"

"I taught you about sculpting. I taught you how to look beyond Ms Baehr and see what else you can do."

"And you think you deserve to be paid back? You think I owe you something? Friendship doesn't work that way. Friends are friends because they like each other, not because they're in debt," I said. I was angry, but I didn't raise my voice. I didn't want to upset the Rodowskys.

"I *do* like you," replied Ashley, and for the first time since I'd met her, I thought she looked, well, not in control. Her chin quivered and her voice quivered and her eyes filled with tears. "I do want you to be my friend," she added.

"But you want me to devote my life to art. And that's not fair. You shouldn't make up conditions for friendship. Besides, there's more to my life than you and art. I'm not giving anything up."

Ashley regained her cool as quickly as she'd lost it. "You mean, you're not giving anything up *just for me*. Because I'm not important enough to you. That's what you're saying, isn't it? Well, I'll tell you something, Claudia Kishi. You are ungrateful. And foolish. And you don't know a thing about being a friend."

With a swish of her hair, her eyes flashing, Ashley spun around and marched down the steps and across the yard to her house. She left me standing on the Rodowsky's porch, feeling like an empty sack that had once held something nice, like dried flowers, and was now slowly being filled with rocks. And each rock was an unpleasant thought:

Clunk: She's right. I haven't been a good friend. At least, not to Stacey and the other members of the Babysitters Club.

Clunk: Everyone must hate me.

Clunk: I wish I could talk to Stacey, but I'd be surprised if she ever speaks to me again.

"Hey, you guys," I called to Jackie, Shea, and Archie. "Come on inside, okay? Red Light, Green Light wasn't a very good idea after all. It looks like it's going to rain."

The boys came inside with only a little grumbling. I settled them in front of the TV in the playroom, and then went to the living room to think. I needed to be alone for a while. What had happened to me over the past couple of weeks? Somehow I'd allowed myself to be swept away by Ashley. Did I have any other friends now? Before Ashley came along, I'd call Stacey when I was upset about something. Now I couldn't do that. And what about the art show? Ms Baehr expected me to enter. I'd told my parents I was going to enter. And I didn't even have a subject for the sculpture.

"Claudia?"

My thoughts were interrupted by Jackie. He approached me with one sneaker on, the other in his hand, the laces bunched into a huge tangle.

"Can you help me?" he asked, holding out the sneaker. He was smiling his great smile.

"Of course," I answered.

And as I worked at the knot, I suddenly thought: Jackie. I'll sculpt Jackie. He'd be a great subject. I've been wanting to sculpt something "alive" all along.

I gave Jackie a grin and was rewarded with another of his gap-toothed ones.

12th CHAPTER

What an interesting afternoon this turned out to be. I was sitting for the Rodowskys' and Claudia came over. This was totally unexpected. I'm pretty sure she didn't know I was going to be there. (After all, when was the last time she looked at the appointment calendar in the record book?) Claudia tried to hide her surprise when I answered the door. And I tried to hide my annoyance. We both succeeded Anyway, it turns out she wants to sculpt Jackie. She had just started making a sketch of him when the doorbell rang again. This time it was Ashley! I think Claudia and Ashley had had a fight. Then they sort of had another one in front of Jackie and me. Things were getting "curiouser and curiouser." Thank goodness Claudia filled me in on everything, or I would have died from wondering....

When Mary Anne wrote "What an interesting afternoon this turned out to be," she sure was right. I think it was more interesting for me than it was for her, though. Once I got the idea to sculpt Jackie, my mind began working overtime. And my fingers began itching to start the project. I went over to the Rodowskys' the very next afternoon so that I could make some sketches of Jackie to work from, since he couldn't model for me hour after hour. Also, I wanted to ask Mrs Rodowsky for permission to do the sculpture, and of course I had to ask Jackie himself whether he was interested in being my model.

Boy, was I surprised when I rang the Rodowskys' bell and Mary Anne answered the door! For some reason, I just hadn't expected another club member to be there. I don't know why.

"Claudia!" exclaimed Mary Anne when she saw me on the stoop. The faintest of frowns flickered across her forehead.

"Oh . . ." I said. I was almost speechless. "Um, hi."

"Are you supposed to be sitting?" Mary Anne asked, looking confused.

"Oh, no," I replied. I held out my sketch pad. "I wanted to sketch Jackie. I mean, I want to sculpt him, but I have to sketch him first. Oh, and I have to ask if he can do it."

"We-ell," said Mary Anne slowly. "Mrs Rodowsky isn't here, of course, but why don't you ask Jackie? *He's* here." Mary Anne sounded a little frazzled.

"Is it one of his bad days?" I asked.

"You could say so. He didn't *mean* to exactly but he knocked over a ten-pound bag of dog chow, and then got nail polish all over a pair of socks."

"Gosh, what is it with socks, anyway?" I wondered out loud.

"What?"

"Never mind. It's a long story. How did he get nail polish on his socks?"

"That's a long story, too. Why don't you come on in?"

I stepped inside and was greeted by an excited Jackie. "Hi!" he exclaimed. "I'm the only kid here today. Shea's at his piano lesson and Archie's at his tumbling class."

"Don't you like to take lessons?" I asked Jackie.

"Yeah, but I break too many things. Mrs Schiavone said so."

"Who's Mrs Schiavone?" Mary Anne and I asked at the same time. We glanced at each other and I could tell she was debating whether to hook my baby finger and say "jinx." I knew because I was wondering the same thing. But we didn't do it.

"Mrs Schiavone's the piano teacher," Jackie replied. "She lets Shea go to the house because he didn't break her metronome. Or her umbrella. Or her doorbell."

"How did you break her doorbell?" Mary

Anne wanted to know.

Jackie frowned. "I'm not sure. But it's broken all right. It used to play 'Somewhere Over the Rainbow.' Now it just goes 'boing, boing, bonk.'"

I tried hard not to giggle. Jackie wasn't laughing and he gets upset about his accidents sometimes—because they really are just accidents. Mary Anne hid her smile, too.

"Jackie," Mary Anne said when the laughing danger was past, "Claudia came over because she wants to ask you something."

"What?" replied Jackie.

He plopped down on the couch and I sat next to him. I explained about the sculpture and the sketches and the art show.

"You want to make a statue of *me*?!" he exclaimed finally.

I couldn't even look at Mary Anne then. "Well, yes. Sort of. Except that I'm not going to sculpt all of you. Just your head."

"Sculpt my head?" he repeated. "Will it hurt?"

"Not a bit. I won't even touch you."

"And I'll be in a show? Where everyone will see me?"

"Yup."

"Oh, boy! Oh, boy!" was all Jackie could say.

"Do you want to start now?" I asked him. "I need to make some drawings of you."

"Is it okay?" Jackie asked Mary Anne.

"Fine with me," she replied.

I posed Jackie at one end of the couch, settled myself at the other, and began sketching. At first, Jackie sat almost motionless. He didn't smile, didn't even blink his eyes.

"Jack-o, you can relax a little," I told him. "You can even move around if you want. I mean, don't stand up, but—"

"How about if I get him a colouring book?" suggested Mary Anne.

"Oh, great," I replied.

While Jackie was colouring and I was sketching, Mary Anne sat in an easy chair. At first she just watched. Then, after what seemed like a very long time, she said, "So, um, how's Ashley?"

I shrugged. "Okay, I guess."

Mary Anne gathered up her courage to ask me an important question. I can always tell when she's doing that. Gathering her courage, I mean. She starts to fidget, then she starts breathing heavily, then she's silent for a few moments, and finally she clears her throat. "Ahem."

"Yes?" I replied.

"Claudia, I was wondering. Is Ashley your, um, best friend now?"

"She most certainly is not."

"She isn't?"

"No way."

"But I thought—"

"I thought we were friends, too," I interrupted her. "I thought nobody understood me the way Ashley did, but I guess I was wrong." I paused. "You know what I was wishing yesterday? I was wishing I could talk to Stacey. Stacey—and the rest of you guys—understand me in *other* ways. Ways that mean nothing to Ashley. But Stacey's probably mad at me, too."

"Too?"

"Yeah." I didn't say anything else. I didn't feel like telling Mary Anne about the fight with Ashley just then.

"Claudia?" Jackie spoke up. "You and that girl who wears the long dresses are mad at each other, aren't you?"

"I guess so," I replied. I flipped a sheet of paper to the back of my pad and started a new drawing.

"Mummy says when you're mad, you have to tell the other person why. Did you do that?"

"I tried to."

"You know what happens when you do?"

"What?"

"Then the other person tells you why he's mad, then you say something, then he says something, and *then* . . ."

"Yes?" I prompted him.

"I don't know. It's funny, but sometimes you're mad all over again."

I smiled at Jackie and he shrugged.

The doorbell rang then. For the first time

I noticed that it sounded like *boing, boing, bonk.*

"Hey, did you break this one, too?" I asked Jackie as Mary Anne got up to answer the bell.

"Sort of," he replied sheepishly.

A few seconds later, Mary Anne, wearing a huge, fierce frown, returned. Ashley was right behind her. Mary Anne didn't utter one word. She just stood aside, folded her arms, and looked from Ashley to me as if to say, "Well? What's going on?"

"Ashley!" I cried. "What are you doing here?"

Ashley leaned over to look at the sketch I was working on. "I saw your bike outside. What are *you* doing here? I couldn't believe you were baby-sitting again . . . and I see you aren't."

"Nope. I'm starting my sculpture for the show. That should make you happy."

"Not if you're going to sculpt *him,*" replied Ashley, pointing.

Jackie's eager face fell.

"*Him* has a name," I told her. "He's Jackie. And he's one of my good friends."

Jackie's smile returned cautiously.

"So you lost your nerve," Ashley went on, as if she hadn't heard me. "You're going to sculpt a person."

"Right."

"Why?"

"Because I'll sculpt what I want to

sculpt. I'll sculpt what I do best, and I do people best, even though I still have a lot to learn."

"I'll say. Well, you're not going to learn it from me," retorted Ashley, and she headed for the front door. Her parting words were, "You're ruining your career, you know." Then she let herself out.

"Whoa," said Mary Anne under her breath. "Intense."

Jackie was looking at me worriedly. "It's okay," I told him. "Really."

"Are you still going to put my head in the show?" he asked.

"You bet. That is, if I finish on time."

"Hey, Claud, you know you really stood up to her," said Mary Anne, looking impressed.

"I suppose. I mean, I know. But I don't think it did any good. She still doesn't understand what I'm saying."

"She doesn't *want* to understand," Mary Anne corrected me. "And that's a big difference. She knows you don't agree with her."

I nodded thoughtfully.

"Are we going to see you at the next club meeting?" Mary Anne asked carefully.

"I think so. Not today's, because I'm behind in my homework and I got a D on a spelling test. And there's this library project I haven't even begun yet. So I'm going to hit the books."

"But couldn't you come back from the library by five-thirty?"

"Usually, but . . . just not this time." The problem was, I didn't think I'd be welcome at the meeting. Even if it was in my own room.

"All right," said Mary Anne briskly. "I'll tell the others."

"Okay." I gathered up my pencils and closed the pad. "I've got enough sketches for now, Jack-o," I told him. "Thanks a lot."

It was time to go. I had a lot to do. And I mean a *lot*.

13th CHAPTER

One of the best things to do when you have a *lot* to do, is make a list. Then you can cross things off as you complete them. Also, you won't forget anything. After dinner that evening, the first thing I did was go to my room and make a list of lists to make. That's how behind I was!

This is what my first list looked like:

<u>List of Lists of Things to Do</u>

1. Freinds
2. Schoolwork
3. Scupture ~~[illegible]~~ show

This is what my second list looked like:

<u>Things to Do: Freinds</u>

1. Call Aslhey -- try to explian
2. Call Stacey -- aplogise
3. Call Kristy -- aplogise. Tell her will try to be at next meeting

This is what my third list looked like:

<u>School Work To do</u>

1. Ask Mrs. Hall if I can take speling test agian
2. GO TO THE LIBRARY AGAIN!!! Work on project abot War of 1812.
3. Finish <u>The 21 Ballons</u>
4. Start <u>A Wrinkel in Time</u>

This is what my last list looked like:

<u>Thing to Do: Scupture Show</u>

1. Think very carfuly about how much time I need for new sclupture.
2. Talk to Mr. Bear?
3. Talk to mum and dad?

I sat on my bed and looked at all my lists. Then I threw away the first one since I'd made the other three lists. I felt very organized—and very panicked. How could I get everything done?

I didn't know, but the best thing to do was jump right in. The number-one item on the Friends list was to call Ashley. So I did. I closed the door to my room, curled up on my bed, and dialled her number. I'd called her a lot lately, so I knew her number by heart.

"Hi, Ashley," I said, after Mrs Wyeth had called her to the phone. "It's me."

"Who?"

"*Me*. Claudia."

"Oh."

"Well, it's nice to talk to you, too," I said sarcastically.

"Look, I'm really busy—" Ashley began.

"Tell me about it," I replied, glancing nervously at my lists. "Listen, I'm calling because I have to tell you something. I want you to try to understand this."

"What?"

"That my life is very . . . big. I mean, there's a lot to it. I have friends and my family and school and art and pottery and baby-sitting. Maybe someday I'll decide I want to narrow things down, but not right now. I like to try new things. I like, what do you call it? Variety, I suppose. I'm happiest when I'm busy, even if sometimes I'm too busy.

"I really like you, Ashley, but I can't spend all my time with you, working on sculptures even if you are the most talented person I know. Do you see what I mean?"

"Yes," replied Ashley after a pause, "I do."

And then she hung up on me.

For a moment I sat and stared at the receiver. I wanted to cry. Ashley didn't like me any more. She probably didn't value me as an artist any more, either. But what had I really lost? Certainly not a friend. A real friend would have listened and tried to understand. A real friend would not have hung up on me. Ashley was not a real friend. It wasn't that she was a mean person or a bad person; it was that art was the only thing that truly mattered to her. So if I wasn't going to be as serious an artist as Ashley, then I didn't much matter to her. Ashley's only friend was art.

I hoped my theory about a real friend not hanging up on me was true—because I was about to call Stacey. If she hung up on me, I'd be crushed. But I dialled her number anyway. I'd just crossed item number one off list number two and I had to move on to item number two.

Stacey answered the phone before the first ring was finished. She must have been sitting on her bed. (She has a phone extension in her bedroom, but not a private, personal phone number like I do.)

"Hi, Stace," I said tentatively.

"Claudia?"

"Yeah, it's me. Stacey, I'm calling to apologize. I know I've been a really rotten friend. I got all carried away with Ashley because she studied at the Keyes Art Society and said I had talent." For five minutes I explained everything to Stacey. When I finished, she was still on the other end of the phone.

"Claudia," she said, and she sounded as if she were trying not to laugh. "Reach under your pillow."

"My pillow? Okay." I felt underneath it and my fingers closed over a wadded-up piece of paper.

"Did you find the note?" she asked.

"Yeah."

"Then read it, ignore it, and throw it away."

The note said: In my breadbox of friends, you are a CRUMB.

It was kind of funny, but I didn't laugh. I threw it away as Stacey had instructed.

"Did you write that?" I asked.

"Yes. But I only meant it a little. Claud, we're still friends. At least, I still want to be your friend. But I think we have some things to talk about."

"I agree," I told her.

We decided to try to find a time to talk in person. Maybe in school or before the next meeting.

I crossed item number two off list number two and phoned Kristy.

Karen, Kristy's little stepsister, answered the phone. "Claudia!" she exclaimed. "We're having a terrible night over here! Ben Brewer's ghost hypnotized Boo-Boo, and—"

"Karen," I interrupted, "I'm really sorry, but I have to talk to Kristy. Can you get her for me, please?"

Karen grew all huffy, but she brought Kristy to the phone. When Kristy was on, I started my little speech all over again. Then I told her that I was probably going to spend my lunch periods in the Resource Room making up work, but that I would definitely be at the next club meeting.

"Okay," said Kristy shortly. "Great." She sounded as if she didn't believe me.

"I really will be there."

"Fine."

"I'll even call Dawn and tell her she can go back to being the alternate officer again."

"O*kay*."

"Okay."

" 'Bye."

" 'Bye."

That wasn't much of a start, but it was something. I'd just have to be patient, and I'd certainly better turn up at the meeting.

I spent the rest of the evening and a lot of that weekend doing homework and looking at the sketches I'd made of Jackie. By the time I went to bed on Sunday, I'd reached an important decision.

"Ms Baehr?"

"Yes, Claudia?"

Another art class was over. Ashley had sat in the front of the room. I'd sat in the back. With the sketches of Jackie spread across the table, I'd begun my sculpture. Now, the rest of the students were gone. I'd just called Ms Baehr over to look at my work.

"I like the subject you finally chose," she said, smiling approvingly.

"Me, too," I replied. "But I'm not going to be able to finish this in time for the show. I've only got one more week. I have schoolwork to catch up on—you know how my parents feel about that—and other things to do, too. So I'm not going to enter anything in the show. I'll talk to Mum and Dad tonight. I'll work on this sculpture for class, but it won't be ready for the show."

"Claudia, I wish you'd re-think this," replied Ms Baehr. "If you work hard, I think you *could* finish in time."

"Only if I drop everything else, and I don't want to do that."

Ms Baehr nodded. "All right. I respect your decision."

"Thanks," I said. "Thanks a lot."

I did talk to my parents that night. They were surprised that I'd decided not to be in the show, but they have this thing about school. They think it is very, *very*, VERY important. So when they heard that I was putting school before art, they were delighted. Even though they tried not to show it.

After I had finished talking with my parents I went to my room, settled myself at my desk, and looked over the lists I'd made the night before. I'd done everything on the Friends list so I threw it away. I'd done everything on the Sculpture Show list so I threw it away, too. My School Work list was not in such good shape, which wasn't surprising. Hardly anything having to do with schoolwork is in good shape if I'm involved.

However, I had asked Mrs Hall if I could take the spelling test again—and she'd said yes! I reached into my pencil jar so I could cross off item number one. I pulled out a pencil with a piece of paper wrapped around it.

I sighed. Another note.

I unrolled the paper. The note was in Kristy's handwriting. It said: Famous jerks—Benedict Arnold, the Wicked Witch of the West, Claudia Kishi.

I threw away the note and crossed off number one on the list. I couldn't cross off two, three, or four, though. But that was all right. Soon I'd be able to. I was almost finished with *The Twenty-One Balloons* and I'd taken *A Wrinkle in Time* by Madeleine L'Engle out of the library. While I was thinking about it, I opened *A Wrinkle in Time* and read the first sentence. "It was a dark and stormy night." Well, that didn't sound so bad. In fact, it sounded kind of like the Nancy Drew books I like so much. And the titles of the first three chapters were "Mrs Whatsit," "Mrs Who," and "Mrs Which." They sounded like fun! I looked longingly at the book as I put it aside to start studying for my spelling test. Maybe finishing up my School Work list would go quickly after all. I smiled.

And tomorrow I would go to a meeting of the Babysitters Club.

14th CHAPTER

The next day, I packed a lunch (something I hardly ever do) and at lunchtime went to the Resource Room. I'd done that the last couple of days, too. This time, I brought *The Twenty-One Balloons* with me. I had finished reading it, and now I needed someone to test me on the spelling of the hard words so I could get ready to retake the spelling test. One of the Resource Room teachers worked hard with me during the whole lunch period. I was proud of myself. Maybe I wouldn't get an A on the test, but I thought I could get a C or even a B.

After school, I had to do a chore. Well, maybe chore isn't the right word, but I *had* to do something I didn't *want* to do. That certainly sounded like a chore.

As soon as I got home, I jumped on my bike and rode over to Jackie Rodowsky's house. The Rodowskys weren't expecting me, so Jackie's mother was a little suprised to see me standing on the doorstep.

"Claudia!" she said. "Has there been a mix-up? Did I—"

"Oh, no," I interrupted. "I came to talk to Jackie. Is he home from school yet?"

"He got here a few minutes ago. Come on in, honey."

Mrs Rodowsky led me inside just as Jackie came bounding downstairs, leaped over the last three, stumbled against a table as he landed, and knocked a vase to the floor. Luckily, it landed on the rug and didn't break.

"Whoops," said Jackie.

Mrs Rodowsky shook her head. But all she said was, "Jackie, Claudia's here to see you." Then she disappeared into the kitchen.

"Claudia!" Jackie exclaimed. "Are you going to start sculpting my head?"

"Not today," I replied. "That's what I wanted to talk to you about. Come and sit with me." I sat down on a sofa and patted the cushion next to me.

Jackie charged across the room and threw himself down on the couch, accidentally kicking my right knee.

"Ow!" I couldn't help crying out.

"Oops. Sorry."

"Jackie," I began, rubbing my knee, "I came over to tell you something. I'm really sorry but I'm not going to be able to put you in the show after all."

Jackie had been bouncing and wiggling around. Now he stopped. "You're *not*?" he said. His eyes began to fill with tears.

"No," I replied. As simply as I could, I explained how I'd run out of time.

Jackie didn't say anything. He poked the end of his shoelace inside his sock.

"I'd still like to sculpt you, though," I told him.

"You would?"

"Yup. I showed the drawings of you to my teacher and she really liked them. She wants me to sculpt you, too."

"But no show?"

"No show. . . . Would you like to be my model anyway?"

Jackie screwed up his face in thought. "Yes," he replied at last.

"Great!" I said. "I'm sure you're going to be a terrific model. I am sorry about the show, but I wanted you to know the truth if I was going to sculpt you."

Jackie nodded. "You know what, Claudia?"

"What?"

"I love you." Jackie wrapped his arms around my waist and I hugged him back.

I was glad I'd been honest with him. A smile spread across my face as I realized something. I hadn't been baby-sitting much lately and I *missed* little kids. Only someone Jackie's age would hug me and thank me when I'd just disappointed him.

When I left the Rodowskys' I rode over to the public library. I worked on my War of 1812 project again. But when the clock over the front door said 5.10, I gathered up my papers and notebook, hopped on my bike, and rode home. I reached my house at 5:31 and ran to my room. Kristy, Mary Anne, Dawn, and Stacey were already there.

"Hi, everybody!" I exclaimed. "I'm back!"

I flopped onto the floor and looked around. Kristy was sitting in the director's chair, drinking a Coke and wearing her visor. Mary Anne and Dawn were lying across my bed on their backs. Stacey was perched on my desk.

"Hi," the others replied. They didn't look at me.

"Any calls yet?" I asked.

"Nope."

"Good. Then it's time for . . ." I reached under my bed and pulled out a crisp bag, only I knew there weren't any crisps in it. I held the bag out. "Everyone has to take one, even you, Stacey."

"But I can't—" she began.

I held up my hand for silence. Then I offered the bag to Kristy. She reached in and pulled out a folded piece of paper. Everyone else did the same.

"Now," I said, "who has the paper with the number one on it?"

"I do," said Dawn, unfolding the note.

"Okay, you read yours first. Then whoever has number two, read yours. And then three and then four, okay? Dawn?"

Dawn cleared her throat. " 'Friends,' " she announced, reading the title. " 'Long ago in another time, I had four friends and they were mine.' " Dawn stopped and looked around.

"Oh," said Stacey. "Um, 'Then I found an artist who said I am good and so are you.' "

" 'So I followed her here and there,' " read Kristy, " 'and round and round and everywhere.' " She giggled.

" 'But,' " went on Mary Anne, " 'she was false and it took you to show me friends that are really true.' "

When Mary Anne finished, no one said anything.

"I guess," I spoke up, "that's my way of saying I'm sorry. And that I kind of learned the hard way who my real friends are. I, um, really missed you guys. And baby-sitting. And meetings. And I'm sick to death of animated objects or whatever they're called. I know you're still mad, but I hope we can be friends again. Someday."

"Oh, that is so sad and lovely!" cried Mary Anne and burst into tears.

At *that*, Kristy burst out *laughing*.

"Lunatics," said Stacey. "We have a club full of fools."

"Club of fools!" I repeated, and then everyone laughed, even Mary Anne.

"I'm not asking you guys to forgive me right now," I went on. "I know it'll take time—"

"Claudia, Claudia, Claudia," said Stacey. "Save your breath. We forgive you."

"You do?" I asked.

"We do?" Kristy asked.

"Yes," said Stacey firmly, glaring at Kristy, "*we do.*"

I began to feel teary-eyed myself then. "I don't deserve friends as good as you," I choked out. "I'm too lucky."

"Oh, Claudia!" wailed Stacey. She slid off the desk and ran over to me and we hugged.

"Hey, are you wearing new perfume?" I asked her, sniffing.

"Yeah!" she exclaimed. "Do you like it? It's called Moonlight Mist."

"It's fabulous."

"Let me smell," said the others, crowding in.

"Ooh, nice," breathed Dawn.

"Heavenly," added Mary Anne.

"It's okay—if you want to smell like a rosebed," said Kristy.

We were all talking at the same time.

"What's wrong with a rosebed?" Mary Anne wanted to know.

"Can I try some?" I asked.

"Sure, I've got the bottle right here in—"

Ring, ring.

The phone!

"Oh, can I get it? Puh-*lease*? It feels like years since I've taken a job call," I exclaimed.

"Go to it," replied Kristy.

"Hello, Babysitters Club," I said, picking up the receiver. "Yes. . . . Yes. . . . Oh, no problem. . . . Sure. Okay, call you right back. 'Bye." I hung up the phone and faced the others. Mary Anne was holding the record book in her lap, pencil poised.

"Who was it?" asked Kristy.

"Mrs Newton. She needs a sitter for Jamie and Lucy next Thursday evening. It won't be a late night. They'll be back by nine."

"Let's see," said Mary Anne. "You're free then, Claud. Want the job?"

"Sure!" I replied. I called Mrs Newton back to give her the information. As I was talking, I began to feel like a real, official club member again. "Boy," I said when I'd hung up. "It sure is good to be back with you guys."

"Claudia?" asked Mary Anne seriously from the spot on my bed. "What happened?"

"What happened?" I repeated. "What do you mean?"

"I mean with Ashley and the club and us."

"Oh. That. . . . I just got carried away, I

guess. You have to understand something. Hardly anybody ever tells me I'm *really* good at something. I mean, actually *talented*. When you're me, that just doesn't happen often."

"We always say how good you are in art," Mary Anne pointed out, looking hurt.

"I know. And that means a lot. But the things is, if you'll excuse me for saying this, you guys don't know much about art. So your comments are nice but . . . when Ashley came along, and she *was* an excellent artist and she had even studied at Keyes, well, her comments meant a *lot*. Suddenly I felt very important. At least I did when I was with her. And I didn't want to lose that."

Mary Anne and Stacey were nodding slowly.

"I see," said Stacey. "I understand."

"But it turned out that Ashley only liked my talent," I went on. "I mean, she liked the person she *thought* I was, and she doesn't really want to hang around anyone who isn't an artist. But that's not what makes a friendship, is it? I mean, if *we* didn't like baby-sitting, we would still be friends."

"Right," said Stacey.

"Right," said Dawn, Kristy, and Mary Anne.

"And now," added Kristy, "let's get down to business. Where's the treasury? We have money to count, subs to be paid."

We all got to work.
And I thought, I'm back, I'm really back!

15th CHAPTER

"Oh, I am so nervous. I am so nervous!" I kept exclaiming.

"Relax, Claud, you're going to give yourself apoplexy," said Kristy.

I was even too nervous to ask Kristy what apoplexy was.

It was 7.45 in the evening. Milling around in front of Stoneybrook's new art gallery were a bunch of students from the Arts Centre and their families and friends. I was there with Mum and Dad, Mimi, my sister Janine, and the members of the Babysitters Club.

In exactly fifteen minutes, the front door was going to open and everyone would be allowed inside to see the new gallery—and the Arts Centre sculpture show. I wasn't nervous about the opening of the gallery. That was exciting, but it wasn't enough to give me appendicitis, or whatever Kristy had said. No, I was nervous because of a phone call I'd got that afternoon. I'd picked up the receiver, and Ms Baehr had been on the other end of the line.

"Claudia?" she'd said.

"Yes?" I replied, trying to get over my shock. (You just never expect a teacher to call you at home.)

"I have to tell you something. I'm not sure I should have done this, but I did, so it's too late." She paused. "I entered your sculpture of Jackie in the art show."

"You what?!" I cried. "But it isn't finished! It's, maybe, half-finished."

"I know. I entered it as a work-in-progress. It's wonderful, Claudia. I want people to see it. . . . Claudia?"

"I'm still here. I—don't know what to say."

"Don't say anything. Just come to the show tonight. Bring your family. By the time the gallery opens, the prizes will have been awarded."

So you can see why I was nervous. I didn't think I'd won an award. Not for a work-in-progress. But that half-finished piece was going to be on display. And I didn't want anyone laughing at it.

Oh, I thought now, I should never have mentioned the show to my friends. Why had I done that? (Maybe because I'd still been in shock.) Of course they'd wanted to come—Mary Anne had even brought her father—and now they'd be around to see the laughers.

A new worry came to me. Ashley would be there and she'd see the laughers, too, only she'd probably join them.

I shook my head. What a mess.

A murmur in the crowd made me stop worrying. The front door was opening. People were streaming inside.

My heart began to beat as loudly as a train running down a track. I could feel it pumping in my throat.

"I think I'm going to faint," I said to Stacey.

"Oh, Claud, you are not," she replied. Nevertheless, she reached out her hand and I grabbed it. We entered the exhibition like two little kids on their first day of kindergarten.

My family, my friends and I stood in a group and looked around. The new art gallery was lovely. It was all carpeted and quiet and everything was grey or white—so that it didn't distract from the art that was on display. Usually, I guessed, paintings would be hung on the movable partitions that divided the gallery into rooms, but now our sculptures stood proudly on brown pedestals. I could see about twenty in the room we had entered. The rest must be in other rooms. Ms Baehr had said about sixty pieces were on display.

Still gripping hands, Stacey and I began

walking from sculpture to sculpture. Some of them were hard to see because of the crowd, but we waited patiently or stood on tiptoe until we could get a glimpse of each one. I was determined not to miss a thing.

"Look! There's something by Mary Drabek!" exclaimed Dawn. "She's in my maths class."

"Hey, she got a third-prize ribbon!" said Kristy, wiggling her way closer to the sculpture.

"This is very impressive, honey," my mother said to me. "I think the new gallery is wonderful. You should be proud to be in its first exhibition."

I nodded my head. I was afraid to speak. Where was my sculpture of Jackie? I didn't hear any laughing. . . .

Stacey and I had finally dropped hands. Soon I got separated from my family and the club members, so I wandered around by myself. I made a complete tour of the first room and didn't find Jackie.

I entered the next room.

The first piece I saw was a boxing cow by John Steiner. It hadn't won an award.

The next piece was Fiona MacRae's. It was the stag she'd been working on. The second-prize ribbon was attached to it.

I passed a rabbit, two little girls holding hands, a man reading a newspaper, and a baseball player.

And then I reached a small crowd of

people. They weren't laughing so they couldn't have been looking at Jackie. I edged closer, squeezing between a man who smelled of tobacco and a woman with a baby in her arms. There on a brown pedestal was Ashley's fireplug. The blue first-prize ribbon hung jauntily in front of it.

I was amazed. Somehow, Ashley really had managed to make that hydrant come to life. And the judges must have appreciated what she'd done.

"It's an animated inanimate object," I heard a voice explain.

Ashley.

There she was.

Our eyes met.

I smiled. "Congratulations," I mouthed to her.

Ashley nodded at me and then smiled back.

I left the room. Suddenly, I wasn't very interested in finding my sculpture. I didn't care where it was or whether anyone was laughing at it. Maybe I should have listened to Ashley more. Maybe I really could have learned from her.

But just at that moment, I heard an excited squeal behind me.

"Claudia!" Kristy cried. She had grabbed my arm and was jumping up and down. "Come see what I found!"

Kristy led me into a third room. Then she picked up her pace and pulled me straight through it, nearly knocking a bunch of people over.

"What *is* it?" I exclaimed, half-annoyed, half-amused.

"It's . . . this sculpture!"

In front of me was Jackie. Kristy had been the first of us to find it. Right away, I noticed two things: no one was laughing at it, and a green ribbon had been fixed to the pedestal.

"You got an honourable mention!" said Kristy.

"For a work-in-progress," I marvelled.

"You would have won first prize if you'd finished," someone spoke up behind me.

It was Ms Baehr.

"I would have?"

She nodded. "The judges were very impressed."

"You'll have to tell Jackie," said Kristy.

"I'll say."

The next half hour was one of the most exciting I've ever known. My parents and sister and Mimi and Mary Anne and her dad and Dawn and Stacey all crowded around to look at and exclaim over the half-finished sculpture of Jackie. Then a *Stoney-brook News* photographer took a picture of all the winners, even the three of us who just got honourable mentions. She said that the photo and an article about us and the gallery would appear in the paper a few days later.

All that night people kept congratulating

me. Even my sister, who wants to be a physicist and whose head is usually in the clouds, said, "This must be most rewarding for you. You're among very talented company." And Mimi hugged me to her and said, "I love you, my Claudia."

The next day I was sitting with my friends in the lunch hall. We were back to our regular old lunch routine. Kristy and Mary Anne had bought the hot lunch, Dawn had brought a health food lunch from home, and Stacey and I had bought sandwiches.

Kristy was saying, "You know the smell of trainers after gym class? And you know the smell of Cuthbert Athlete's Foot Creme? Well, if you mixed those smells together, wouldn't they smell just like this pot roast?" and Mary Anne was practically gagging, when I glanced up and saw Ashley walk by our table with her tray. She was alone as usual, looking for a place to sit.

I'm not sure what got into me, but I jumped up and ran to her. I touched her arm. "Ashley?"

"Yes?" she replied, turning around. "Oh . . . Claudia."

"Um, I was wondering. Do you have somewhere to sit? I mean, would you like to sit with my friends and me?"

"With you?" Ashley glanced at the members of the Babysitters Club who were, of course, watching us curiously. "Well . . ."

"Oh, come on," I said. I knew perfectly well that Ashley and I would never be best friends. And I knew she would never understand my interest in baby-sitting. I would never understand how she could think *only* of art. But we did have things in common. I felt that we could be friendly. I wanted to give it a try, at least.

I pulled Ashley over to our table. "Go ahead. Sit down," I said.

Ashley did, somewhat reluctantly.

Kristy scowled at me, and I knew why. Ashley looked just plain weird in her outfit—a long knitted vest over an even longer shirt which she was wearing tails-out over a skirt that didn't match much either the vest or the skirt. And there were those hiking boots again.

But the first thing Ashley did when she sat down was sniff at her lunch and say, "You know what this meat smells like?"

"Old trainers and athlete's foot creme?" suggested Kristy.

"Well, I was going to say turpentine, rubber cement, and acrylic paint," replied Ashley. "I guess that's pretty much the same."

Kristy grinned. "Yeah, I guess so."

And then we began to laugh. All of us. Afterwards, Ashley and I got into a discussion about sculpture, and my friends listened. Then my friends and I got into a discussion about baby-sitting for kids who don't like baby-sitters, and Ashley listened.

When lunch was over, we left the lunch hall together.

After that day, Ashley sometimes sat with us but often sat alone. Either way, it was okay. She and I had become sometimes friends, and that was okay, too. Like Jackie Rodowsky's accidents, those things just happened—sometimes.

The Babysitters Club

Need a babysitter? Then call the Babysitters Club. Kristy Thomas and her friends are all experienced sitters. They can tackle any job from rampaging toddlers to a pandemonium of pets. To find out all about them, read on!

1 **Kristy's Great Idea**
2 **Claudia and the Phantom Phone Calls**
3 **The Truth About Stacey**
4 **Mary Anne Saves The Day**
5 **Dawn and the Impossible Three**
6 **Kristy's Big Day**
7 **Claudia and Mean Janine**
8 **Boy-Crazy Stacey**
9 **The Ghost At Dawn's House**
10 **Logan Likes Mary Anne!**
11 **Kristy and the Snobs**
12 **Claudia and the New Girl**
13 **Goodbye Stacey, Goodbye**
14 **Hello, Mallory**
15 **Little Miss Stoneybrook ... and Dawn**
16 **Jessi's Secret Language**
17 **Mary Anne's Bad-Luck Mystery**
18 **Stacey's Mistake**
19 **Claudia and the Bad Joke**
20 **Kristy and the Walking Disaster**
21 **Mallory and the Trouble With Twins**
22 **Jessi Ramsey, Pet-Sitter**
23 **Dawn On The Coast**
24 **Kristy and the Mother's Day Surprise**
25 **Mary Anne and the Search For Tigger**
26 **Claudia and the Sad Goodbye**
27 **Jessi and the Superbrat**
28 **Welcome Back, Stacey!**
29 **Mallory and the Mystery Diary**
30 **Mary Anne and the Great Romance**
31 **Dawn's Wicked Stepsister**
32 **Kristy and the Secret Of Susan**
33 **Claudia and the Great Search**
34 **Mary Anne and Too Many Boys**
35 **Stacey and the Mystery Of Stoneybrook**
36 **Jessi's Babysitter**
37 **Dawn and the Older Boy**
38 **Kristy's Mystery Admirer**
39 **Poor Mallory!**

40 Claudia and the Middle School Mystery
41 Mary Anne Vs. Logan
42 Jessi and the Dance School Phantom
43 Stacey's Emergency
44 Dawn and the Big Sleepover
45 Kristy and the Baby Parade
46 Mary Anne Misses Logan
47 Mallory On Strike
48 Jessi's Wish
49 Claudia and the Genius Of Elm Street
50 Dawn's Big Date
51 Stacey's Ex-Best Friend
52 Mary Anne and Too Many Babies
53 Kristy For President
54 Mallory and the Dream Horse
55 Jessi's Gold Medal
56 Keep Out, Claudia!
57 Dawn Saves The Planet
58 Stacey's Choice
59 Mallory Hates Boys (and Gym)
60 Mary Anne's Makeover
61 Jessi and the Awful Secret
62 Kristy and the Worst Kid Ever
63 Claudia's ~~Freind~~ Friend
64 Dawn's Family Feud
65 Stacey's Big Crush
66 Maid Mary Anne
67 Dawn's Big Move
68 Jessi and the Bad Babysitter
69 Get Well Soon, Mallory!
70 Stacey and the Cheerleaders
71 Claudia and the Perfect Boy
72 Dawn and the We Love Kids Club
73 Mary Anne and Miss Priss
74 Kristy and the Copycat
75 Jessi's Horrible Prank
76 Stacey's Lie
77 Dawn and Whitney, Friends For Ever
78 Claudia and Crazy Peaches
79 Mary Anne Breaks the Rules
80 Mallory Pike, No1 Fan
81 Kristy and Mr Mum
82 Jessi and the Troublemaker
83 Stacey vs the BSC
84 Dawn and the School Spirit War
85 Claudia Kishi, Live on Air
86 Mary Anne and Camp BSC
87 Stacey and the Bad Girls
88 Farewell Dawn